MW00652597

Reading Mary Alongside Indian Surrogate Mothers

The Bible and Cultural Studies

The Bible and Cultural Studies series highlights the work of established and emerging scholars working at the intersection of the fields of biblical studies and cultural studies. It emphasizes the importance of the Bible in the building of cultural narratives—and thus the need to intervene in those narratives through interpretation—as well as the importance of situating biblical texts within originating cultural contexts. It approaches scripture not as a self-evident category, but as the product of a larger set of cultural processes, and offers scholarship that does not simply "use" or "borrow" from the field of cultural studies, but actively participates in its conversations.

Series Editors: Hal Taussig and Maia Kotrosits

Titles:

Reading Mary Alongside Indian Surrogate Mothers: Violent Love, Oppressive Liberation, and Infancy Narratives
By Sharon Jacob

Reading Mary Alongside Indian Surrogate Mothers

Violent Love, Oppressive Liberation, and Infancy Narratives

Sharon Jacob

First published in 2015 by
PALGRAVE MACMILLAN®
in the United States—a division of St. Martin's Press LLC,
175 Fifth Avenue, New York, NY 10010.

Where this book is distributed in the UK, Europe and the rest of the world,
this is by Palgrave Macmillan, a division of Macmillan Publishers Limited,
registered in England, company number 785998, of Houndmills,
Basingstoke, Hampshire RG21 6XS.

Palgrave Macmillan is the global academic imprint of the above companies
and has companies and representatives throughout the world.

Palgrave® and Macmillan® are registered trademarks in the United States,
the United Kingdom, Europe and other countries.

ISBN: 978–1–137–54252–6

Library of Congress Cataloging-in-Publication Data is available from the
Library of Congress.

A catalogue record of the book is available from the British Library.

Design by Newgen Knowledge Works (P) Ltd., Chennai, India.

First edition: August 2015

10 9 8 7 6 5 4 3 2 1

For my wonderful husband Madhu Rao and
my son Arth Aadrian Rao
Who have inspired me to never give up on my dreams.

The threefold terror of love; a fallen flare
Through the hollow of an ear;
Wings beating about the room;
The terror of all terrors that I bore
The Heavens in my womb...
What is this flesh I purchased with my pains,
This fallen star my milk sustains,
This love that makes my heart's blood stop
Or strikes a sudden chill into my bones and bids my hair
    stand up?
                —W. B. Yeats, "The Mother of God"

Contents

Acknowledgments

This project would not be possible without Dr. James Vijaykumar, and Dr. Gnana Robinson, who encouraged and supported me to begin my studies in the Masters of Divinity Program at Lancaster Theological Seminary. I want to thank my faculty and friends in Lancaster Theological Seminary, especially Dr. Greg Carey, professor of New Testament, who challenged me to have faith in my voice and use it with pride to read the Biblical Text. This project would not have been possible if my mentor, my teacher, and my friend Dr. Stephen D. Moore, professor of New Testament at Drew University, had not shown faith in my work. It was his belief and support in my little, out-of-the box idea that encouraged me to truly believe and have faith in my own vision. His ability to push boundaries and engage in cutting edge scholarship that pushes readers to read and engage in new perspectives that constantly bring to the surface new interpretations has been an inspiration not only in my scholarship but also in my personal life. I would also like to thank my dissertation committee members Melanie Johnson-Debaufre, Althea Spencer Miller, and Tat Siong Benny Liew, who helped me think through tough questions and motivated me to keep pressing on and not give up on this project. My project would not have seen the light of day without two women in particular, Katie Van Heest and Maia Kotrosits. Their guidance and faith in my work has been overwhelming and humbling. I want to thank them for taking the time to read my work and helping me edit and shape my book. I want to thank my family back in India who, in spite of not fully understanding my work, have stood by me and supported m with their unconditional love. I would also like to thank the new addition in my life, my son, who continues to remind me to enjoy my motherhood, not take myself too seriously, and enjoy the simple pleasures of life. I would like to thank my husband Madhu Rao, who has always inspired me and brings out the best in me. His unconditional support and faith in me, even when

I doubted my own ability has given me the courage to never give up on my ambitions and my dreams. Without him this project would never have seen the light of day and for having the belief in me, I thank him very much.

Introduction

In a fictionalized narrative of the medical tourism industry in India, Kishwar Desai's novel *Origins of Love* tries to expose the dark underbelly of infertility clinics and the practices they use to exploit the poor Indian surrogate mother looking for extra income in order that she too can dream of better opportunities for herself and her family. One of the main characters in Desai's novel is Dr. Subhash Pandey, a successful doctor turned businessman, running his own hospital specializing in in-vitro fertilization treatments in Gurgaon, New Delhi——aptly named the Madonna and Child clinic. Desai's impulse to name the hospital "Madonna and Child" is a subtle remark on the androcentric hypocrisy underlying the successful nature of surrogacy in India——the recreation of a conception that does not involve physical intimacy, but is thought to serve a higher purpose. Mary, the mother of Jesus, of course, has evolved culturally and textually into a savior-carrier, unblemished by the stain of intercourse, her body being used for a higher purpose. Even though Desai comes very close to making a literary connection between the Christian infancy narratives and the surrogacy industry in India in her novel, she leaves unprobed, this close association which links the bodies of these mothers separated through history.

The sudden boom of the reproductive tourism industry in India has taken everyone by surprise. The availability of English-speaking doctors, cheap medical costs, and exotic locations has made India an ideal destination for reproductive tourism, which, in 2012, was projected to be a $450-million-dollar industry in India alone.[1] Sadie Stein, a journalist, writes that Indian surrogacy is very affordable (relative to the prices in Western countries), the industry is unregulated, and the potential carriers are quite willing because "the fees can make the difference between poverty and relative economic stability."[2] Discussions about the reproductive tourism industry in India often depict the surrogate mother in dichotomous categories of victim or hero. The use of dichotomies, while helpful in capturing or constructing some of the realities, whereby Indian surrogate mothers willingly enslave or economically liberate themselves by becoming gestational carriers for wealthy western couples, fails to fully acknowledge the ambivalent complexity present in their *choice to purchase opportunity for equality i*n a free market system.

On the surface, the contextual body of the Indian surrogate, and the textual body of Mary may appear unrelated. There are, however, many similarities between the two. To name a few, both conceive without the physical presence of a male; their conception takes place only after their *consent*; they are impregnated by a third party who hails from a superior realm; and, finally, their *willingness* to participate in an anomalous birth is driven by their desire to better the situation of their people or their families. Thus, when these two partial subjects are placed alongside each other, a more complex picture of choice emerges. Resisting traditional interpretations of Mary, I read her textual body as a site of contradiction fluctuating between the poles of violence and love, and constructing her motherhood as performative of a violent love, that, in the end, leaves her in ambiguity and uncertainty, a symbol of oppressive liberation: She is never fully freed, nor yet fully enslaved. My approach is interdisciplinary in that it is informed by intersecting theories of race, empire, and nation, along with the "real life" experiences of the Indian surrogate mothers. These lenses, when applied to the textual character of Mary in the New Testament infancy narratives, will enable me to (re)produce a Mary who is relevant to the lives of the modern Indian women, and bring to light her contradictions and her ambiguity as a "victimized hero." At the same time, Mary's choice to become a *mother for the other* captures the complexity of living in a globalizing economy, where choice promises a conditional freedom. By highlighting the ambiguities of agency that beset the Indian surrogate mother, living in a postcolonial India and a neocolonial world, I am also highlighting the effects of globalization on the bodies of Indian women in general.

Similar to the dichotomized hero/victim terms within the Indian context, feminist biblical and theological scholars have argued that in the Christian tradition the figure of Mary as a virgin goddess mother, elevated within the church, has led to the subjugation of actual women. Rosemary Radford Ruether observes:

> Mary represents the original, good matrix of nature before its alienation from the Spirit. She preserves that original nature that God blessed and called "very good" in the beginning. She exemplified the primordial potential for good of created existence undeformed by sin. In this

theology of the male feminine, we sense the hidden and repressed power of femaleness and nature as they exist both beneath and beyond the present male dualisms of matter and spirit. Precisely for this reason we cannot accept this theology on male terms——This very effort to sunder us from our mortal bodies and to scapegoat women as cause of mortality and sin is the real sin.[3]

It is important to note that the elevation of goddess mothers is not only dependent on the repression of female sexuality, but also constructs these somewhat mythological maternal figures as altruistic heroes. As a result, altruism and motherhood often become synonymous with one another. In other words, motherhood defined as an act of selfless love, constructs an unachievable narrative that hinders women from becoming fully human and living dignified lives. This prompts a redefinition of motherhood that resists the stringent dichotomies between mythology and reality, and constructs a maternal subjectivity reflective of an ambivalent love that is closer to the realities of everyday women. This book, therefore, seeks to understand and interpret the character of Mary in the Matthean and Lukan infancy narratives through a different lens, one informed by the lived realities of the Indian surrogate mothers working and surviving in a postcolonial India. Such an interpretation, I argue, deconstructs the holy mother myth that controls women's bodies and constructs their *love for the other* only through an altruistic lens.

Additionally, the popularity of surrogacy or reproductive tourism in India has created a new class of proletariat in India. In their book titled *Empire,* Michael Hardt and Antonio Negri argue for the changing definition of the proletariat in a capitalistic economy. They observe:

Some labor is waged, some is not; some labor is restricted to within the factory walls, some is dispersed across the unbounded social terrain; some labor is limited to eight hours a day and forty hours a week, some expands to fill the entire time of life; some labor is accorded a minimal value, some is exalted to the pinnacle of the capitalist economy.[4]

In this book, the meaning of labor is redefined as the maternal body of the Indian surrogate mother laboring (in both sense of the term) for another in exchange for a price in the free market system. Gayatri Chakravorty Spivak observes:

The product of a woman's body has been historically susceptible to idealization——just as, in the classical Marxian argument, the reason why the free (male) laborer becomes a "proletarian" under capitalism is not that he has nothing but his body but that, his product, being a value-term is susceptible to idealization. The commodity, by the same token, is susceptible to being transformed to commodity-capital.[5]

Not only are the Indian surrogate mother's reproductive capabilities idealized by capitalism, but also, in recognizing her potential, the Indian surrogate mother idealizes her own maternal body by objectifying it and selling her services in the free market. However, the idealized body of the Indian surrogate mother, and her willingness to participate in an act that not only promises her economic freedom but also skillfully exploits her reproductive capability, is a serious ethical dilemma.

Hardt and Negri depict the ways in which colonialists have used binaries to create a homogenous narrative of the colonized other. They write: "Colonialism homogenizes real social differences by creating one overriding opposition that pushes differences to the absolute and then subsumes the opposition under the identity of European civilization. *Reality is not dialectical, colonialism is.*"[6] Although Hardt and Negri comment and draw attention to the use of binaries in contexts of colonization, such categories continue to play a major role within postcolonial contexts such as India. For example, the categorization of the Indian surrogate mother as an exploited victim or an altruistic hero seeking to eke a living in a capitalistic economy, constructs a homogenous narrative that then subsumes those moments that peek through the cracks.

Commenting on the marketing skills that surrogacy clinics in India employ to attract clients from overseas, Deonandan observes:

> The perception of Indian women is a subtle and largely immeasurable point. Poor, village-based Indian women are often perceived in some circles as being ideal surrogates due to their global image as demure and submissive. Indian women are perceived to be less likely to drink alcohol, to smoke, and to engage in other practices seen to be detrimental to a successful pregnancy. In other words, it is their powerlessness relative to men and to the structures of their society that make them attractive to this trade. Maternal surrogacy is where India's dominance in the world ART [Artificial Reproductive Technologies] market truly manifests, given her abundance of young, poor women.[7]

Although Deonandan's observation is significant, it relies on a one-dimensional perspective of the surrogate mother as powerless and, therefore, vulnerable to exploitation. Chandra Talpade Mohanty argues against this homogenous characterization of third world women in her essay titled "Under Western Eyes: Feminist Scholarship and Colonial Discourses." She writes:

> [W]omen are defined systematically as the victims of male control—the "sexually oppressed." Although it is true that the potential of male violence against women circumscribes and elucidates their social position to a certain extent, defining women as archetypal victims freezes them into "objects-who-defend-themselves," men into "subjects-who-perpetrate-violence," and (every) society into a simple opposition between the powerless (read: women) and the powerful (read: men) groups of people.[8]

A simple binary construction of the Indian surrogate mother, therefore, as a powerless victim forecloses the possibility of bringing to the surface her agency demonstrated in a predominantly patriarchal and a capitalistic society such as India. In other words, while there is no doubt that the Indian surrogate mother is being exploited by the wealthy couples and the technologically advanced reproductive tourism industries, the notion that these mothers are fully aware of their choices, and the repercussions of those choices, must not be brushed aside or ignored. Arguably, these mothers perform an *exploited-exploitive motherhood* as they use their own bodies and use the system that dared to prey on their powerlessness and poverty.

Meanwhile, supporters of surrogacy highlight the altruistic motivation that drives the Indian surrogate mother to participate in the business of surrogacy. Adrienne Arieff notes, "At one end of this world, there is one woman who desperately needs a baby and cannot have her own child. And at the other end, there is a woman who badly wants to help her own family. If these two women want to help each other, why not allow that? They're helping one another to have a new life in this world."[9] Constructing surrogacy as a win-win situation that promotes women helping other women, not only describes this industry as a noble profession, but also depicts the Indian surrogate mother as a noble hero who enables all those around her to draw happiness from her sacrifice. However, one is unable to hide the monetary motivation that drives these mothers into becoming surrogates for wealthy couples. As journalist Adriana Janowhich reports:

> Nazma, 28, has three children, ages 9, 6 and 3½. Her husband is unemployed. She is not pregnant. Through Kaur, she tells Fryhover [the client looking to hire a surrogate] she would like to carry her child. She also says, "If I had the money, obviously I wouldn't do it." Kaur says

all the surrogates agree. She [Nazma] also says, "All would do it again." Translating for Nazma, Kaur says: "She's saying surrogacy is not a bad thing: I'm getting money, and the other person is getting a child. She says I'm doing it for your happiness. I'm doing it for money, but I want to see happiness on your face."[10]

Doctors supporting the business of surrogacy also argue that it is a valid means of employment that offers poor and low caste women a shot at success. Dr. Indira Hinduja argues: "That's right, you give her [the Indian surrogate] the money, tell me when she is starving on the streets, her children are dying in hunger, her house has collapsed in the heavy rain, who is going to help her, is [the] government helping her? Are you and me going to help her? I would say to have a child ."[11] Both Deonandan and Hinduja agree that the motivation for the poor and low caste Indian mothers to become surrogate mothers is primarily a financially driven desire. But while Deonandan construes this financial motivation as luring the Indian surrogate mother to submit to an act of exploitation exacerbated by her powerlessness and disparate economic circumstances, Hinduja interprets this incentive as a stimulus for an act of self-empowerment by highlighting the woman's agency and suggesting that this mother transforms herself into a surrogate so that she can take care of her family. Although both these interpretations play an important role in the larger discussions of the impact of the surrogacy business on the bodies of Indian mothers and the success of the reproductive tourism industry in India, they fail to take into account, and perhaps even overshadow the real issue that lies at the center of these dichotomous interpretations of the Indian surrogate mother.

Neither Deonandan nor Hinduja discuss the complicated subjectivity of the Indian surrogate mother as she vacillates between being a subject of empowerment and an object of exploitation. I argue that forcing the Indian surrogate mother to fit into preordained social categories of exploited victim or empowered mother causes her already split self to rupture even further. This divided body of the Indian surrogate mother never fully fits into the dichotomous categories preordained either by Indian or western societies. Her motherhood ambiguously oscillates between the poles of love/violence, liberation/oppression, and hero/victim. The Indian surrogate mother performs a motherhood that encapsulates her ambivalence as her maternal subjectivity erupts between categories of violence and love, promising a liberation that is contingent upon her oppression. As a result, these hybrid moments captured, brought to light, and maybe even acknowledged by the vocal voices discussing the ethical implications of surrogacy in India could, perhaps, lead to a fuller picture of a maternal identity rooted in an ambivalent love that obscures the barriers between being an unselfish mother to a genetically different child and becoming a professional mother selfishly daring to dream about a better future for her own children.

The task of mothering placed exclusively on the bodies of women becomes an ideology that both elevates, and, at the same time, oppresses women-mothers. In her article titled "Relinquishing the Halo: Portrayal of Mother in Indian Writing in English," Sangeeta Dutta remarks: "Motherhood as a social practice, dialectically unites discourse and activity. The role places the virtuous self-abnegating mother on an exalted position while depriving her of real power—of control over material resources and of rights over her children."[12] Maternal subjectivity, then, is defined as a selfless vocation. In other words, motherhood as a performance of an altruistic love becomes a trait that not only defines a good mother, but also raises her above those women who are unable to become mothers or make a choice not to do so. Ketu Kartrak similarly argues, "Patriarchal ideology, in supervaluing motherhood, paradoxically contains and controls women."[13] The notion of pitting women against women by creating a false hierarchy that becomes a tool through which women's bodies are controlled by societies is not new phenomenon. As Dutta rightly points out, "In India, a long history of mother-goddess worship legitimizes woman's glorification/deification as the divine mother, the source of energy, power and fertility while the same motherhood is an institutionalized form of oppression and subjugation of women."[14]

Throughout history, scholars and lay people in the Christian churches (and occasionally outside them) have pondered the historical and the textual character of Mary, the mother of Jesus, as found in the canonical gospels. Discussions surrounding Mary have, for the most part, been dominated by male scholars hailing from the West. Their interpretations have often featured androcentric or patriarchal observations about her character. Their constructions of this holy mother have concentrated heavily on historical and physical issues that revolve around her virginal conception. They have frequently transformed her into a virgin mother goddess, who humbly and willingly, subjects herself for the service of humanity. In his book *Mary Mother of the Lord: Theological Meditations,* Karl Rahner illustrates this tendency: "The divine motherhood of the blessed Virgin is therefore God's grace alone, and her own act inseparably. It is not simply a physical motherhood, it is her grace and her deed, placing her whole self, body and soul, at the service of

God and his redemptive mercy to mankind."[15] The narrative of a young virgin parthenogenetically conceiving the future savior of the Western world has classically been construed as a prototype for all women, in that her purity, humility, and subordination have been glorified and placed on a pedestal. The virginal body, fetishized by male scholars in the dominant theological tradition, has been fantasized as a maternal object whose elevation among women occurs only through her submission to the masculine ideal. Kari Borresen critiques this notion when she observes: "The figure of Mary is a patriarchal construct: virgin, wife, mother and adjunct to the male. She embodies the essential connection between femininity and subordination forged by the patriarchal mindset. To make her the model for free women is absurd, until that connection is broken."[16] Juxtaposing themselves against the patriarchal narrative, feminist scholars have more recently read and reinterpreted the textual body of Mary and deconstructed the myths surrounding the mother of Jesus in order that she might become more relevant to the lives of everyday women.

In their attempts to create a *Mary for all women,* feminist reinterpreters of this virgin-mother-goddess most often produce the story of a woman who is heroic on some readings, manipulated or exploited on others. Therefore, the attempt to construct a *Woman's Mary* in opposition to a *Mythological Mary*, while successful in resisting androcentric interpretations, usually splits her character into hero or victim, and thereby constructs a partial interpretation of Mary's virginity and motherhood.

Although my own reading of Mary stands firmly within a feminist hermeneutical tradition, my social location and my personal experience compel me to redirect my reading of this powerful mother. Solidarity with the feminist readings, my social location, and my personal experience compel me to interpret this powerful mother differently. As an Indian immigrant living in the United States, torn between feelings toward the land that has mothered me and the land that now sustains me, I find myself inhabiting a hyphenated space that at once belongs to both but at the same time, belongs to none. My hyphenated identity, defined through visas, immigration papers, borders, growing up within the Indian caste system and now having my otherness defined through race in the United States, permits me to live in between the lines and labels that seek to define me. This in-between space, my social (dis)location, social location, my interpretive lens, enables me to reinterpret the textual character of Mary, imprisoned within the black and white pages of the ancient infancy narratives. My goal is not to liberate the character of Mary for all women, but to merely use her textual body to reflect the blurred complexities present in the lives of many women in today's globalized, neocolonial economy. In other words, this interpretation of Mary's motherhood is based in the reality of globalization and neocolonial contexts. Within these contexts, Mary can no longer be seen as a hero or a victim, but rather a complex human mother whose ability to hold the dichotomies of her splintered character in tension with each other, personifies her divinity. Such a construction of Mary seeks to provide his transforming her subjectivity into that of a *victimized-hero* whose motherhood is performative of a *violent-love* as the crux through which all of humanity is saved.

This book is not only a homage to feminist scholarship on the biblical character of Mary, but is also my attempt to find a space for my own voice, my own interpretation of this *Mother of God*, as told from my complex sociocultural location. I survey some of the feminist interpretations of Mary's virginity in the New Testament——attempts to reject, defend, or explain that virginity and to liberate Mary from the interpretations of male scholars and theologians. I argue that these feminist interpretations regularly dichotomize Mary, as her body is presumed to fit into the predetermined societal categories of hero or victim. It seems to me that by shifting our focus away from the agenda of liberating the textual Mary for all women, we can begin to find ways to interpret this Biblical character differently——as her motherhood embodies an ambivalent love toward the Other. Mary's motherhood reflects the complexities of an *oppressed-liberation* that seems to be a reality for many women living in the global South.

It is important, however, to note that I am by no means seeking to liberate the character of Mary from the patriarchal or androcentric interpretations that have dominated the construction of this Holy Mother within the Christian tradition. Such a task has been taken up successfully by my feminist theological and biblical mothers and sisters who, drawing on their experiences and sensibilities as women, have constructed a more "gynocentric" versions of Mary.[17] Neither does my book seek to pronounce ethical judgments on the choices of the postcolonial Indian surrogate mothers by proposing that their actions be read through a lens either of exploitation or agency. Rather, I am arguing that decisions made by these mothers must be read more complexly and that the ambivalence performed in their maternal agency must be highlighted in order that the powerful binaries subjecting their maternal bodies into either/or interpretations can begin to be dismantled. Hardt and Negri, quoting Homi K. Bhabha, write: "The affirmation of difference and hybridity is itself, according to Bhabha, an affirmation of community: 'To live in the unhomely world, is to find its ambivalences and ambiguities in the house of fiction, or its sundering and splitting performed in the work of art, is also to affirm a profound desire for social solidarity.' "[18]

In exegetical terms, my intention is to highlight the ambivalence in the maternal choice performed by the textual character of Mary in the Matthean and especially the Lukan infancy narratives. The significance of such an interpretation is that it shifts the focus away from a homogeneous reading and pushes toward the redefinition of binary categories such as liberation versus oppression, where freedom almost always is contingent upon one's enslavement and choice, a reflection of systemic oppression that almost, but not quite, promises hope. But just as the Indian context will shed light on the gospel text, so too will the gospel text shed light on the Indian context. My reading of Mary's motherhood will work to shed light on the violent space in which women living under globalization find themselves——a violent space because it supplies a vision of hope but simultaneously demands that its participants embrace a different version of oppression. I reimagine early Christian images of Mary in ways that make her more relevant and fully adequate to the deep complexities, contradictions, and ambivalences of the lived realities of postcolonial Indian women. Such an interpretation is yet to be found in the works of feminist biblical and theological scholars.

Feminist discussions of Mary in the gospels of Matthew and Luke argue for interpretations informed by the lives of real women, so that the textual and traditional figure of Mary can be relevant to all women. However, the construction of such a Mary is possible only when her textual body is opened up to the contradictions of the lived realities of everyday women. These infancy narratives expose the vulnerability and empowerment of Indian women living in a globalized economy.

Feminist biblical and theological interpretations of Mary (the Lukan Mary, in particular) often find themselves divided over the interpretations of her consent. While one group interprets Mary's choice as being symbolic of her agency, as we shall see, and chooses to read her textual character as an independent woman who makes a choice about her own body, another group reads her consent to participate in this anomalous birth as signaling her manipulation and her victimization at the hands of patriarchy. Although both these interpretations are relevant and extremely poignant in resisting and highlighting the androcentric and patriarchal versions of Mary that have continued to dominate the Christian tradition, it seems to me that feminist discussions surrounding

Mary's choice or consent, gestures to a deeper issue. The dichotomous interpretations connected to Mary's description as a victim or a hero are intimately tied into the feminist biblical and theological scholar's own need to see Mary's motherhood through a dialectical lens. In other words, Mary's choice becomes fundamental for those feminists who read her conception as symbolic of her liberation because she *chooses* to participate in a reproduction that occurs outside the patriarchal norms of society.[19] In contrast, others interpret her participation in an anomalous birth as indicative of her oppression. They argue that the body of a young peasant woman is victimized and seduced by the powers of patriarchy as her reproductive capabilities are exploited so that the telos of salvation for all Israel may be achieved.[20] Such either/or interpretation fails to recognize the ambivalent agency performed in Mary's motherhood that subverts powerful binaries and constructs her maternal subjectivity differently.

The overarching framework of this book is not embedded only in a contextual and cultural biblical hermeneutics based on my sociocultural location as an Indian woman. I also use the globalized industry of surrogate motherhood in India both to explore the complex experiences of women living in a contemporary India (an India standing in the crosshairs of globalization and tradition) and to elucidate the gendered complexities of my chosen texts. More specifically, I listen to the textual voices of surrogate women, obtained through interviews and other articles in print media, to shed new light on questions surrounding Mary's choice, agency, and empowerment in the texts. In addition to using contextual and cultural criticism as my framework, I employ gender theory nuanced with categories of race, nation, and empire to interpret these primary texts.[21]

Throughout, the book critically surveys studies of Mary by both male and female biblical, theological, and philosophical scholars. I also examine the history of Mariological discourse as it pertains to the work of these scholars. Additionally, I highlight and address at length the gaps in the readings of Mary's maternal performance in the infancy narratives of Matthew and Luke, which I have begun to discuss above. Chapter 1 is divided into two sections titled "Surrogacy in Colonial India" and "Surrogacy in Postcolonial India"; as these titles suggest, this chapter looks at the history of surrogacy during both the British Empire and the current neocolonial Empire that is bound up with globalization. In colonial India, the practice of hiring wet nurses was well established and extremely popular. The close proximity between the Indian wet nurse, commonly known as the *ayah,* and the British child was the cause of much colonial anxiety. This is because representatives of the British Empire in India constantly worried about the contamination of the colonial subject by the Indian wet nurse. The next section looks at the growth of surrogacy in modern-day India, where the combination of technology and cheap labor construct it as the perfect destination for the reproductive tourism industry. This section also looks at the way the overt exploitation of the Indian women's bodies under the colonial empire has now become a subtle and more covert seduction of the post-colonial Indian woman. Globalization has created a new form of slavery in which the Indian surrogate mother is promised partial freedom on the condition that she willingly enslaves her body to the rich and powerful Western couples looking to hire her reproductive services.

Chapter 2 analyzes the infancy narrative of Matthew, in particular the five mothers present in the genealogy of Jesus. By placing those women, not least Mary herself, alongside Indian surrogate mothers, I begin to dismantle some of the binary interpretations that have confined these maternal figures in categories of victim or hero. This deconstructive reading sets the maternal performance of each of these women in an ambivalent light and depicts them as mothers who willingly submit to exploitation, so that they in turn may exploit the powers of patriarchy. Chapter 3 analyzes the infancy narrative of Luke, who places on Mary's lips a canticle exalting the Lord who has impregnated her. Here I read the character of Mary more single-mindedly, alongside and through the body of the Indian surrogate mother living and working in a postcolonial context, to focus on the ambivalence of her consent.

Finally, I look at Matthew's and Luke's Synoptic Marys together, in the context of the powers acting upon them, around them, and through them. The character of Joseph, present in Matthew's narrative has his own, rather, gendered concerns, which are echoed in the roles that surrogate mothers' husbands play today in India. The English-speaking fertility doctor acts as a hybrid subject, much as Luke's angel envoy pronounces to Mary, in the language of empire on behalf of the Hebrew Lord they both serve. Reading Mary's motherhood through the capitalized body of the Indian surrogate mother transforms Mary into a victimized hero, whose love for the other promises her only a partial freedom that both oppresses and liberates her at one and the same time.

As I discussed above, previous feminist readings of Mary, while helping to construct a *Mary for all women*, trimmed her character so that it neatly fits into binary categories—hero/victim, oppressed/liberated, violence/love etc.——and held her up as an object of identification for contemporary women. However, the question is whether such a dichotomous interpretation of Mary can indeed serve as an object of identification for women living lives that are incredibly complex, blurred, and, by no means clear-cut, such as women in contemporary India. Subjectivities formed in contexts of globalization are especially complex, blurred, and ambivalent as definitions of community and society expand from the local to the global.[22]

The expansion of technology and the ability to outsource labor has led to the development of a global community, in which, cultures and economies freely interacting with one another produce identities that can no longer be understood as linear or singular. A postcolonial reading of the Matthean and Lukan infancy narratives, performed in the context of globalization, resists binary depictions of Mary as it strives to construct her textual character as an ambivalent figure who mirrors the complexities of women under globalization. In other words, rather than liberate Mary for *all women*, a postcolonial reading of Mary, set in the context of globalization transforms her into the *all-woman* or global woman, with all the internal differences, contradictions, and ambivalences that entails. In this book, I am attempting to articulate a Mariological discourse shaped by my experience and relevant to me personally—a postcolonial Indian woman living in the United States and negotiating my identity in a global economy. Such a reading of Mary is yet to be found among feminist Mariological discourses.

Choice is ordinarily defined as the opportunity or privilege of choosing freely, and reflects individual freedom; but what if the freedom to choose promises an independence contingent upon one's enslavement? Mary, read through the living bodies of Indian surrogates, reflects a mother who resists the attempts to polarize her actions/choices into binary categories. She is a victimized hero who *willingly chooses to be used* by both God and her people. Interpreting Mary through the Indian surrogate's experience enables reflection on issues of choice, agency, and empowerment, especially in a global context. For both Mary and the Indian surrogate, choice promises freedom contingent on victimization. Thus, *choice* is never merely personal, but is also material and driven by the desire for a better life both for themselves and their families/people.

CHAPTER 1

Breast, Womb, Empire

Outsourcing is often understood as an invention of modern Empire, a byproduct of globalization. However, the notion of hiring racially othered laborers from a certain socioeconomic class under the guise of economic development and "civilizing" expansion is a concept as old as colonization itself. The modern surrogate mother living and working in a postcolonial India catches glimpses of herself in the reflection of the textual body of the *amah* and the *dhaye/ayah*.[1] These women living in colonial India and hired by the Empire, particularly the British memsahibs,[2] become foster-mothers to the future progeny of the Empire. Thus, while for the modern surrogate mother it is the womb that marks the point of contact between the self and the other, for the colonized *amah/ayah* it is the brown breast/body that binds the oppressor with the oppressed, uniting them and making them one.

The colonized surrogate mother played a significant role in the growth of the British Empire. However, that same maternal body hired to perform the duties of a surrogate becomes the site for constant suspicion, anxiety, and control, given the *ayah*'s high degree of access to the infant—its body and its growing psychological sensibilities. As Chaudhuri writes, "Although the sheer sense of need for help in raising infants forced memsahibs to hire Indian servants, nonetheless the memsahibs could not overcome their racial prejudice. They were always apprehensive of the intimate relationship between the ayah and the infant."[3] The colonized mother's ability to slip through boundaries of race, class, and gender by sliding back and forth between the public sphere and the private sanctum of imperial power caused a stir in the colonizer's consciouness. Indrani Sen notes that the female *ayah* and the female wet nurse specifically made the memsahib's household authority less than total. They enjoyed intimacies with the up-and-coming colonial generation that the memsahib had, it was true, abdicated, but nonetheless, her shortcomings—the inability to do it all—were nowhere more exposed than in the nursery.[4] While these maternal figures were seen as being necessary for the growth and the maintenance of the Empire, their presence also risked the potential corruption of the imperial mind resulting in the disintegration of the Empire.

Scholars have often subjected the narratives of the colonial and the postcolonial Indian surrogate mothers to independent interrogation and as a result the development of the surrogate practice in India has been for the most part ignored. For this reason, tracing the entire history of surrogacy in India sheds light on some of the connections between past and present maternal bodies. One such connection that comes to light, as we shall see, is both surrogate mothers (colonial and the postcolonial) are hired by the Empire to serve as gestation sites for the colonizer.

The purpose of this chapter is twofold. First, it attempts to reconstruct the historical figure of the colonial surrogate mother in India. Second, it tries to show that the impact and the implications of surrogate motherhood in postcolonial India are illuminated when set against the backdrop of the "colonial anxieties" precipitated by the colonial surrogate. In other words, these residual colonial anxieties are implicitly addressed under the pretext of technology in the contemporary business of surrogate motherhood in India. The ideology behind the business of surrogate outsourcing in India is better understood when read in the light of the colonial surrogate mothers hired to "m/other" the British Empire.

At Home in the Empire: The Private Mimics the Public

Constructing the history of the colonial surrogate mother relies heavily on one-sided accounts penned by the British memsahibs. This means that while the Empire acknowledges the presence of the colonized *amah/ayah*, her voice, unfortunately (but not surprisingly), has been erased from the pages of Indian colonial history. The erasure of the Indian surrogate from texts not only allows for a partial historical construction of the colonized mother, a fetishized object who is at once feared and desired, but also points to the imbalance of power in an already oppressed group—that is, women, in the colonial arena. While European men asserted themselves at the top of all hierarchies—racial and gender, most obviously—their female counterparts occupied grayer spaces, enacting colonialism but being subjugated within the very power structure that they were imposing.[5] The ambiguous position of the European woman becomes apparent as she oscillates between being an oppressor to being oppressed. These roles are continuously redefined in her ability to move back and forth between the private and the public realm. The one place that, in effect, transforms the white woman from a *Memsahib* (lady boss) to a *Sahib* (the male boss) is her colonial home. The image of the memsahib as a forlorn woman—having traveled far from her home community and all of that community's industrial luxuries—vulnerable to the dangers of an unknown world narrates only half of *her-story* in the *his-story* of British colonialism in India. In other words, the British memsahib's role in the Empire is one of ambivalence because as her subjectivity oscillates between points of being a passive victim and an active dictator, she moves from being the one who is victimized to the one who can now victimize. The domestic sphere becomes for the British memsahib, a miniature Empire in which she rules over the native servants with absolute and unconditional imperial authority with little or no interference from her largely absent husband, all the while remaining subordinate to the white male in the public realm.

Evidence of the public subservience of the memsahibs to the Empire is found in colonial narratives. For example, similar to the Indian surrogate mother whose significance to the Empire was rendered invisible, the British memsahib's role is reduced to a stereotype in the male narratives. Thus, the importance of the British memsahib in the national ideology of the Empire is thereby underplayed.[6] Rudyard Kipling, Denis Kincaid, Suresh Ghosh, and others depicted the memsahib as a lazy and passive woman whose sole purpose was to find a husband or to be a respectable wife, and those are the dominant historical (even if fictional) voices on the matter because household duties over which a memsahib might have exercised total authority tend not to be documented in any official way.[7] In addition to this, the British memsahib also gets the reputation of being a "colonial separatist." The white female body was a lightning rod for the fear of contamination and corruption, prompting "the white communities to tighten their ranks, clarify their boundaries and mark out their social space."[8] As a result, efforts to protect the British memsahibs from the imagined, unbridled sexuality of the natives are stepped up as lines pertaining to race, class, and gender are redrawn, usually to the exclusion of nonwhites, who are suspected of wanting to violate the white man's prize, the white woman. The sexuality of the white woman living alone in an alien land and being surrounded by natives is continuously threatened.

As the object of the "brown gaze," the British memsahib is constructed as a fetishized passive subject whose safety must be ensured at any cost. However, her protection is intimately intertwined with the sentiments of nationalism and imperial ideology, which configure the brown-black man as a sexual predator.[9] The white female body of the memsahib becomes the passive object exposed to the colonized man's active and penetrating gaze. Sequestering the British memsahib away from the native men becomes a key feature of nationalist imperialism[10] and so the European woman—fetishized by white men vicariously, through their fetishization of nonwhite men's fabled lusts—is constructed as a passive object powerless not only under the active gaze of the natives, but also incapable of exercising control over her own self. Thus it was pertinent that "male colonizers positioned European women as the bearers of a redefined colonial morality" (Ann Stoler: Making the Empire Respectable).[11] The question one needs to ask is, does the production of the passive British memsahib, anxious about her sexuality and the lustful eyes of the "Other," reprise a historically accurate role in the colonial Empire?

Colonial homes in British India served a dual purpose in that they not only protected the sexual purity of the British memsahib, but became places where the memsahib could exercise her imperial authority and power over the natives, as she tries "to replicate the empire on a domestic scale."[12] At the same time, restructuring the domestic sphere to resemble the power structures of the Empire permitted the conversion of the British memsahib from a passive object into an active subject. In other words, the colonial home becomes a space where the gaze is displaced as the once "observed object" now becomes the "observing subject."[13] The British memsahib's displaced gaze, then, constructs the native who is disciplined, fashioned, and styled to satiate her visual pleasure. The deconstruction of the native Indian enables the reconstruction of a new Indian identity, a subject who is more Anglo in nature and therefore less threatening to the Empire.

The responsibility of producing a native subject styled, educated, and formed in the Imperial ideology rests solely on the delicate, white shoulders of the memsahib. This also means that the once sexually aggressive native threatening to penetrate the memsahib, now becomes the penetrated object exposed to the piercing white gaze of the memsahib as his/her body is disciplined to perform as an "Anglicized Indian." Similarly, the walls separating the public from the private also mark the transition in the role of the British memsahib. In other words, the passive *gori mem*,[14] exposed to the sexually aggressive brown-black man outside her home, fulfills her national duty to the Empire by becoming an active dictator within her home and creating copies of Anglicized native Indians.[15]

Colonial women played a significant role in furthering the imperial agenda of the Empire. The production of children for the growth of the Empire was seen as the primary responsibility of the British memsahib, the ability to run a household that replicated the workings of the larger Empire was seen as being equally important: "there are doors to be locked; corridors to be periodically dusted; rooms to be fumigated and made free of pests; children (i.e., 'natives') to be doctored, educated, clothed, and disciplined; accounts to be kept; boundaries redrawn and fences mended."[16] As we have already seen, the colonial home was not only a site that protected the British memsahib, but was also a space that allowed for the transformation of the European woman from powerless victim to an imperial dictator: "Housekeeping in the colonies is often represented as a military/imperial campaign."[17] The politicization of the domestic sphere constructs colonial women as guardians of imperial culture. The representation of the Anglo woman as a brave soul, faithfully following the calling of her country, contradicts the textual narratives that often describe her as an appendage to the colonial Empire:

> What would India be without England, and what would the British Empire be without Englishwomen? To these women are due gratitude not only of their country but of the civilized world. Fearlessly the woman of British birth looks in the eye of danger. Faithfully and with willing sacrifice she upholds the standard of the King-Emperor—the standard of culture and of service to humanity.[18]

At the same time, the responsibility of the British memsahib as the bearer of tradition does not stop with her embodiment of the imperial culture, but her service lies in her ability to spread and teach the ways of the Empire to the natives.

The colonial home therefore becomes a site that aids in the conception of minds created to imbibe the imperial culture and mimic it as Homi Bhabha has so well explicated.[19] While Bhabha's work exposes and focuses on the mimic man performing his "Britishness" in the public domain, my work emphasizes on the construction of the domesticated Anglicized woman/man solely produced by the British memsahib. The colonial home mirroring the British Empire mimicked its imperial and racial power structures by regulating behaviors and maintaining distance between the colonizers and the natives. The invisible yet powerful lines demarcating the colonizer from the colonized based on race, gender, and class become the premise upon which the colonial home is erected. Domestic spheres strived to mimic the larger Empire by reproducing the racial binaries and creating power imbalances between the colonizer and the colonized, with the servants' dwelling placed far from the colonial homesteaders' bungalows.[20] Sen writes that the "safe distance" between living quarters "racialised the compound and reinforced race/class hierarchies."[21] The object of racial binaries in the colonial home not only meant the separation of the subject from the object, but also the elevation of the once-inferior white woman to a superior British memsahib:

> The fact that Western women were considered the inferior sex in the superior race meant that there was a lot at stake in feminists' quest to identify themselves and their cause with British national-imperial enthusiasm, politics, and glory. Primarily it worked to undermine the Victorian construction of woman as Other by identifying her with the Self of nation and empire.[22]

The racial superiority of the British memsahib in the colonial context not only constructed the natives as the "inferior" other, but also justified the Empire's need to duplicate the white colonizer's morality on the home turf.[23] The private mimicking the public is where the white identity of the British woman is constructed as subjectivity.

The selfhood of the British memsahib is further enhanced when her imperial authority is used to discipline and punish the natives under her rule. As a creator of the Anglo-Indian subject, the mimic man of the Empire, the British memsahib needed to closely monitor the excess slippage,[24] which at times could lead to the eruption of the Indian native. It was moments of such slippage—any exaggerated Britishness, any behavior that made the empire seem foolish or, God forbid, eccentric—that called for the strict discipline and punishment of the natives. The servants in the colonial home were depicted as childlike beings that needed to be guided in their domestic duties by the British memsahibs. In a 1904 colonial tome *The Complete Indian Housekeeper and Cook*, Anne Flora Steel and Grace Gardiner write:

> The first duty of a mistress is, of course, to be able to give intelligible orders to her servants; therefore it is necessary she should learn to speak Hindustani....
>   The next duty is obviously to insist on her orders being carried out... "How is this to be done?"...The secret lies in making rules and keeping to them. The Indian servant is a child in everything but age......[F]irst faults should never go unpunished.[25]

The Anglicized Indian man speaking the language of the colonizer is described as an intelligent mimic man enthusiastically absorbing the qualities of the "better" culture. On the contrary, the British memsahib's attempt to speak the Indian language is described more as an act of necessity, or "as motivated by an unpolitical, often purely aesthetic/linguistic, interest in an alien culture."[26] The best example of this can be seen in Maud Diver's colonial guide to home management in which she writes, "Surely no sight could be more pitiful and ludicrous than that of a woman who has given place to wrath, and is powerless to put into words; nor can any one ever hope to keep a retinue of a dozen servants under control."[27] The native language then becomes a tool that is used to control the mind of the "savages" and create harmony in the colonial home; it is the language of necessity spoken only to communicate orders. This is unlike the imperial language, the language of sophistication, culture, and superiority taught to the colonized in order to civilize them and teach them the imperial ways.

The infantilization of the native servants led to the creation of harsh punishments and rewards. Steel and Gardiner write, "But it will be asked, How are we to punish our servants when we have no hold on their minds or bodies?—when cutting their pay is illegal, and few, if any, have any sense of shame. The answer is obvious. Make a hold."[28] Likening the workings of the Indian household to the Indian Empire, a chaotic domain, this domestic manual compared memsahibs to "public servants in India."[29] As a part of their duty the manual instructed them to "go on a regular inspection round the compound,"[30] "maintain monthly audits," and keep "written accounts showing their total yearly receipts and expenditures,"[31] and manage the servants of the house by creating a system of "balance of rewards and punishments."[32] The punishments administered to the servants by the British memsahib created a hierarchy among the natives. Steel and Gardiner note:

> This is considered a great joke, and exposes the offender to much ridicule from his fellow-servants; so much so that the words, "Memsahib tum ko zuroor kaster ile pila dena hoga" (The Memsahib will have to give you castor oil), is often heard in the mouths of the upper servants when new-comers give trouble. In short, without kindly and reasonable devices of this kind, the usual complaint of a want of hold over servants must remain true until they are educated in some sense of duty.[33]

The memsahib ensured the smooth running of her household by balancing the punishments with proper rewards. Marangoly George observes

some of the methods employed by the memsahib to create a successful system of rewards: "The trick is to engage servants at the lowest
rate possible and then offer some extra as—buksheesh—conditional
on good service."[34] The infantile state of the native servant is further
enhanced with the incorporation of rewards and punishments by the
British memsahib. The giving of rewards in the form of "buksheesh"
exposes the greedy nature of the native servants and reinforces the colonial stereotype of the native—a greedy, lustful caricature of a savage,
who must be controlled through punishment and rewards. A successful
household in the colony also meant learning when to relax the reins
of domesticity by disavowing some of the actions of the natives and
tightening the controls by acknowledging their mistakes: the memsahib
must "learn not to see all that comes in the ways of her eyes; for with
natives, as with children, the art of not seeing, practiced sparingly and
judiciously, will go far to preserve domestic peace."[35] The discipline of
the natives by the memsahib under the guise of "civilizing the Indian
man into mimic Anglo man" not only helps in producing a domesticated replica of the Empire but eases the "white" anxiety of the colonizer constantly threatened by sexual prowess of the brown-black man.

Homes to the Empire: Nursing the British Raj

In her essay "'Breastgiver': For Author, Reader, Teacher, Subaltern,
Historian...," Gayatri Chakravorty Spivak dismantles the stringent categories of history and literature. Spivak points to the short stories written by Mahasweta Devi as examples where history imagined into fiction
permits the subaltern to move away from being viewed as a historical
object to finally becoming a subject.[36] Colonial surrogate motherhood[37]
in India blurs the lines between fact and fiction as voices of colonized
mothers lost in the pages of history surface as fictional subjects in literature, film, and art. Spivak notes, "Fiction of this sort relies for its effect
on its "effect of the real. The plausibility of a Jashoda ('Stanadayini'
or 'Breast-giver'), a Draupadi ('Draupadi'), a Birsa Munda (Aranyer
Adhikar) is that, they could have existed as subalterns in a specific historical moment imagined and tested by orthodox assumptions."[38] As a
result, while the use of wet nurses in India was a "reality," the entrance
into their world necessarily relies on the "imaginary." Indrani Sen writes,
"Medical handbooks, without fail, obliterated the 'native' from their
discourse. Medical handbooks or medical manuals written by colonial
physicians were used as guides that helped colonial subjects navigate the
treacherous and the unpredictable terrains of the East.[39] It is striking

how Indians were completely invisibilised in medical manuals, the sole 'native' to find mention being the wet nurse, also referred to variously as the *dai* or *amah*."[40] While the mere presence of the *dai/amah* in such manuals bears witness to their historical existence within the Empire, their lack of voice in these writings is proof of their marginalization and subaltern status. The body of the Indian wet nurse is transformed into an object under the Empire's gaze, her breasts are used to provide nourishment and sustain the imperial infant, but her voice silenced, erased, and kept out of history ensured that she never attained her subjectivity. Spivak writes, "If 'the need to make the subaltern classes the subject of their own history [has, among other] themes . . . provided a fresh critical thrust to much recent writing on modern Indian history and society,' then a text about the (im)possibility of 'making' the subaltern gender the subject of its own story seems to me to have a certain pertinence."[41] As a result, the Indian wet nurse appearing in fictional narratives such as Devi's *Breast Giver*, and Mary Sherwood's *Little Henry and His Bearer*, and *Lucy and Her Dhaye* permits these fictional mothers to become subjects of their own history. Therefore, it seems to me that in order to acknowledge these colonized mothers as historical subjects and step out of their subaltern statuses we must, as Spivak says, allow "history and literature to critically interrupt each other, and bring each other to crises."[42] In short, the body of the Indian wet nurse, objectified, silenced, and erased from colonial history, reappears in literature as her voice, critically interrupting our postcolonial imagination in order that we may visualize her as a subject of her own story.

Motherhood in the colonial Empire was placed at the "center of . . . empire building" as we have seen; this meant that childbearing was depicted as a woman's "national, imperial, and racial duty."[43] The British memsahib as the generator of the future progenitors of the Empire played a vital role in the preservation of Imperial power. Because it was so much more precarious an endeavor outside Britain,[44] giving birth in the alien land increased the memsahib's nervousness. The colonizer perceived India as an exotic yet dangerous land representing the potential death of the British body. The blistering heat of the tropics becomes a topic of fear and dissension as it takes on its own character in colonial writings. As Edward John Tilt[45] observes, "We could conquer India, but we succumb to its climate." He also notes the climate's adverse effect on women's health by highlighting "a marked effect on the reproductive organs of British women" living in India, suggesting that they became easy targets to miscarry, especially "during the hot season." At the same time, while some argued that the heat threatened the existence of the

British memsahib and affected her ability to conceive, others pointed to the benefits of the tropical climate especially on British infants. One of the memsahibs argues, "In many respects, India is a more healthy country for very young children than England. How rarely is there an instance of bronchitis, croup, or any lung disease, and how slight in general are the infantine disorders of measles and whooping-cough."[46] However this view was countered by other authors who continued to hold the opinion that the Indian climate had adverse effects on women's health and threatened their existence.

Into this climate came British women who, by virtue of the advances in Western obstetrics, were more divorced from the mechanics of childbirth than ever before. The lack of Western medicine enhanced India's image as a backward, superstitious land and justified the unequal power relationship. This "flexible superiority"[47] of the West over the East constructed power on a slippery slope that needed to be defended by the colonizers. In other words, the West's inability to control the climate and the diseases of the East meant that it was not only a *flexible* but a *fragile* superior power in need of constant vigilance and protection. This fragility of the British Empire is exposed when the topics of infant mortality and colonial motherhood in India are discussed.[48] It is for this reason that the preservation of European life in the colonized tropical climate, intertwined with the conception and protection of the future race of imperial subjects, becomes a significant task for both the Empire and the British memsahib.

This perception of India as a land symbolic of death and destruction threatening the existence of the colonizer needed to be countered with a view of an insider: a person who could at once belong to both the colonizer and the colonized. The nineteenth-century Anglo-Indian newspaper *The Pioneer* describes the role of the ayah (wet nurse/nanny) as follows: "The Ayah smooths down the rough surfaces of life in India . . . [T]he servants see their mistress through the Ayah . . . and the mistress sees the servants humanized through the intelligible womanly instincts of the Ayah."[49] The ayah's ability to seamlessly transgress the boundaries between the self and other constructs her as a site/sight of colonial anxiety.

Colonial motherhood is constructed through a dialectical relationship as the two mothers (one of the Empire and the other for the Empire) are pitted against each other. While the British memsahib is credited for the conception and delivery of the future of the Empire, it is the Indian wet nurse who is responsible for the growth and the nourishment of the white subject. Quoting from the source titled "Domestic

Guide to Mothers in India" Chaudhuri writes, "While critical of using Indian midwives, physicians had no hesitancy in strongly recommending Indian wet nurses: '-no infant thrives so well as those fed by these women.' "[50] The "weak" imperial infant needed the Indian wet nurse to guarantee its survival. At the same time, the pink/white mouth of the colonizer sucking on the brown breast of the Indian wet nurse becomes a site/sight where interactions between the colonizer and the colonized overturn relationships of race, power, and superiority as the symbiotic relationship between the self and the other is established.

The brownish-black nipple connecting the colonizer to the colonized needed to be brought under the white gaze of the Empire via Western medicine. Prior to being hired, the *ayah* would need a detailed checkup of her body. In her fictional narrative "The Breast Giver," Mahasweta Devi fantasizes about the body of the *ayah* metamorphing into a sacred human-animal being: "Mrs. Haldar [Jashoda's mistress] believes that the more the cow eats, the more milk she gives. Jashoda's place in the house is now above the Mother Cows. The Mistress's sons become incarnate *Brahma*[51] and create progeny. Jashoda preserves the progeny."[52] While Devi explicitly links the body of Jashoda to the cow—the holy animal worshiped and revered by Indian society—and openly threatens to dismantle the barriers separating the human from the animal, this connection is far more subtle within medical handbooks of colonial physicians.

Sen, quoting from Joseph Ewart's "Goodeve's Hints for the General Management of Children in India, in the Absence of Professional Advice," writes, "Goodeve advised that she [the *amah*] should have 'smooth, sleek skin ... well-nourished frame; a clear eye; a clean tongue; good appetite ... and also urged that she should be 'temperate in her habits, both as regards food, drink and smoking.' "[53] The examination of the *amah* does not end with the close examination of her body; in fact this inspection is extended to her offspring: "the amah should look 'young and healthy and her infant fat and well."[54] At the same time, the amah bearing a child also meant keeping a close watch on the relationship of the Indian mother and the child by making sure that the brown breast hired to feed the white subject of the Empire does not divert its attention into suckling the native child.[55] Moreover, the colonial anxiety unleashed onto the body of the amah and her child now gets redirected to the breast of the Indian wet nurse, the source that produces the milk for the Empire.

The colonized breast of the Indian wet nurse becomes a site/sight of vigilant scrutiny by the western physicians as they suggest that "the amah's breasts should ideally be plump, full and firm ... with nipples of sufficient size and length."[56] In addition to the breast, the milk produced by the wet nurse is also subjected to colonial control: her milk should "flow freely, on the nipples being gently compressed, whilst it should be of a bluish color, and yielding a generous cream on being collected in quantity and being allowed to cool in the open air."[57] The medical inspection of the wet nurse was justified by the Empire by highlighting her greedy and manipulative behavior. Colonial physicians warned mothers against "common deceptive practices adopted by prospective wet nurses such as passing off of someone else's healthy baby as their own, or presenting their breasts full of milk by not drawing out the milk for hours before 'inspection' and so on."[58] Some of the physicians advised the memsahibs to protect themselves from deceptive *amahs* by providing the following solution: "In all cases the amah should be made to draw of half a wineglassful of her milk at her first examination in the presence of the mistress, every attention being at the time paid to the nature of the flow."[59]

While on the one hand the wet nurse was depicted as being integral to the Empire, she was also portrayed as a servant who manipulated her importance within the Empire.[60] British memsahibs complained about the outrageous demands of the wet nurses, which began with salary hikes and spread into caste complications of the amah that further disrupted the workings of the colonial home. From one of the letters of a memsahib:

> The amah is a caste woman, and her whims are the plague of my life: I am obliged to keep a cook on purpose for her, because her food must all be dressed by a person of her own caste; and even then she will sometimes starve all day rather than eat it, if she fancies anybody else has been near it: she has a house built of coca-nut leaves in the compound, on purpose to cook her food in.[61]

For the most part, the wet nurses within the Empire belonged to low-caste Hindu or Muslim communities.[62] However, the hire of wet nurses from lower caste or other religions did not solve the complications of the caste system. Emma Roberts, an English author who had traveled to India and wrote a book titled *Scenes and Characteristics of Hindoostan in 1835*, makes the point that Muslim wet nurses also followed caste prejudices that they had "acquired from their Hindoo associates."[63] In addition, Roberts also complained that these wet nurses would use the excuse of "pollution from the touch of the European infants in order to extract extra compensatory money for purchasing their reinstatement to caste."[64] It is important to note that while the demands of the *amah* enabled depiction of her as a manipulative, tyrannizing servant, her ability to negotiate the terms of her employment gives the readers a glimpse into her relative independence within the colonial home.

In other words, the "milk mother" to the Empire now becomes the mother who milks the Empire in return for her services. By recognizing the importance of her milk to the Empire, the *amah* constructs her own space within the colonial home by exercising her freedom to negotiate her terms of slavery. The fact is that the powerlessness memsahibs felt[65] reflects the great value of what the *ayahs* provided to these outsiders who had chosen to dwell on Indian soil, with Indian climates, customs, and infrastructure. It is important to note, however, that while the manipulations of the Indian wet nurses gesture to their "freedom" to negotiate their role within the Empire, their "independence" cannot be recognized without acknowledging the harsh reality that these womens' breasts, brought under the control of the colonial economy, become objects that pay the price of liberation. In short, the breasts of the wet nurses as "objectified Subjects" enable the partial liberation of these women.

The milk produced by the objectified body of the native woman becomes the life force of the Empire, but it is at the cost of the Indian infants born to these professional milk mothers. In her discussion of the text "The Life" written by Mrs. Mary Sherwood, Joyce Grossman notes that the *ayahs*' breastmilk being diverted meant that their own babies often went malnourished or even died.[66] Mahasweta Devi's narrative of the "Breast-Giver" also plays on the concept of the "borrowed breast." The protagonist redefines her breasts as objects of value, transforming them into a site of economic gain. Jashoda, a Brahmin woman,[67] uses her breasts as a working tool that feeds the children of her masters. Devi writes, "Jashoda was a mother by profession, professional mother. Jashoda was not an amateur mama like the daughters and wives of the master's house. The world belongs to the professional."[68] The professional motherly role is not only accepted by Jashoda wholeheartedly, but also becomes a way of constructing her motherhood as being complete and a source of pride. The conversion is something Spivak has theorized: once a body or body part is seen to hold worth, it is first idealized and then commodified.[69] The surplus milk sold by Jashoda and other Indian wet nurses to the Empire's/Master's offspring incorporates their breasts within the colonial economy by placing them in a direct relationship between demand and supply.

One source of relief for the British memsahib with the wet nurse was the latter's short-term presence in the colonial home.[70] The use of the surrogate mother as a mode of survival is always accompanied with an anxiety that threatens to contaminate the "colonizing self." For example, in the tale *Henry and His Bearer,* Henry is cared for by a male surrogate named Boosy. Grossman writes, "—although Boosy's title as 'bearer' identifies his job as that of hoisting a palanquin, he superintends Henry's care."[71] The close relationship between the British child and the Indian surrogate parent becomes a constant source of worry to the British mother and is made frighteningly vivid when the memsahib starts seeing Boosy as effeminate, someone who bore her child— meaning that her child is raised in a gender-confused, culture-confused relationship.[72] The fusion between Henry and Boosy leads to the fear that too much contact with the "degenerate" natives could transform the male colonizer into a degenerate, feminized body. While Boosy is depicted as being solid and unimpressionable in that he does not take on the identity of Henry/Empire, the body of Henry is illustrated as being fluid and impressionable, thereby necessitating protection from the Indian surrogate. As Stoler suggests, "Servants could steal more than the sexual innocence of European children. They could redirect their cultural longings, the smells they preferred, the tastes they craved and their sexual desires."[73] Thus the separation of the child from its surrogate mother (or in this case its surrogate father) becomes an important step in the construction of the colonizer's identity. The Indian surrogate becomes a site of contradiction needed/desired and at the same time repelled/feared by the Empire, constructing them as ambivalent bodies that are at once disdained and loved.

The colonial fear that the intimate relationship between the *ayah* and the British child could lead to the construction of a "British subject" who was not quite white was a real one.[74] In particular, the Indian language flowing from the mouth of the British child threatened to contaminate not only the child's mind but also the subjectivity of the British self, the British "I."[75] The British mother's own lack of facility with the Indian language estranged her from the child's relationship with his primary caregiver, further increasing her apprehension and her growing sense that the child would need to be sent back to the British Isles for education and health reasons.[76] The British mother and her *lack* of knowledge of the Indian language places her subjectivity outside the realm of formation. The common language shared between the Indian *ayah* and the British child constructs them as the "I" differentiating the English-speaking mother as the "Non I/You." This would mean that the subjectivity of the British child constructed through the Indian language transforms it into a menacing hybrid (Indian-British) threatening the hierarchical binary oppositions on which Imperial power depends.

The intensifying ideology of race, of blood, coincided with a sense that native influences could corrupt otherwise "pure" English people—whose authority in fact rested in the idea of full racial superiority.[77] In the historical context of imperial India, the "contaminated tongue" of the colonial child pitted against the "pure tongue" of the Mother-Empire threatens its existence and its right to rule over those natives who now become a part of the Empire as opposed to being apart from it. The very "foundations of empire" were at stake in the blurring of cultural boundaries between European children and their Indian caregivers.[78] It is this emergence of a British subject as a hybrid, degenerate native that causes anxiety within the mind of the Mother-Empire. Thus the history of surrogate mothers in India under the British rule was constructed around their ability to play host to another's body, as their subjectivity revolved around their capacity to produce milk and become maternal caregivers. This transformed them into sometimes glorified, sometimes derided, and always ambiguous subjects of the Empire.

Conclusion

The sight of the white infant latching onto the brown breast or body of the *ayah/amah,* symbolizes that the colonizing other has found a native home in the body of the *ayah/dhaye.* In other words, the hired body of the colonial *ayah/amah* living in the colonial home, figurative of a "home within a home," locates the sight/site of simultaneous colonial anxiety and colonial control. At the same time, the private *oikos* as a reflection of the public *polis* under the reign of the British memsahib is brought under the control of Empire, and as we see this control extended to the retinue of servants working in her colonial home. Spivak notes that one of the most important critiques of Marxist theory of labor by feminist groups is its inability to take into account "sexual reproduction . . . when speaking of social reproduction or the reproduction of labor-power."[79] The sexual reproduction of the *ayah/amah* brought under the colonial control allows for the appropriation of her body into the colonial economy of the Empire.[80] The lactating breast of the *amah,* as well as the motherly gestures of the *ayah* in the colonial home "extracted and appropriated" by the colonial Empire within the "extended domesticated economy," allows for the insertion of women's sexual reproductive power into the economy of labor. However, this interjection of the colonial surrogate mother into the power structures of the Empire is only possible through the domestication of the colonial home.

At the same time, this absorption of the *ayah/amah/dhaye* into the colonial home and the appropriation of her services by the Empire intensify the anxieties of the colonizer. In that, the construction of the colonial home as a microcosm of Empire is threatened by the native surrogate mother who is hired to "house" the colonizing British subject. Therefore the "domestic within the domestic" becomes a space immune to colonial control, thereby risking the contamination and therefore the degeneration of the infantile mind of the British subject and, by extension, the British Empire. While British memsahibs were credited for the conception of the future of the Empire, it was the "hired bodies" of Indian wet nurses/maternal caregivers that nourished the progeny of colonial power. This resulted in the body of the colonized surrogate mother becoming a kind of necessary evil, both desired and derided by the British Empire. As we shall see in the next chapter, this colonial anxiety persists in the new postcolonial Empire of globalization to construct the Indian surrogate mother through an ambivalent lens of desire and disdain.

CHAPTER 2

Desired Mothers, Discounted Mothers: The Postcolonial Surrogate Mother Emerges

While colonial contexts prided themselves in separating the colonized from the colonizer using racial, economic, and geographical boundaries, the new global Empire, disguised under the prospect of economic progress, shatters barriers of such separation and creates desire for a new kind of liberation among Third World countries. This liberation, while promising economic emancipation and racial equality, is contingent upon the voluntary submission to exploitation. At the same time, penetrable borders cause anxiety for the global Empire as it allows for an unsupervised mixing leading to the creation of heterogeneous subjectivities. As Michael Hardt and Antonio Negri point out, "The dark side of the consciousness of globalization is the fear of contagion."[1] Contaminated subjects, as a result, become excellent sites for economic opportunity as their hybrid subjectivities make them desirable subjects that at once belong, but not quite, to the new Empire.

Countries such as India and China have enthusiastically embraced the phenomenon of globalization with the hope for economic stability and an opportunity to compete with the First World. This has especially been the case with India whose economy under globalization has blossomed as outsourced labor from the First World, creating employment opportunities for Third World individuals, thus promising hope for an economic liberation. Thus with India's ability to fashion itself as a country that provides cheap, reliable labor to First World multinational companies, the seamless transition from outsourcing physical labor to actual reproductive labor comes as no surprise as the business of surrogacy in India begins to boom. Women's bodies have played and continue to play an important role in a capitalistic, consumer-driven market. In an economy that is predominantly driven by needs, wants, and desires, financially desperate individuals find themselves participating in the capitalistic mind-set as they *will* the exploitation of their own bodies in the hope for a temporary economic emancipation.

Culturally we are trained to revere mothers, as motherhood is depicted as the hardest, most selfless job in the world, a job, nevertheless, women ought to want in order to complete themselves and become whole. I do not mean to suggest that the role of mothers and their sacrifice is insignificant in our society, nor am I trying to say that all women become mothers in order to complete themselves. But it is important to point out that motherhood in our society is socially constructed as the true vocation of womanhood, and as a result women's bodies are pressured (sometimes subtly and sometimes not so subtly,) to accept this role wholeheartedly. In her book *Politics of the Female Body* Ketu Kartrak argues that women living in postcolonial contexts often become contradictory sites of oppression and resistance. She points to the struggle that the woman faces in traditional societies such as postcolonial India,in attempting to seek an identity outside the role of being a mother. Motherhood, in the Indian context, is seen as a blessing, a gift from God, and the only true identity of a woman. Kartrak remarks, "Female lives are governed by anticipation and attainment of motherhood."[2] It is this social need to feel complete that causes women to enact their desires in some of the most bizarre fashions. In her essay "Outcast Mothers and Surrogates: Racism and Reproductive Politics in the Nineties," Angela Davis exposes the economic factors in reproductive technologies that deepen the racial and poverty lines in our society, dividing woman against woman. Davis writes:

> Women who can afford to take advantage of the new technology—who are often career women for whom motherhood is no longer a primary or exclusive vocation—now encounter a mystification of maternity emanating from the possibility of transcending biological (and socially defined) reproductive incapacity. It is as if the recognition of infertility is now a catalyst—among some groups of women—for a motherhood quest that has become more compulsive and more openly ideological than during the nineteenth century.[3]

The heady combination of money, technology, and choice leads women to aggressively seek out bodies of other women who can help fulfill their desire for motherhood. Davis continues:

While working-class women are not often in the position to explore the new technology, infertile women—or the wives/partners of infertile men—who are financially able to do are increasingly expected to try everything. They are expected to try in vitro fertilization, embryo transplants, surrogacy. The availability of the technology further mythologizes motherhood as the true vocation of women."[4]

It is this expectation to fulfill the need for motherhood that causes a rise in the practice of surrogacy in the Third World context. In other words, Third World countries provide the perfect context, as the combination of technology and cheap labor creates the ideal breeding ground for the consumer-driven business of reproduction. While the surrogacy business, especially in India, tailors itself as an industry in which *women help women*, the reality of a racial, economic, and class/caste divide between the Third World and the First World illustrates a more sinister operation hidden under the disguise of globalization. "The global politics of difference established by the world market is defined not by free play and equality," Hardt and Negri write, "but by the imposition of new hierarchies, or really by a constant process of hierarchization."[5] The presence of the New Empire casts an ambiguous light on issues of exploitation and liberation, as the lines of separation are not as clear as they seem. Davies likewise observes, "This commodification of motherhood is quite frightening in the sense that it comes forth as permission to allow women and their partners to participate in a program that is generative of life."[6] The body of the Indian surrogate offering her services to financially superior women (from both First and Third Worlds) blurs the lines between oppression and liberation, as her womb, exchanged for a price, is placed at the center of global economy.

As we have already seen, surrogacy is not an entirely new phenomenon. As a matter of fact one can catch glimpses of these women throughout the pages of history. For example, one can trace the existence of surrogate mothers in the Hebrew Bible, the most famous one being that of Sarah, the wife of Abraham, who engages the services of Hagar, her Egyptian slave, to conceive a child (Gen. 16). Additionally in the Hebrew Bible, we find the character of Rachel, the barren wife of Jacob, who hires her maid Bilhah to serve as her surrogate so that the lineage of her husband may continue (Gen. 30:1–8). Evidence of surrogacy is also found in Hindu mythology: "In the Bhagvata Purana, Vishnu heard Vasudev's prayers beseeching Kansa not to kill all sons being born. Vishnu heard these prayers and had an embryo from Devaki's womb transferred to the womb of Rohini, another wife of Vasudev.

Rohini gave birth to the baby Balaram, brother of Krishna, and secretly raised the child while Vasudev and Devaki told Kansa the child was born dead."[7] A common link connecting these surrogate mothers (apart from the glaring lack of their consent or choice) is their genetic connection to the child. The ancient surrogate mother hired to conceive the child was also its biological mother. This meant that the genetic connection shared by the mother and the child disrupts the commodification of motherhood because it inserts emotions into the business of surrogacy. In her essay "Of Likeness and Difference: How Race Is Being Transferred by Gestational Surrogacy," Heléna Ragoné looks at the medical, economic, and ethical reasons driving surrogate mothers to choose in vitro fertilization methods over and above traditional surrogacy. She observes:

> Overall, the women interviewed who elect to become gestational surrogates tend to articulate the belief that traditional surrogacy, even though it is less medically complicated, is not an acceptable option for them because they are uncomfortable with the prospect of contributing their ovum to the creation of a child. They also cannot readily accept the idea that a child who is genetically related to them would be raised by someone else. In other words, they explicitly articulate the position that in traditional surrogacy (where the surrogate contributes an ovum) the surrogate is the mother of the child, whereas in gestational surrogacy (where she does not contribute an ovum) she is not.[8]

Thus, the success of modern surrogacy depends not only on finding a perfect surrogate, but also on eliminating (notionally, at least) any emotional or physical connection between the surrogate mother and her child, as their relationship is strictly defined through a monetary lens.

Surrogacy in India is intimately linked to the economics of demand and supply. The laboring body of a woman becomes a site for economic progress and prosperity. Louis Althusser writes, "The reproduction of labour power requires not only a reproduction of skills, but also at the same time, a reproduction of its submission to the ruling ideology for the workers ."[9] The body of the Indian surrogate, hired to reproduce for her client, duplicates her submission on multiple levels as she reproduces physically as a mother while mentally she reproduces her submission by opening up her body to others. At the same time, the reason for her submission is conditional to her need for economic liberation that is available to her only when she willingly submits herself to the need of the other. Thus, it should come as no surprise that surrogate women not only come from the Third World, but also belong to a certain class and racial background. As Davis remarks, "Because domestic work has been primarily performed in the United States by women of color, native-born as well as recent immigrants (and immigrant women of European descent), elements of racism and class bias adhere to the concept of surrogate motherhood as potential historical features, even in the con-temporary absence of large numbers of surrogate mothers of color."[10] Bodies of low caste and lower middle class women are used as gestation sites in the business of surrogacy in India. Continuing further, Davis points, "Those who opt to employ a surrogate mother will participate in the economic as well as ideological exploitation of her services. And the woman who becomes a surrogate mother earns relatively low wages."[11] While I agree with Davis, it seems to me that even though the practice of surrogacy is an exploitation, we cannot ignore the fact that surrogate mothers participating in this act are fully aware of their exploitation and choose to do so because they are hoping for that one moment of lib-eration that will temporarily solve their economic difficulties. In other words, the money received by the surrogate for selling her womb is used to provide an economically bright future for her own children. Thus the lines that once demarcated race, class/caste, and geography are crossed, even as a new form of exploitation, temporary freedom, is promised to citizens of this new global Empire.

If we understand a mother to be a woman who not only births, but also nurtures and socializes a child, the colonial *ayah/dhayee* can also be understood as a surrogate mother. In that even though the colonial *ayah/dhayee* is not the biological mother of the British infant, her ability to nurture, feed, and socialize the child constructs her as a mother— a surrogate mother, if you will, one hired to *m/other* the child of another. In this regard, both the colonial Indian surrogate mother (the *ayah/ dhayee*) and the postcolonial Indian surrogate mother are quite similar. Their respective maternal bodies, hired and inserted into the economy by the Empire, help commodify the nature of motherhood. As Karl Marx writes: "Every owner of a commodity wishes to part with it in exchange only for those commodities whose use-value satisfies some want of his. Looked at in this way, exchange is for him simply a pri-vate transaction."[12] Surrogacy, therefore, not only becomes a way to insert another aspect of women's labor into the market, but also con-structs motherhood as a commodity that, when produced in surplus, is exchanged for a price. The consumerization of this act, at the same time, deconstructs the altruistic nature of motherhood.

Although there are many distinctions between the colonial wet nurse/*dhayee* and the postcolonial surrogate mother living in contemporary India, especially in terms of their historical conditions of existence, there still appears to be strong similarities that help connect the bodies of these two mothers separated through time. While the method to commodify, exploit, and insert women's labor into the economy is shared by both the colonial and postcolonial surrogacy practices in India, the intensity of this commodification varies greatly in the two historical epochs. With regard to the colonial *ayah/dhayee,* the surrogate mother is represented by the British memsahib as purely an employee hired to fulfill the needs of the future imperial subject. In contrast, the postcolonial Indian surrogate mother, also an employee, is manufactured in fertility clinics run by Indian doctors, and is customized and trained to fit the needs of her clients. Their lives are highly regimented and their bodies placed under constant surveillance. As Tina, a surrogate mother tells Amrita Pande about her daily ritual in the surrogacy hostel:

> Everything works like clockwork. We wake up at 8 a.m., have tea, take our medicines and injections, and go back to sleep. Then we wake up at noon, bathe and eat lunch. We basically rest. That's what is required of us. We are allowed visitors, but not for the night. In the evening we pray. Then the English tutor comes and teaches us how to speak in English. We will be learning how to use a computer next.[13]

In addition to this, the practice of surrogacy in postcolonial India takes on a contractual nature where behaviors, remuneration, and emotional attachment are spelled out in legal terms under the pretext that the interest of both the client and the surrogate mother are being protected. Furthermore, the contractual nature of motherhood in postcolonial India leads to the mass production of surrogate mothers in fertility clinics. So where as at one time the hire of a wet nurse/*dhayee* was a sign of luxury and wealth,[14] the cheap labor provided by Indian surrogates to women from First World nations makes this practice affordable. Indeed the business of surrogacy in both colonial and postcolonial India rests on its ability to hire women from underdeveloped countries who can, and are willing to provide cheap maternal labor to women from the First World.

As we have already seen in the previous section, the brown breast/body of the Indian *ayah* exposed to the colonizer becomes a point of concern for the British Empire, the colonizer constantly agonizing over the close bonds that were being formed between the future imperial subject and his/her native maternal figure. This anxiety is implicitly dealt with in the postcolonial world in that postcolonial surrogate mothers impregnated through invitro-fertilization treatments are bound by law to give up the custody of their child at birth. The brown belly of the Indian woman, subjected to the vigilant gaze of the colonizer, controls the interaction between the surrogate mother and the child. The practice of postcolonial surrogacy in India, streamed through the language of legality, economic power, and choice, is put into place not only to protect the couple hiring the surrogate and the surrogate mother herself, but also to implicitly address some of the concerns surrounding the construction of a pure imperial subject. By limiting the time a surrogate mother spends with her child, the neocolonial Empire is able to ensure the creation of subjects who are not tainted or influenced by the thoughts, likes, or behaviors of the colonized Other.

In what follows, I will trace the development of postcolonial surrogacy in modern India and work to uncover some of the racial and economic agendas of the global Empire concealed under the guise of modern technology. The insertion of these lenses into the definition of motherhood constructs it in an ambivalent light in which surrogate mothers, unable to fit into dichotomous categories of heroes or victim, create their own space in society. This section is divided into three parts; the first part looks at the commodification of motherhood in postcolonial India, where fertility clinics, as factories, enable the lower costs in maternal labor through the mass production of surrogate mothers. The second part of this section questions the nature of choice and works to uncover the true nature of a woman's free choice in her decision to become amother to an/other. The third section looks at the importance of race and the concept of whiteness that is inserted into the wombs and the minds of the postcolonial Indian surrogate mothers.

Marketing the Womb

India is truly a land of contradictions, where, on the one hand, the tentacles of globalization are intimately intertwined with the development and progress of urban centers, while, on the other hand, small towns and villages still continue to struggle to achieve basic necessities such as water and electricity in order to maintain a decent standard of living. India embraced the phenomenon of globalization with the hope that outsourced jobs, technology, and modernization would ultimately lead to its evolution and earn it the title of a developed nation in the world. However, as is often the case with any nation running in the race to become a part of the first world, the price for its development is often paid, literally, through the bodies of its women. Amartya Sen notes: "Nothing, arguably, is as important today in the political economy as an adequate recognition of political, economic and social participation and leadership of women."[15] Women's bodies have played, and continue to play, a significant role in the development and modernization of nations. Gayatri Spivak asks, "Are the new diasporas quite new? Every rupture is also a repetition. The only significant difference is the use, abuse, participation, and role, of women."[16] As one begins to see, the practice of postcolonial surrogacy in a globalized India works hard to distance itself from colonial surrogacy by highlighting the exploitation of women under the British Raj. However, it seems to me that the only significant difference between the two mothers is the time of their actual historical existence; exploitation differently labeled and disguised is packaged and sold under different brand names in both colonial and neocolonial Empires.

The capitalistic success of surrogacy in the global market not only depends on the low cost of production of surrogate mothers, but also hinges on the creation of a perfect surrogate mother-worker,[17] that is, a woman/mother who can be emotionally distant and yet biologically intimate with the surrogate child. Therefore the success of globalization and the development of Empire are intimately tied to production through women's labor. "The lifestyles of the First World are made possible by a global transfer of the services associated with a wife's traditional role—child care, home making, and sex—from poor countries to rich ones," as Barbara Ehrenreich puts it.[18] Women's labor, especially around maternal roles, is not only about monetary benefit, but rather, it is also deeply enmeshed in cultural constructions of love and selflessness. Ehrenreich continues, "Today, while still relying on Third World countries for agricultural and industrial labor, the wealthy countries also seek to extract something harder to measure and quantify, something that can look very much like love."[19] One of the traits of a developing nation is found not only in its ability to provide cheap labor, but also in creating a labor service that is imbricated in love. Amrita Pande, likewise argues, " The perfect commercial surrogate, like the perfect laborer of global production, is not found ready made in India. The perfect surrogate—cheap, docile, selfless, and nurturing—is produced in the fertility clinics and surrogacy hostels."[20] The production of the postcolonial surrogate, therefore, read through the shadowy figure of the colonial *ayah/dhayee,* brings to light some of the anxieties of the Empire. In other words, while the manufacture of the surrogate mother in postcolonial India ensures the creation of a professional surrogate mother, trained to fulfill the needs of her clients, the colonized *ayah/dhayee* hired by the British Empire is depicted as an unprofessional and a high maintenance surrogate mother, incapable of being civilized or disciplined by the white memsahib. This lack of training is aptly illustrated by Kate Platt in her medical manual when she writes,

> [The] Indian ayah has many good points; she surrounds her charges with an atmosphere of love and devotion and has infinite patience....Taking into consideration her home surroundings, her entire lack of training in European customs...it is wonderful that she is as satisfactory as she is found to be, but too much should not be expected of her.[21]

The British memsahib's longing to hire a professional stand-in mother, qualified in the European ways, is fulfilled centuries later through the body of the postcolonial surrogate. The postcolonial surrogate mother working in a global economy, carefully selected and trained by the fertility clinics, not only leads to the creation of a perfect "mother-worker," but also smoothes silently the lines of worry etched in the colonizer's forehead.

Commodification of the human body is not a new concept.[22] The human body inserted into the economy becomes a production site that is exchanged for a price. By the same token, bodies of colonized people and women become valuable commodities that provide human labor to developed countries. As Leslie Sharp observes: "The fragmentation of the body, and the subjectification of colonized subjects all potentially dehumanize individuals and categories of persons in the name of profit. It is for this reason that slavery and colonization so frequently emerge as metaphors for a host of commercialized and exploitative practices."[23] Thus, while the human body is traded in the market as a commodity, some bodies are depicted as being more valuable, and therefore fetch a higher price in exchange than the others. Sharp remarks: "Certain categories of persons—whether strangers, children, virginal or fertile women, laborers or others considered hardly or otherwise accomplished—may be viewed within their respective societies as possessing more power than others in particular contexts, and thus their body parts may be highly prized."[24] This rings especially true in developing countries such as India, where half of the population lives below the poverty line. However, it is ironic that in a country where the birth of a girl child, even today, is considered as an inauspicious occasion and female infanticide is a reality, women's bodies are celebrated because of their ability to turn themselves into revenue sites that helps uplift their families as well as the society in which they live. So while modern societies participating in a global economy reinforce the commodification of women's bodies, women belonging to these developing nations also wholeheartedly embrace their objectification because the survival of themselves and their families depends on it.

Although neocolonial Empire fashions itself as a modern, technologically advanced, and more humane alternative to old-fashioned imperialism, the question we must ask is, is it really? Power relationships formed in the new Empire may often appear to be subtle but are far more sinister than those found in contexts of colonization.[25] This is especially the case when looking at the role women's bodies play in both colonial and neocolonial Empires. Women's bodies serve as contact zones for both colonial and neocolonial Empires. However, I would argue that while the contact between the breast and the colonial Empire was more literal and less driven by consumerism, the connection between the womb and the postcolonial Empire, though subtle, is far more sinister. In her article "For Love and Money: The Political Economy of Commercial Surrogacy," Deborah Spar observes,

> In the past, the only way for surrogate mothers to produce children was to engage physically in sexual relations with the prospective father—a messy business under any circumstances and one that had little appeal for the wives of the husbands involved. With AI [Artificial Insemination], however, conception was removed from sex, making it possible for a man to impregnate a surrogate without meeting her.[26]

By eliminating the physical contact between the surrogate mother and the prospective father, the postcolonial Empire constructs the business of surrogacy as a more civilized, more altruistic form of motherhood, a motherhood that benefits and fulfills the need of both the infertile couple and the surrogate mother. Spar continues, "In economic terms, then, the emergence of commercial AI enhanced both the demand for and supply of surrogate mothers. Once demand and supply were in place, the market followed readily."[27] The success of surrogacy in globalization depends on creating an atmosphere of consent, where the surrogate mothers of the postcolonial empire willingly concede to the use of their bodies and the commodification of their wombs. Thus while the practice of surrogacy in the colonial period was depicted as being more technologically backward and blatantly exploitative (especially considering their lack of choice/consent) of women's bodies and their wombs, the neocolonial Empire's penetration of women's bodies subtly disguises their use/abuse under the façade of technology, consumerism, and legal contracts, making it a far more sinister operation.

Understanding the business of surrogacy through the eyes of capitalism in the neocolonial Empire brings to light a more dangerous use/abuse of women's bodies, one that constructs and identifies them only through their ability to reproduce. The surrogate mother living in the neocolonial Empire is reduced to a womb, one that not only generates life but also defines the identity of Third World women. Capitalism in the neocolonial Empire, therefore, fragments the Third World female bodies as their commodified wombs are hired to manufacture the future citizens of the First World.

The mass production of commodified bodies of Indian women redefines the traditional meaning of women's labor-power.[28] Women's labor, especially maternal labor, has often been relegated to the domestic sphere and is constructed as the ultimate altruistic act performed by a female. However, with the introduction of commercial surrogacy and the technological commodification of women's bodies, the understanding of maternal labor-power as a private affair performed by a specific gender begins to get deconstructed. Gayatri Spivak observes, "It is the body's susceptibility to the production of value which makes it vulnerable to idealization, and therefore, to insertion into the economic. This is the ground of the labor theory of value. It is here that the story of the emergence of value from Jashoda's labor-power infiltrates Marxism and questions its gender-specific presuppositions."[29] Maternal labor-power inserted and introduced into the economy as a commodity can only be exchanged and appropriated when it is produced in surplus. The commercial surrogate mother living in postcolonial India is required to have her own child before being hired as a surrogate mother. Fertility clinics in India question the legitimacy of the consent given by the Indian surrogate mother if she has never experienced childbirth before, additionally, it is also a way for the clinics to be assured that the surrogate can achieve pregnancy.[30] The maternal labor-power of the Indian mother used to produce her own child/children is of "use-value," a domesticated labor that is not exchanged for a price. At the same time, the labor-power of the newly transitioned surrogate mother employed to give birth to another's child not only constructs her labor-power as "surplus-value," but also allows for its appropriation in the market. As a result, maternal labor-power transformed into commodity moves from the private into the public sphere.

Commodified labor-power as an integral part of a laborer's self enables the transition of maternal labor-power from the private *oikos* to the public *polis,* thereby allowing for the transformation of maternal labor from being a "use-value" commodity to a "surplus-value" commodity that is exchanged and appropriated in the market. According to Marx, rather than laborer selling his commodity in the market in which his labor is incorporated, the laborer must be coerced or manipulated to sell that labor power that cannot exist apart from himself.[31] Commercial surrogacy in postcolonial India works hard to extricate the womb from the female body by constructing it as a separate entity. As Trinh Minh ha observes: "Men name 'womb' to separate a part of woman from woman (to separate it from the rest that forms her: body and mind), making it possible to lay legal claim to it. By doing so, they create their own contradiction and come round to identifying her with their fabrication: a specialized, infant producing organ."[32] Surrogate mothers living in postcolonial India are hired in the belief that only their wombs are inserted and appropriated in the market. In fact, I would argue that the identity of the Indian surrogate mother is just that, an object, a womb, and a space that is rented out for nine months by another subject. Khanderia, one of the surrogate agents, tells Pande:

> I have to educate them about everything because all these women are poor and illiterate villagers. I tell them, "You have to do nothing. It's not your baby. You are just providing it a home in your womb for nine months because it doesn't have a house of its own. If some child comes to stay with you for just nine months, what will you do? You will take care of it even more, love it even more than you love your own, because it is someone else's. This is the same thing. You will take care of the baby for nine months and then give it to its mother. And for that you will be paid." I think, finally, how you train them—that is what makes surrogacy work.[33]

The comparison of the surrogate mother's womb to a house not only depicts the transient nature of the commodified maternal labor-power of Indian surrogate mothers, but also constructs the womb as a separate entity, fracturing the subjectivity of the Indian surrogate mother. In her article titled "Is Woman's Labor a Commodity?" Elizabeth Anderson points to the strangeness of maternal labor in surrogate transactions where the surrogate mother, as a professional, must work hard to not bond emotionally with the child that she is carrying.[34] The consumerization of the surrogate enterprise prides itself in effectively extricating the womb from the female body of the Indian surrogate, thereby alienating maternal labor power from the very experience of motherhood. However, as many scholars argue, these lines of separation are not as distinct as they seem. From talking to mothers, reading articles on motherhood, and my own experience of giving birth, I understand that unborn children are able to hear and recognize the voices of their mothers. Additionally, the fetuses also develop a taste for the food of the mothers, that reaches them through the umbilical cord. Thus, fertility clinics may place the body of the Indian surrogate under constant supervision, but how does one supervise the fetus that has come to recognize and understand the native dialect of the Indian surrogate and has developed a palate for the native food? Can the emotional bond be truly severed? Or does the unborn fetus living in a surrogate womb become a hybrid subject even before it sees the light of day?

Rengachary Smerdon's words evoke the reality of motherhood, illustrating that pregnancy is not an isolating experience but rather an experience that integrates the body and mind of a woman. While fertility clinics run their business under the principle that it is only the womb that is capitalized in the market, the reality is that the complete body of the surrogate mother is employed by the surrogate agency. As a result, the practice of surrogacy depends on a woman's ability to not only commodify her maternal labor-power, but also commodify her whole self.

Does Yes Truly Mean Yes?

The success of the surrogacy business in postcolonial India depends not only on constructing motherhood as a commodity, but also on employing women who willingly consent to the consumerization of their wombs. Choice, as a result, plays an important role in the business of postcolonial surrogacy. Fertility clinics claim that women who serve as surrogate mothers are willing and eager participants of this process. Najima Vohra, the potential surrogate of Jessica Ordenes, tells Abigail Haworth, "I have been so excited since Dr. Patel chose me to be a surrogate, that I haven't been able to sleep since."[35] The business of surrogacy highlights the eagerness of surrogate mothers in the hope that it may distance itself from accusations of exploitation and oppression. However, the nature of this "free choice," so willingly performed by Indian surrogate mothers, must be interrogated.

Womanhood is defined by Indian society only through the ability to become a mother. "Womanhood and motherhood become inextricably and dangerously merged in her one body almost to the extent that her identity as mother overwhelms her womanhood and ultimately claims her life," as Ketu H. Kartrak explains.[36] This intricate fusion between motherhood and womanhood also exiles those female bodies that are unable to experience the joy of reproduction. Kartrak continues: "In most traditional societies, women who do not become mothers almost automatically carry—the stigma of infertility. This severe social and psychological prejudice exiles the woman further from her body that has failed to provide the visible physical marks of pregnancy and child-birth."[37] While I do agree with Kartrak that the "stigma of infertility" is prevalent in traditional societies, it seems to me that such a stigma can also be found in Western, more progressive societies. In her book *Maternal Encounters: The Ethics of Interruption*, Lisa Baraitser points to the prominent role of the mother even in Western society. As a culture, the mother is placed above all women, motherhood is set up as an ideal that women even in the west are coerced, manipulated, or seduced into achieving.[38] It is this need to feel complete that drives women to break barriers pertaining to race, class, caste, and economics and find bodies of other women willing to help make them complete.

The practice of surrogate motherhood has often been defended as an act that helps form a global sisterhood among women: "Oprah Winfrey declared in front of eight million viewers in 2007 that Indian surrogacy was a case of 'women helping women.' "[39] Maternal labor is thereby constructed as an ultimate act of benevolence and women who partici-pate in surrogacy are hailed as real life heroes who unselfishly sacrifice themselves for the benefit of others. Mary Warnock observes that the common notion surrounding postcolonial surrogacy denotes that, "the labor of the surrogate mother is said to be a labor of love. Her altruis-tic acts should be permitted and encouraged."[40] Rituja, a real-life sur-rogate, tells Kritivas Mukherjee, "It's true I'm doing this for money, but is it also not true that a childless couple is benefiting?"[41] Similarly, Raveena, a former surrogate and currently a surrogate counselor tells Pande: "Of course, I also want the best deal for the surrogates. I know how painful this thing is. I have been there myself. But I teach my sur-rogates one crucial thing: don't treat it like a business. Instead, treat it like God's gift to you. *Don't be greedy.*"[42] The performance of surrogacy therefore not only becomes an altruistic act, but also transforms itself into a divinely ordained act. Parvati, a surrogate at one of the fertility clinic argues: "We can't really call surrogacy 'work.' I personally feel it's nothing strange to us Hindus; it's in our religion. It's something like what Yashoda Ma did for God Krishna. And Krishna loved his Yashoda Ma, didn't he?"[43] On the surface, the modern day surrogate does seem to resemble the mythological character of Yashoda; however a closer look reveals many troubling inconsistencies between the two narratives. First, the bond between the mythological surrogate mothers, unlike in real-life modern surrogate mothers, is never founded on a monetary relationship. Second, Devaki and Yahsoda stand on the same rung of the social ladder. While Devaki is a queen and Yahsoda is a cowherd's wife, the fact that Devaki is in prison not only causes her to lose her royal status, but also, in some ways, makes her seem lower than Yashoda. Rengachary Smerdon notes: "Fertility tourism has been compared to *The Handmaid's Tale* by Margaret Atwood, whereby wealthy infertile couples treat third parties from disenfranchised groups as "passports" to reproduction."[44] The arrangement of postcolonial surrogacy is between two women who are economically and racially unequal. Apart from all of these inconsistencies, the most glaring difference between the mythological and the postcolonial surrogate mothers is that of choice. Yashoda unknowingly becomes a surrogate mother to Krishna; she is never depicted as being a consenting individual who willingly decides to mother the child of another. In contrast, surrogacy in postcolonial India can only occur when the consent of the Indian surrogate mother is presented in a written form.

Fertility clinics in India depict the postcolonial surrogate mother as a free agent whose will is never coerced or directed by an outside influence. In an article titled "Womb for Rent: Surrogate Mothers in India," Abigail Haworth comments on the dangerous and fast-paced growth of the surrogate industry in India, where the number of Indian women willing to carry an American child is growing on a daily basis. She writes:

> [Dr. Nayna] Patel reports to Haworth that the "surrogacy business" has taken off beyond her imagination. She says that she has about 150 "foreign couples" who are currently on the waiting list, and every day, at least three new Indian women sign up to be "potential surrogates." However, Dr. Patel is quick to explain that unlike other doctors who are interested in exploiting women, she is interested in the welfare of the Indian surrogates. She explains that most women who apply to her clinic hail from lower middle class, poor and low caste families. Patel says that she feels good about helping these women, as long as she is aware that these women are not being coerced into this act by their husbands or their in-laws.[45]

Patel fashions herself as a woman who stands up for the rights of other women and protects them from exploitation. She notes explicitly that it is the willingness of the Indian surrogate mother that makes her a consenting participant in this form of motherhood. Once the Indian surrogate mother gives birth to the child, she signs away her parental rights; her name does not appear on the birth certificate;this mother, erased from sight, soon becomes a vague memory haunting only our unconscious postcolonial minds.[46] The gesture of signing away the rights to the child works as a way to protect the rights of the couple that uses the services of the surrogate woman. In almost all of the published interviews, the reader is told explicitly by the doctor and the surrogate that this act is not an act of exploitation and the women participating in it are agents of their own free will. However, it seems to me that this act of willingness can be seen either as a gesture that truly liberates the Indian surrogate mother because it depicts her ability to use her agency, or as an act that camouflages a sinister oppression that manipulates a woman to use her agency and enslave her body as a receptacle for the other.

Choice plays an important role in the business of surrogacy in postcolonial India, because it allows the surrogacy industry to distance itself from the accusation of exploiting women. Surrogacy is constructed as a win-win situation for women, as the maternal longing of one woman fulfilled by another is argued to be a noble gesture. Motherhood itself is depicted as an altruistic act, and the task of unselfishly carrying a child for another woman, without any conditions, takes on a divine meaning. In fact, the Indian surrogate mothers translate the act of surrogacy in precisely such terms. However, the insertion of economics and commerce within the business of surrogacy casts a shadow over this "global sisterhood," where the line between the rich and poor, widened, maintained, and deepened, questions the acts revolving around issues such as agency, choice, and willingness.[47]

A woman's ability to make a choice about her body by becoming a surrogate mother is not only emblematic of her freedom but also gestures to her agency. The conscious decision to become a *mother to another* turns into a decision of women's empowerment, rather than exploitation. However, such a characterization seems to simplify the complex nature of choice dominant in the concept of Indian surrogacy. This is because, while on the one hand, choice is the mark of individual freedom, on the other hand, the ability to make a choice in the Indian context of surrogacy gestures to a deeper reality of enslavement and exploitation. In their article titled, "Globalization and Cross-border Reproductive Services: Ethical Implications of Surrogacy in India for

Social Work," George Palattiyil, Eric Blyth, Dina Sidhva, and Geeta Balakrishnan remark that the surrogacy industry is growing and currently is estimated to be a US$445 million enterprise. The Indian surrogate receives US$3000–6000, which is an attractive fee for a woman whose annual income is around US$500.[48] So choice in the Indian context of surrogacy, constructed around a financial or an economical need, illustrates an individual's exploitation under the guise of freedom or agency. As Salma, one of the surrogate mothers tells Pande: "Who would choose to do this? This is not work, this is *majboori* [a compulsion]. It's just something we have to do to survive. When we heard of surrogacy, we didn't have any clothes to wear after the rains— just one pair that used to get wet—and the roof of our house had collapsed. What were we to do?"[49] The eagerness of the Indian surrogate mother must not be misconstrued as an act of freedom but rather must be understood as a mode of survival that stems from systemic poverty and the resultant vulnerability of impoverished women to exploitation. As a result, within the context of modern surrogacy, choice must be redefined, as it reflects a woman's freedom that is contingent upon her enslavement. Choice for the modern Indian surrogate mother creates a space wherein controlled exploitation allows for a possible measure of economic freedom. However, the question we need to ask is this: how far is the Indian surrogate mother willing to go to get a glimpse of or partake in this economic freedom, however transitory it may be?

The Production of Whiteness

The womb of the postcolonial surrogate mother is splintered as the brown belly swollen with the fetus of an economically superior couple not only becomes the embodied site/sight of a globalizing economy and outsourced labor, but also becomes the space where whiteness (re)produced and maintained continues to haunt the once colonized consciousness of brown subjects living in India. In her book *Desiring Whiteness: A Lacanian Analysis of Race,* Kalpana Seshadri Crooks, using Lacan's theory of sexual difference to understand the concept of race, argues that different races can define themselves only when they refer back to the master signifier, that is, Whiteness. She writes: "By Whiteness, I refer to a master signifier (without a signified) that establishes a structure of relations, a signifying chain that through the process of inclusions and exclusions, constitutes a pattern for organizing human difference. This chain provides subjects with certain symbolic positions such as "black", "white", "Asian", etc, in relation to the master signifier."[50] The term "whiteness" not only refers to the physical characteristic of being white, but rather focuses on the hegemonic constructions of whiteness in postcolonial contexts as well, whereby residues of whiteness continue to haunt the liberated yet colonized minds of the Indian subjects. Alfred J. Lopez gestures to this hegemonic construction of whiteness in postcolonial contexts in his essay entitled, "Introduction: Whiteness after Empire:" "It would seem a simple enough assumption that the end of colonialism ushers in the end of whiteness, or at least of its unrivaled ascendency. Yet the cultural residues of whiteness linger in the postcolonial world as an ideal, often latently sometimes not."[51] The body of the Indian surrogate mother read through the theory of whiteness not only uncovers the real motif of racism hidden under the technological advancement of modernization, but also exposes the trauma of postcolonial whiteness as the *symbolically lacking* subject bleaches his/her unconscious mind and engages in the reproduction of whiteness. The insertion of whiteness into the colonized bodies of Indian women serves a dual purpose as the distinct racial lines drawn in the wombs of the Indian surrogate mother not only makes it possible to distinguish the offspring from its surrogate mother, but also links whiteness to racial superiority and economic success. Race plays a significant role in the act of commodifying surrogacy in that not only are women of color easier to commodify, but it is also easy for a surrogate of color to separate herself from a white child as it bears no racial resemblance to her.[52] Additionally, constructing and reinforcing whiteness as the cultural norm not only racializes the Indian body further, but also creates within it a desire to be bleached by the absorption of economic success. Whiteness, then, in postcolonial surrogacy becomes the master signifier that not only distinguishes the non-white other, but also creates a desire in that other to become a part of the master signifier.

As we have already seen, the close relationship between the Indian *ayah/dhayee* and the British children caused quite a stir in the white consciousness of the colonizer's identity.[53] The close proximity between the Indian *ayah/dhayee* and the young British child was believed to corrupt the fragile colonial mind of the infant-subject, as the development of the white British subject was interrupted by the brown-black language spoken by the native. The British memsahib agonized over the possible corruption of the white tongue speaking the brown-black language of the native other. The interaction between the Indian *ayah/dhayee* and the young British infant had to be controlled because it not only helped in preserving and protecting the colonial consciousness, but also maintained the racial barriers between the British subject and the Indian object.

Language in the postcolonial context also dismantles the barriers that separate the subject from the Indian object. However, the language of the white subject in the postcolonial context gestures to a sign of prosperity and economic growth, as opposed to the degeneration of the white mind speaking the native dialect in the colonial context. In other words, learning to speak the English language in postcolonial India not only provides for better economic opportunities, but also becomes a way through which whiteness in postcolonial contexts can be performed and mainatined. The outsourcing industry in India is on the rise because of the number of English educated individuals, in fact the availability of English speaking doctors in India is also one of the reasons why the surrogacy industry in India is on the rise.[54] Lopez remarks in his article:

> Here we may think of any number of colonial-era discourses and practices, from the adoption of the erstwhile mother tongue (whether English, Spanish, French, or some other) as the new national language, to the persistence of color-based socioeconomic caste structures in former colonies such as Jamaica and the Dominican Republic. These examples and many others point to the stubborn persistence of whiteness as a cultural norm in many of the postcolonial world's official and unofficial cultural practices. Further, what emerges in the relation between former colonizers and colonized, now fellow citizens in a postindependence state, is their common dependence upon—and complicity with—the ideology of whiteness, or more specifically of white (hence Western) superiority.[55]

Even though India has many vernacular languages, the English language continues to take precedence in the minds of postcolonial Indians. One surrogate mother, Diksha Gurung, 28 explains that she will "earn $7,500 for nine months' work, allowing her to buy a house, motorbike and English-language education for her sons."[56] Another surrogate, Najima Vohra, explains "that the money she will receive as a surrogate will be used to educate her daughter and fulfill her dreams of becoming a school teacher."[57] For both the surrogate mothers, the future of their children does not just lie in their education, but rather in their English education. The notion that English-educated individuals attain better economic opportunities is a common sentiment that is shared in postcolonial India. Additionally, the reality of globalization and the sudden increase in multinational corporations and call centers in India illustrate the demand for English speaking individuals and better economic opportunities. The desire to learn English must be read as an economic opportunity; however, it also unearths the hidden desire present in the Indian mind to become a part of the colonizing subject through the medium of language. Thus, while the white child speaking the brown language of the native Indian threatened the future of the British Empire in colonial India, the brown child speaking the white language of the colonizer signifies a promise of a better future in postcolonial India.

The brown breast of the Indian *ayah/dhayee* served as the contact zone that linked the colonizer to the colonized in colonial India. In contrast, the connection between the infant subject and the colonized maternal object in postcolonial India is one that is far more literal and intimate. The womb of the Indian surrogate mother becomes a space where the genetic disconnection between mother and child is literalized in her body. In other words, the sperm and the egg of a privileged nation/family is inserted into the under- privileged womb of an Indian woman. This insertion not only helps preserve the genetic connection between the child and its biological parents, but also safeguards the racial boundaries that both create and maintain the distance between the self and the other. This racial divide is also observed by Ragoné in the United States; she points out that post World War II, children born to single mothers from a Euro-American background were seen as more valuable than those children born to mothers of color. Ragoné notes that such a racial divide still exists as social workers are advised not to place children of color with white or European individuals.[58]

It is interesting to note that even though US society tends to frown upon the construction of interracial families, insertion of white fetuses into the brown wombs of the Indian surrogate mothers does not appear to stir the censure.

On the Indian side, the lack of a genetic connection not only makes it easier for the mother to give up her child, but allows her to racially distinguish herself from the white subject. Rengachary Smerdon makes a point of this by saying: "Some surrogates themselves have noted that differences in skin color enable them to distance themselves emotionally from the child they are carrying. As one Indian surrogate remarked on the white child she would bear, '[i]t won't even have the same skin color as me, so it won't be hard to think of it as [the commissioning mother's]."[59] The ability to distinguish herself from the child she carries, not only allows for an early separation between the mother and the child, but also helps protect the subjectivity of the "white" child formed in the brown belly of the Indian surrogate mother. Ragoné makes a similar observation in her article when she interviews two women Carol and Linda, the former an African-American woman and the latter a Mexican-American woman, both surrogate mothers carrying babies that are racially different: "Cultural conceptions such as this about the connection between race and genetics deserve further exploration. Although she [Carol] knows that the child is not genetically hers, certain boundaries become blurred for her when an African-American couple is involved, whereas with a Euro-American couple, the distinction between genetic/nongenetic or self/other is made more clear."[60]

Whiteness has been inscribed and reinscribed in the Indian consciousness to such an extent that it has become not only a cultural norm of economic prosperity but also a standard of beauty. Phrases such as *gora sahib* or *gori memsahib* (white master or mistress) were not mere words used to stereotype the British, but also contained in them a deep resentment. This resentment was very much a part of the fabric of pre-independent India.[61] As Roshni Johar writes: "In recent past, it was the *gora* British who ruled over Indians described as 'dark natives.' The *goras* were the sahib log, our lords and masters, who set our social standards."[62] It is interesting to note that the word *gora,* once used to describe the British/other, is now absorbed into the Indian self and has become a standard that must be achieved. One look at the Indian matrimonial column not only betrays the white/dark divide present in the Indian context, but also highlights the deep-seated racism that is projected onto the bodies of women. "Just read any matrimonial advertisement looking for brides. Invariably, all of them mention that fair-complexioned girls are required for eligible sons."[63] Cosmetic procedures and skin bleaching products allow women to achieve this standard of beauty and fulfill their desire to become a part of the other. The fairness industry in India is estimated to be a $140 million dollar industry.[64] The success of this industry in India not only gestures to the unconscious racism unleashed upon itself by the brown Indian body, but also highlights the identification of the bleached white skin with the economic success of globalization. As Seshadri Crooks observes, "Whiteness is the 'object of desire' (of recognizing or fantasizing a lack in the symbolic order of race) . . ."[65] The practice of bleaching allows for an escape from backwardness and poverty. The bleached Indian skin promises to fill the "fantasizing lack," but never quite becomes completely white.

The white skin is also linked to economic prosperity and hope. Leistikow points out that advertisements selling fairness products deliberately link fair skin to economic growth, prosperity, purity, and success, creating in the mind of the viewer a desirability to become *White.*

It is quite common to see commercials of a woman cursed for her gender and her inability to find a job suddenly finding success in her professional and private life after using a fairness product.[66] Commercials selling fairness products in India, targeting female consumers, often deal with two themes: first, fairness leads to economic prosperity and is intimately linked to the body of a female; second, fairness/whiteness in India allows women to transgress traditional gender barriers.[67] Thus, in a patriarchal society such as India where female infanticide, violence against women, and dowry deaths are a reality, the little box of bleach containing a hope for equality and recognition is one offer that is too tempting to pass up.

One of the most important aspects in the practice of surrogacy in the Indian context is the notion of race. But it is important to note that within the practice of surrogacy boundaries begin to be erased. In many parts of India caste system is a reality. Lower caste people are often depicted as untouchablesand, as the name suggests, this discrimination, based on their imagined impure and dirty status, encourages people to not touch them. It is interesting to note that issues revolving around fertility and childlessness create an environment of no boundaries, as lines separating race, class, religion, etc. begin to disintegrate.[68] Caste can also be added to this list of difference. Infertility, then, erases differences because it plays on emotions of desire, acceptance, and touchability. In such a context, the image of a low caste surrogate mother being hugged by a white Western woman is not just a sign of gratitude but becomes a sign of empowered violence. The touch of the Other empowers the Indian surrogate mother by making her feel accepted and touchable, and at the same time, violates her as First World fingers of capitalism and greed close around her womb. The idea of a superior woman willingly touching an inferior woman not only becomes an image of power, but becomes a sight of violence— a seductive violence that manipulates the Indian mind to think that it is a desired subject. Lopez writes: "The demise of colonialism brings with it the beginning of the end of whiteness as well; but it is also true that one of the cultural residues left in the wake of empire is precisely this ideal of or aspiration to whiteness, what we might call a postcolonial 'will to whiteness' that lurks in the burgeoning state's national racial unconscious. The eagerness of the low caste surrogate to perform motherhood for the white woman betrays her own desire for whiteness and plays on her emotions of wanting to be touched. This psychology of the surrogate Indian woman is manipulated not only by the western couple, but also by the Indian-Western doctor who offers to sell her womb to the other. As a result, constructing the practice of surrogacy within the Indian context through the binaries of touchability and untouchability, allows for the emergence of the practice of surrogacy as a *performance of motherhood* that is both liberating and oppressing.

The brown body of the surrogate mother in the global Empire becomes a site/sight where an oppressive-liberation/violent-love is performed. While the exploitation of the Indian surrogate mother at the hands of the global Empire is self-evident, the choice to serve the Empire is also symbolic of her liberation. In other words, in exchange for her womb the Indian surrogate mother is paid a nominal fee, and it is this money that provides an economically bright future for her own children. However, I do want to be careful with my own analysis of this temporary emancipation of the postcolonial surrogate mother and not romanticize this notion. This is because, at the end of the day, the broken body of the Indian woman becomes a site that helps fulfill the dreams of white and brown subjects alike. So the practice of surrogacy within the Indian context performs a liberation that is both emancipating and enslaving. As surrogacy allows the Indian mother to transgress poverty, make a choice, and hope for a better future, it simultaneously enslaves her body thorough misogynistic and colonial notions of labor. The discourse of postcolonial surrogacy in India, understood through the hybrid lens of *emancipated-enslavement*, constructs the body of the postcolonial Indian surrogate mother within the hyphenated space between oppression and liberation.

Conclusion

The body of the Indian mother objectified by Empire, both colonial and postcolonial, becomes a site/sight through which powers of colonization and slavery continue to dominate and subjugate the minds of people living in developing nations. However, while the colonization of the Indian surrogate mother/wet nurse serving the British Empire is an obvious subjugation, the colonization of the postcolonial surrogate mother living under the new Empire of globalization, is a far more subtle, and to some extent, even more damaging subjugation. This is because the new form of colonization called globalization constructs oppression through an ideology of liberation. This is especially true in the Indian context where outsourced jobs provide economic liberation in lieu of dependency, exploitation, exhaustion, and domination. At the same time, postcolonial surrogacy in India provides economic and racial freedom for the economically deprived women, as it allows them to participate in, and experience, the white culture. Unlike the colonial surrogate mother/wet nurse, who was treated with suspicion and never allowed to participate in the imperial whiteness of the memsahib, the postcolonial surrogate mother, through language and monetary benefits, is allowed to participate in, and perform, whiteness within the Indian context. This postcolonial Indian surrogate mother then becomes a fetishized maternal object, one whose body is no longer the site of fear and derision, but is transformed into an object of white desire.

CHAPTER 3

Exploited Exploiters, Victimized Victimizers: Reading the Matthean Mothers alongside the Contextual Body of the Indian Surrogate Mother in Postcolonial India

The phenomenon of outsourcing has taken on a new meaning in the surrogacy industry, as infertile couples (both Indian and non-Indian)[1] with considerable financial resources seek out and hire the local wombs of poor Indian women for the purposes of generative labor. Sentiments regarding the ethical and moral nature of this practice are quite often divided. Journalist Sagarika Ghosh documents one such exchange in the television program, *Face the Nation*. Ghosh interviews four prominent women, two of whom are Dr. Indira Hinduja, a gynecologist at a reputed hospital in India, and Kishwar Desai, author of the novel *Origins of Love*. When asked if commercial surrogacy is a practice that exploits the poor women in India, Dr. Hinduja responds: "If the poor woman is carrying a baby to give someone a very meaningful, profound life, meaningful result to its life, if the couple by themselves, by their pleasure—want[s]to compensate those women, what's wrong with that?"[2] Advocates of modern surrogacy like Dr. Hinduja, highlight the business of surrogacy as an altruistic practice by suggesting that such a transaction is a win-win situation for both the women involved. However, as critics have duly noted, such an argument fails to pay attention to the redesignation of "women's labor" as a commodity exchanged in the free market for a price. Constructing her argument along these lines, Desai contends that the practice of surrogacy does not emotionally invest in the lives of surrogate Indian mothers, but rather, treats them as objects whose emotional and physical investment of labor is compensated with monetary resources. She notes:

> [P]artially in a sense that the woman is doing it for the money, there is no other reason that she is doing it. But there is a lot of ethical ambiguity involved in this. Because while I do feel a lot of sympathy for the infertile couple who want their own children, I think we should have equal sympathy and empathy for [those] desperately and I would like to repeat that desperately poor women who are forced to rent out their wombs. It's like a mini factory [producing] children on demand but it's a business, Sagarika, it is an absolute business and there [is] no emotional ground on which these women are being looked after. They are being looked after because of the baby, I mean all the roles that they play in this is of production, as a mean of production.[3]

Although both Hinduja's and Desai's view on the surrogate mother are extremely relevant to the discussion of the reproductive tourism industry in India, their dichotomized interpretations of the already objectified surrogate mother as either a victim or hero fail to fully take into account the complex reality of these mothers entrenched in poverty. These surrogate mothers participating in an ambivalent motherhood inhabit the space between victim and hero, as their ability to transform themselves into *exploited exploiters* or *victimized victimizers* ensures their survival in a globalized economy.

Discussions revolving around the reproductive tourism industry in India often overlook the role of the husband of the Indian surrogate (when he is present) and his influence in helping transform the domestic Indian mother into a professional surrogate mother whose womb is successfully marketed in a capitalistic economy. In a patriarchal society such as India,[4] the enthusiastic consent of the husband actively nudging his wife to become a surrogate for another couple is not only ironic, but never interrogated. This is because the emphatic voice of the surrogate mother placed at the center of discussions of surrogacy draws our attention and drowns out the hushed approval of her husband. For example, Desai remarks in passing on the role of the Indian husband in the business of surrogacy, but she does not fully explore the reason behind the husband's willingness. She writes:

> Straightening her saree, Preeti had given him [Subash, the doctor at the infertility clinic] one last glance from beneath her lashes, a glimmer of excitement in her eyes. "Is everything okay sir? Sharmaji [the broker/

middleman] said you will pay us five lakhs for the baby?" She had asked outright. "That's right. But has Sharma met your husband and explained it to him?" "Yes." "I know his consent is on the file, but I have to be certain." "You're sure he won't object?"—"Absolutely, sir. My sister will be there." The way she said it made Subash wonder if this was a family enterprise. After all, she would bring in more money with just one pregnancy than her husband would earn in his entire life. "So he's okay with it?" "Sir, he's the one who went to Sharmaji and suggested that I come here."[5]

Although Desai's novel is fiction, her words echo the voices of many surrogate mothers who eagerly note that their husbands are generally very accepting of them lending their wombs out to other couples. In most cases, the husbands themselves approach the middlemen/women who serve as coordinators for the big hospitals undertaking this procedure. Hence, given the important role of the Indian husband in this business, it is surprising that the consent of the Indian husband has often been ignored in discussions of this industry.

Helen Pidd reports: "A glance at the Indian media reveals the range of abuse suffered by the nation's women on a daily basis. Today it was reported that a woman had been stripped and had her head shaved by villagers near Udaipur as punishment for an extramarital affair. Villagers stoned police when they came to the rescue."[6] While it is important to remember that not all women in India are subjected to such extreme forms of punishments for transgressing their marital boundaries, the idea of a woman stepping out of her traditional role as a "virtuous wife" in a patriarchal society such as India is thought of as bringing social dishonor not only to her husband, but also to her community. Hence, in such a context, how does one rationalize the role of an obliging, supportive husband approving of his wife's decision to lend her womb to strangers? Modern surrogacy answers this dilemma by recreating a conception that is not only virginal and legitimate, but also fits within the patriarchal mindset. The success of surrogacy in a male dominated society such as India then, lies in its ability to engineer a conception that not only ensures the protection of the sexual chastity of the Indian surrogate mother, but also assures the Indian husband that his social honor remains unviolated and, therefore, intact within his community.

The story of a couple participating in a conception that falls outside the traditional boundary of marriage is not a new phenomenon. In fact, before the business of surrogacy was turned into a capitalistic venture in modern society, the ancients had already found a way to redistribute their reproductive labor to female slaves and foreign women. As Palattiyil, Blyth, Sidhva and Balakrishna state:

> Practices akin to surrogacy have been reported throughout history. The Bible (Genesis 16:1–4) describes a form of genetic surrogacy (where the surrogate is also the genetic mother of the child). However, this—and other Biblical instances—differs from more recent forms of genetic surrogacy in so far as the surrogate conceived following sexual intercourse with the genetic father as opposed to inseminating non-coitally. Second, the surrogate, invariably a household servant, seems to have had little choice regarding her participation.[7]

The examples found in the Hebrew Bible entail a more traditional form of surrogacy, in which conception occurs and is dependent only upon physical intercourse between a man and a woman. A more complex and more intriguing link to the modern business of surrogacy is the virginal conception of Jesus as represented in the infancy narratives of Matthew and Luke found in the New Testament. Desai writes in her novel: "Subhash reflected that globalization had made motherhood complex almost beyond belief—and its boundaries were constantly shifting, as everyone searched for the immaculate conception and birth."[8] Even though Desai makes an implicit connection between Mary and the Indian surrogate mother by openly commenting on the success of the surrogacy industry in recreating a virginal conception, she does not delve deeper nor does she interrogate this connection any further.

On the surface at least, the character of Mary found in the Gospel of Matthew and the Indian surrogate mothers seem to be very different. The Matthean Mary is described as a *parthenos* ("virgin"—Matt 1:23)—in other words, she has never been sexually penetrated by a man—while the Indian surrogate mother is a woman required to have had children of her own in order to participate in this business. Journalist Fred De Sam Lazro observes:

> The moment their pregnancies are confirmed, surrogates are required to move into this home run by Dr. Patel. They're offered skills training in things like tailoring, but mostly it's a quiet, sedentary life. *The women who spend nine months in this surrogate hostel have all experienced childbirth with their own biological children. It's a prerequisite for becoming a surrogate.* What very few of them have experienced with those previous pregnancies is any kind of prenatal care. That's in sharp contrast to the pampering they get here: meals provided and medical attention, should they need it, round the clock. Dr. Patel acknowledges the irony but says

it is part of a thorough surveillance to ensure smooth pregnancies, for both surrogate and parents' sake.[9]

Despite this apparent difference between the ancient character of Mary and the surrogate mother living in modern India, there still appears to be a bond connecting the bodies of these two mothers separated by time. In other words, the participation of Mary and the Indian surrogate mother in a noncoital conception and the consent provided by the men present in the lives of these women illustrates an obvious correlation that, in my mind, is highly significant.

The Matthean infancy narrative and the contemporary context of surrogacy in India have little in common with each other. While the former is an ancient text that narrates the tale of the birth of the Messiah, the latter speaks to the effects of globalization and the growing success of the reproductive tourism industry in India. Additionally, the character of Joseph, a Jewish man betrothed to a virgin, is the foremost character in Matthew's infancy narrative, Mary being accorded a background role, whereas, the husband of the Indian surrogate, a married man who is already a father, is barely mentioned in the interviews. In complete contrast, the readers never hear his voice and know nothing about his characteristics. Although these are significant differences and illustrate the diverse contexts in which these narratives are constructed, there appears to be a connection nonetheless, that links these two conception-and-birth texts together. This connection, I would argue, is the *consent* of both these men that allow their betrothed or wife to participate in an irregular conception, with the hope that such participation will ultimately lead to a better future for their family or community. As a result, the Matthean Joseph's *consent* interpreted in the light of contemporary Indian context, which includes the economics of supply and demand, desire, and survival, not only complicates his participation, but also constructs his righteous, obedient nature in an ambiguous light. To state that the Matthean genealogy and the infancy narrative are constructed from an androcentric point of view is to state the obvious. Janice Capel Anderson writes: "In terms of gender, the genealogy substantiates Jesus' patrilineal claim to the titles. It also locates him in the sweep of salvation history from Abraham to David, from David to the exile and from the exile to the Christ. This salvation history is viewed essentially as a male enterprise. The stereotyped pattern of the genealogy—male δέ ἐγέννησςν τόν male(s)—repeats itself thirty-nine times."[10] In addition to this, scholars note that Matthew's infancy narrative when compared to Luke's infancy narrative, paints Joseph in a much more favorable light. Levine observes: "Unlike Luke's nativity account, which emphasizes women's active roles, Matthew's depicts Mary as entirely passive. This presentation is consistent with Matthew's insistence that familial connections are to be restricted in the new community that Jesus creates. Mary's passivity serves to undercut the privileged position she acquires by being Jesus' mother. Here, Joseph is the model of higher righteousness."[11] Given this androcentric pattern, how does one explain the occurrence of the five women inserted into Jesus's lineage (Tamar, 1:3; Rahab 1:5; Ruth 1:5; Bathsheba 1:6; and Mary 1:16) that apparently disrupts the predominantly male emphasis of the genealogy?

One of the ways scholars have tried to reason with the presence of these unlikely women in Matthew's genealogy is by highlighting their participation in a conception that is irregular and takes place outside the patriarchal tradition of marriage. However, such a connection, while effective in its interpretation, categorizes these mothers as we shall see, into either marginalized women victimized/exploited by patriarchy or mothers who exploit the rules of patriarchy by performing their textual agency and consenting to participate in an "irregular conception" that ensures the survival of both themselves and their families.[12] While such interpretations poignantly illustrate the connection between the women in Matthew's genealogy, they fail to accommodate the complex nature of the participation of these women in an irregular conception that intensifies the ambivalence of their already dichotomized maternal subjectivities as victimized marginal women vs. empowered heroic mothers. In order to bring to light the complexity of these mothers, I will read the ancient textual bodies of these women in conjunction with and through the contextual body of the postcolonial Indian surrogate mother. Such an interpretive move, I argue, deconstructs the binary categories illustrated in the labels such as exploiter exploited and victimized victimizers, and depicts their participation in an *irregular conception* in a new light. These women, pushed to the margins of society, transform themselves into mothers who allow themselves to be exploited in order that they can exploit the powers of patriarchy and ensure the survival of themselves and their families. In short (and anticipating the argument I will develop fully below), the five mothers in Matthew's genealogy are not only connected by their scandalous past, their marginalized positions in society or their participation in an irregular conception, but also linked in their performance of an *exploiter-exploited motherhood* that blurs the boundaries between exploited victims and exploiter heroes, thereby casting their maternal actions in an ambivalent light. The next section of my chapter will begin with the genealogy constructed by the author of Matthew and, in particular, will pay attention to the women included in Jesus's lineage.

Women in Matthew's Genealogy and the History of Their Interpretation

Men, more specifically fathers, take on an important role in the Matthean genealogy as patterns of men begetting other men repeats throughout the narrative, which is broken out into lineage "from Abraham to David" and then "from David to the deportation" and "the deportation to Babylon" (Matt. 1:17). Isaac, Jacob, Judah, Jesse, Jehoshaphat, and Zerubbabel, among others, all merit inclusion. The impression is that every key moment in salient history pivots around a man's choice or a man's experience, making the birth of Jesus, a male child, a natural apex for the Jewish people's story.[13]

This predominantly patriarchal narrative is disrupted, however, by five women who are inserted into the genealogy. The women are not the female consorts of the foundational Israelite patriarchs: Sarah, Rebecca, Leah, Rachel, and so forth. They are Tamar (Gen. 38), Rahab (Josh. 2, 6), Ruth, Bathsheba (2 Sam., 1 Kgs), and of course Mary herself. The presence of the four particular pre-Marian women, in an otherwise perfectly patriarchal construction of Jesus's lineage, has frequently baffled both men and women biblical scholars. If the author of Matthew was carefully weaving a seamless lineage that connected Jesus to the great cultured patriarchs of the past, how does one explain the presence of these female interlopers in an otherwise all male genealogy?

Biblical and theological scholars grappling with this "interruption" have, as a result, constructed three interpretations that help explain the presence of these scandalous women in an otherwise androcentric lineage. They are as follows: (a) the author of Matthew included these women in his genealogy because they are all sinners and Jesus's ultimate mission was to save humanity from their sins,[14] (b) the four women were all gentiles and their presence reflects the larger agenda of Jesus's mission, that he is the Savior of all people, Jews and gentiles alike,[15] and finally, (c) all these women are connected because they participate in irregular sexual unions that fall outside the traditional marital relationship.[16] Although these explanations seem somewhat plausible, scholars, over time, have found certain shortcomings in these theories deeming them unsatisfactory, and perhaps, even incomplete.

If we consider the first explanation—that the women are all sinners—we see that it assumes rather sexist interpretations of these women characters' stories. A feminist hermeneutic—or a hermeneutic at least marginally open to feminism—might stress the adverse circumstances facing these women, and consider their actions as expedient strategies in impossible situations. In place of such a reading, we see here a presumption that women's bodies are sexual and therefore inherently sinful and, as a result, must be controlled by men.[17] Uncritically accepting the notion that women's bodies are sexual and sinful fails to expose the patriarchal agenda present in such an interpretation, and works to justify the subordination of women to men. Furthermore, these female figures were revered during Jesus's time. Both Tamar and Rahab, Raymond Brown tells us, were considered proselytes of a sort, having secured Israel's future: Tamar by continuing her father-in-law Judah's bloodline in spite of his son's death, and Rahab by heroically ensuring the fall of Jericho. Bathsheba is the mother of Solomon, the final king of a united Israel.[18] Although Brown's reading is effective, however inadvertently, in dismantling the androcentric agenda present in Matthew's genealogy, he does not seem to probe their active participation *in an irregular conception* any further and appears content with the explanation that the conversion of these women is symbolic of their faith.

The second interpretation commonly used to explain the presence of these four women in Matthew's genealogy suggests that these women are included because they were foreign, which serves the theological contention that Jesus, himself of mixed heritage, was a savior for all the world, not just the Jews.[19] Although on the surface their outside origins could be seen as a connection between these women, scholars have repeatedly shown that this hypothesis is not without its flaws.[20] One scholarly interpretation takes issue with the claimed foreign status of the four women. In early Jewish tradition, Rahab and Ruth were considered proselytes, and Tamar and Bathsheba are usually considered to be Hebrews.[21] Gender overshadows ethnicity, as the women in Matthew's genealogy are often connected through their womanhood and/or motherhood but their foreignness is never probed further.[22] While Capel Anderson's critique illustrates the importance of a feminist voice in this debate, the question regarding the ethnicity of these women still remains unsolved. While the connection between Rahab, Bathsheba, Tamar, and Ruth can be seen through a foreign lens, the difficulty arises when trying to connect these women to the figure of Mary, who is Jewish. However, through the lens of surrogacy, a connection among these women can begin to emerge.

Finally, the third interpretation notes that all of the five women participated in a birth that falls outside traditional boundaries of marriage, and would have been considered scandalous for their time. The idea is that their inclusion here provides precedent for God intervening in highly irregular ways. Jesus's nativity, while odd and perhaps more extreme than previous aberrations in Israel's patriline, does not violate a pure system but stands out as the most exceptional of the divinely ordained exceptions.[23] In comparison to the first two explanations, most scholars now agree that the third interpretation appears to make most sense and best fits the theological agenda of the author of Matthew.

In addition to these three interpretations there is a fourth interpretation that pushes the boundaries of Christian faith because of its scandalous nature—Jane Schaberg's book *The Illegitimacy of Jesus*. While most biblical scholars (men and women) are content with the explanation that the women present in Matthew's genealogy are connected in their irregular conception,[24] Schaberg pushes this argument further by suggesting that the women in Matthew's genealogy are connected because they all participate in a conception that is not only irregular, but also illegitimate. She writes:

> The problem before Matthew was to make theological sense of the tradition concerning an illegitimate pregnancy. No text and traditions were available to illuminate easily the event and to present it as predicted. No text in the Hebrew Bible vindicates a woman who has been seduced or raped or chooses to become pregnant by someone other than her husband. No text legitimates the child born of such a union (note that the first child born to David and Bathsheba dies) much less prepares for the thought that this might be the origin of a Messiah. Out of fragments easily misunderstood the stories of the four women mentioned in the genealogy, and Isaiah 7:14, elucidated by Deuteronomy 22:23–27—Matthew undertook to understand and present the story of the origin of the illegitimate Jesus as the story of one who relived and lived within Israel's covenant with God.[25]

Reading illegitimacy into the Matthean genealogy has opened Schaberg's interpretation to quite a few misconceptions and criticisms, especially by her male counterparts. One of Schaberg's biggest critics has been her own teacher Raymond E. Brown.[26] For example, in his commentary, *The Birth of the Messiah*, Brown suggests that the arguments laid out by

Schaberg are extremely tenuous, arguing: "She [referring to Schaberg] cannot offer from the first two centuries a single clear Christian affirmation that Jesus was illegitimate. One can debate whether Paul knew the v.c. [virginal conception] when he wrote that Jesus was 'born of a woman'; but he scarcely knew that Jesus was the child of seduction or rape when he wrote that 'he was born under the Law (Gal 4:4).' "[27] Schaberg's interpretation of Mary's virginal conception in Matthew read through the tradition of illegitimacy is understood by Brown to mean either seduction or rape.[28] He continues, "Clearly unlikely is the proposal that Matt and Luke independently happened to create very different stories that apparently stressed Mary's virginity (even though they knew and wanted to convey that she had been seduced or raped) so that all subsequent commentators until Schaberg misread them to refer to a v.c."[29] The problem with Brown's critique of Schaberg's interpretation is that he does not create any textual space for Mary's agency in choice, a conception that falls outside the traditional boundaries of marriage. Schaberg responding to this charge levied by Brown points out, "Astonishing in such a careful scholar is the misrepresentation of my position regarding the possibility of Mary's rape: Brown takes as the essence of my reading the historical claim that Mary was raped, referring to it five times. In fact, I argued that the question whether the pregnancy was the result of the seduction or rape of Mary or the result of her free choice to have sex with someone other than Joseph, must remain an open one historically."[30] By inserting choice into her interpretation, Schaberg expands the definition of illegitimacy to move beyond seduction and rape, asking her readers to entertain the possibility that Mary could have "willingly" participated in a birth that does not fit the patriarchal mindset of her time. Yet, the question regarding the participation of all five women in the genealogy still remains unsolved. In other words, why would five women, marginalized by society, participate in a birth that would have been considered illegitimate/irregular during their time? Thus, reading the narratives of these women alongside the postcolonial context of surrogacy in India will help bring to the surface some of the complexities surrounding their maternal actions to participate in a scandalous conception.

Exploited-Exploiters, Victimized-Victimizers: The Performance of an Ambivalent Motherhood

One possible connection between the postcolonial surrogate mothers in India and the five mothers in Matthew's genealogy is that they are all marginalized women and, as a result of their marginalization, they are forced to act boldly and transgress the patriarchal boundaries that seek to rein in their bodies. In other words, emboldened by their marginal situations, these women—the Matthean mothers and the Indian surrogate mothers take risks with their bodies, that they otherwise might not have taken under different circumstances. The five Matthean mothers are all women pushed outside the patriarchal structure of their time because none of them are properly related to a man through marriage. Tamar (Gen. 38) is a widow and childless;[31] Rahab (Josh. 2, 6), a prostitute by profession, lives in the city of Jericho;[32] Ruth, once again a childless widow refuses to leave her mother-in-law Naomi, and follows her to her homeland;[33] Bathsheba, the wife of Uriah, one of David's soldiers (2 Sam. 11), is seduced/raped by King David,[34] and finally Mary, the mother of Jesus (Matt. 1), is a Jewish peasant woman who is betrothed to Joseph but is found to be with child before their marriage is consummated. Thus, the marginalization of the women in Matthew's genealogy takes place at two levels: first, four of these five mothers are pushed to the brink of society because none of them at conception are connected to a man through the traditional relationship of marriage, and, second, given their status as widows, prostitutes, and/or unmarried mothers, one can infer that none of them belong to the powerful ranks of society. Bathsheba constitutes an interesting exception to both rules, as we shall see, although in other ways her positionality overlaps significantly with the other four women of the genealogy.

Tamar: Genesis 38

The first scandalous mother to be mentioned in Matthew's genealogy is Tamar. The story of Tamar, as Wainwright observes, "challenges the patriarchal understanding of generation and the continuity of the male name. It is a two-edged story in which female power's critique of patriarchy is acknowledged, but that same female power is incorporated into patriarchal structures and androcentric perspectives."[35] Although I agree with Wainwright's point of view that the character of Tamar critiques the patriarchal framework and is descriptive of a widow's female power, I would like to push her analysis even further and argue that the reason why Tamar is able to express her female power is because as a widow, she is marginalized by the society of her time. This is a woman whose economic and social desperation pushes her over the edge and causes her to participate in a controversial conception.

When Tamar was told, "Your father-in law is going up to Timnah to shear his sheep," she put off her widow's garments, put on a veil, wrapped herself up, and sat down at the entrance to Enaim, which is on the road to Timnah. She saw that Shelah was grown up, yet she had not been given to him in marriage. When Judah saw her, he thought her to be a prostitute, for she had covered her face. He went over to her at the roadside and said, "Come, let me come in to you" for he did not know that she was his daughter-in law. (Gen. 38:13–16)

In their book *Narrative in the Hebrew Bible,* David Gunn and Danna Nolan Fewell note: "The woman Tamar, as her widow's garments reminds us, is in a different position. Comforted or not, she is expected to remain where Judah has put her, a widow in her father's house. To get out of her widow's clothes permanently she must put them aside temporarily. Thus, her changing of clothes, which neatly frames her dangerous deception, is symbolic of her larger goal."[36] Tamar's initiative to knowingly (or to use Fewell and Gunn's description "deceptively") engage in sexual intercourse with her father-in-law is a controversial decision for both the ancient and the modern reader. The repercussions of her decision are alluded to in Gen. 38:24: "About three months later Judah was told, "Your daughter-in-law Tamar has played the whore; moreover she is pregnant as a result of whoredom" And Judah said, "Bring her out, and let her be burned." This, raises the question of why a woman who up until now has been described as passive and submissive to the men in her family, crosses the traditional boundaries of her culture and engages in a controversial act that could jeopardize her reputation and probably even her life? Hence, rather than address this question as a historian, I prefer to read this text through a contextual hermeneutic lens. As such, I direct my attention to the postcolonial context of surrogacy in India.

The textual and contextual bodies of Tamar and the Indian surrogate mother are linked together through a number of similarities. First, both Tamar and the Indian surrogate mother are explicitly (in the case of the former) and implicitly (in the case of the latter) accused of participating in prostitution. Palyattil, Blyth, Sidhva, and Balakrishinan, point out, "Surrogacy remains one of the most controversial of current reproductive procedures; primarily because it relies on the reproductive services of a woman acting as a gestational carrier (whether or not she is also the genetic mother of the child she is carrying). Critics have decried it as womb renting and akin to prostitution."[37] Both Tamar and the Indian surrogate mother participate in a conception that not only falls outside patriarchal marriage, but in doing so, choose to walk the fine line between morality and immorality. Pande notes:

> The surrogate-prostitute comparison plays a critical role in the disciplinary project. It is simultaneously challenged and reinforced by the brokers, counselors, and medical professionals at different stages of the labor process. At the time of recruitment and counseling, the surrogates are assured that their role does not involve any "immoral acts" like "sleeping with clients." The bad surrogate, however, is often compared to a prostitute in informal counseling and mentoring sessions. Consequently, the surrogate is under constant fear of crossing the thin line between morality and immorality and disturbing the delicate balance of being a perfect mother-worker.[38]

One can infer from the biblical text and the interviews of the Indian surrogate mother that the decision to participate in a controversial conception is a choice that both Tamar and the Indian surrogate mother make knowing full well about the consequences of their actions. In her article titled "Crossing Bodies, Crossing Borders: International Surrogacy between the United States and India," Usha Rengachary Smerdon contends that most surrogate mothers acknowledge "the psychic costs of service, including missing the children they have while confined at a clinic and missing the child they have relinquished. The fear of miscarriage and fetal disabilities also cause psychic injury and stress for surrogates. In addition, traditional Indian attitudes towards sex and procreation often force a surrogate to hide her pregnancy and/or invent stories about her pregnancy."[39] And yet, in spite of the risks to their physical and mental wellbeing, these mothers, the ancient and the contemporary ones, knowingly and consciously participate in an act that is scandalous, controversial, and a risk to their lives, probing one to interrogate further and deeper into their participation.

While both Tamar and the Indian surrogate mother participate in a controversial conception that challenges their moral character, their decision to do so underscores their need for survival. In one of her interviews with a surrogate named Gauri, Amrita Pande reports: "In the words of surrogate Gauri, 'The only thing they told me was that this thing is not immoral, I will not have to sleep with anyone, and that the seed will be transferred into me with an injection. They also said that I have to keep the child inside me, rest for the whole time, have medicines on time, and give up the child.' "[40] The emphasis on recreating a conception that does not depend on physical intercourse is highlighted by the doctors and the medical staff in order that the Indian surrogate mother can be assured of her chastity and her moral virtue. The implication is that, conception through a needle is more ethical, moral, and socially acceptable than conception through a penis. Although the character of Tamar conceives in a traditional way, there is a similarity between her and the Indian surrogate mother. Both Tamar and the surrogate not only participate in an *irregular conception*, but their decision to do so is intimately entwined with their rationalization for survival.

Explaining the challenges of childless women in the Hebrew Bible, Carol Meyers observes: "The rigors of childbearing notwithstanding, choosing to remain childless was hardly an option. Women responded to their own maternal impulses and to the larger family and societal needs. Thus, having children and caring for them were integral parts of every woman's life (except if she was barren). The variety and complexity of a woman's economic role were surely matched by the demands of her maternal role."[41] As the text of Genesis makes plain, the character of Tamar is pushed to the fringes of society because of her status as a childless widow. This means that the only way she can right this situation is by reinserting herself into the patriarchal framework through her womb. Wainwright illustrates this point: "She [Tamar] is an endangered woman in the hands of the patriarchal law. Because of Tamar's foresightedness, however, it becomes clear that the child Tamar bears is of Judah and she is therefore re-incorporated into the patriarchal clan but in a way that has challenged its structures."[42] Thus, both Tamar and the Indian surrogate mother make a conscious, albeit controversial, choice to insert themselves into their respective communities. While Tamar uses her womb to secure her position as a mother, the Indian surrogate mother voluntarily inserts herself into a capitalistic economy by turning her womb into a commodity that is then exchanged for a price in the free market. However, it is important to note that although both mothers use their wombs quite differently to negotiate their space in society, both mothers, having no material means, are left with no choice but to use the only resource they have as a means for negotiation: their wombs. This illustrates my point that economic marginalization and the fear of social ostracism pushes both these women to trespass moral, ethical, and social boundaries. As a result, in attempting to secure their position in society, both Tamar and the Indian surrogate mother first agree to the exploitation of themselves and their wombs, in order that they can exploit the powerful structures that seek to marginalize their bodies both economically and socially.

Rahab: Joshua 2, 6

The second mother to be mentioned in Matthew's genealogy is Rahab. Wainwright notes, "The biblical story of Rahab (Jos. 2, 6:22–25) stands out in the midst of the military campaign of Israel against the land of Canaan. Within this story, the woman Rahab, designated as a harlot but whose profession receives no more attention in the story, stands out by way of contrast to the male world of conquest (represented by the two Israelite spies) and the world of power (represented by the King of Jericho and his men)."[43] Unlike Tamar, who is married and placed firmly within the patriarchal framework of her time, the character of Rahab is a perpetual outsider living in the margins. Joshua 2:15 states, "Then she let them down by rope through the window, for her house was on the outer side of the city wall and she resided within the wall itself." Although it is not clear from the text whether Rahab's proximity to the margins of the city wall was due to her profession, the profession was considered scandalous by the ancient world. Yet Schaberg argues:

> The narrator makes no comment of scorn or condemnation on Rahab's harlotry. Apparently she was accepted as an outcast who survived in an institutionalized status outside the family unit, beyond the normal social structure and its boundaries and rules. Nor does the narrator comment on the presence of the Israelite spies in her house. The Old Testament discourages unions with prostitutes (Prov 2:16–22; 29:3; 31:3) and warns fathers against their daughters becoming prostitutes (Lev 19:29; cf. Deut 23:17), but it also recognizes that prostitutes were patronized. Their sexual activity, not under the control of a husband or a father, was probably tolerated if not encouraged.[44]

What does the character of Rahab have in common with the postcolonial Indian surrogate mother? On the surface these two mothers could not be further apart. While Rahab is a prostitute from the ancient world, the Indian surrogate mother is a married woman from the contemporary Third world, renting out her womb to rich infertile couples and struggling to make a living in a neocolonial environment. In addition, while the Indian surrogate mother participates in an irregular conception, Rahab does not. However, in spite of these glaring differences, it still seems to me that there is one common trait that connects the bodies of these women: both women, marginalized and placed on the fringes of society, risk their lives for the greater good of their families.

In her article titled "Having Twins with a Surrogate—in India," Adrienne Arieff narrates that her journey to motherhood was brought to fruition in India through surrogacy, and explains to her readers the benefits of this industry, as told to her by surrogate, Vaina. She notes:

> In India, by contrast, the applicable laws were written at a national level, the paperwork more straightforward, and the results far more predicable in practice. I also learned that for my surrogate, Vaina, surrogacy was an opportunity to help her own growing family. She would earn the equivalent of several years' salary, allowing her husband to start a business and to better care for their children. I admit I'd imagined a proto-feminist surrogate, perhaps using her money on her own education, but Vaina is who she is. Dr. Patel's clinic works with its surrogates to protect them, and their fees. Vaina's earnings would go where she wanted them to go.[45]

The notion that the surrogacy laws in India are straightforward and simple is, however, quite problematic, especially when discussing the rights and the protection of the Indian surrogate mother. In addition, note how Arieff draws an implicit comparison between Vaina, her Indian surrogate, and the proto-feminist (read: Western) surrogate. Mohanty argues:

> Feminist discourse on the third world which assumes a homo-geneous category—or group—called "women" necessarily operates through such a setting up of originary power divisions. Power relations are structured in terms of a unilateral and undifferentiated source of power and a cumulative reaction to power. Opposition is a generalized phenomenon created as a response to power—which, in turn, is possessed by certain groups of people. The major problem with such a definition of power is that it locks all revolutionary struggles into binary structures—possessing power versus being powerless. Women are powerless, unified groups.[46]

Although Arieff never explicitly mentions or labels the Indian surrogate mother as a "powerless victim," she implicitly deems this third world mother as being lower than her Western counterpart because of her benevolence toward her family. Such an interpretation, it appears to me, overlooks the agency of the Indian surrogate mother demonstrated in her ability to become a professional mother who is not only exploited by the powerful structures of surrogacy, but, in turn, exploits this industry by turning her womb into a commodity and exchanging it in the free market for a price.

How does this compare with Rahab? Joshua 2:12–14 states:

> Now then, since I [Rahab] have dealt kindly with you, swear to me by
> the Lord that you in turn will deal kindly with my family. Give me a
> sign of good faith that you will spare my father and mother, my brothers
> and sisters, and all who belong to them, and deliver our lives from death.
> The men said to her, "Our life for yours! If you do not tell this business
> of ours, then we will deal kindly and faithfully with you when the Lord
> gives us the land."

Although the means to ensure survival for both Rahab and the Indian
surrogate mother are different, in that the former seeks the protection
of her family through a promise while the latter receives monetary compensation, their ability to use their marginalized, sexualized status as a
tool to negotiate the incorporation of their families into a patriarchal
economy illustrates a connection between the two. Wainwright argues,
"Within the story, however, Rahab is the chief actor. She thwarts the
search for the spies, secures the promise of the spies to contravene the
rule of hērem (Josh 6:17) and thereby guarantees a place for herself and
her family in the history of Israel (Josh 6:22–23,25). The woman who
is outsider to the patriarchal culture generally and outsider to the ethnic
culture of Israel is incorporated into both (6:25)."[47] Although I do find
myself agreeing with Wainwright's interpretation that Rahab is incorporated into the patriarchal and ethnic culture of her time, it seems to
me that the only way she can insert both her family and herself into this
culture is by risking her life.

Both Rahab and the Indian surrogate mother consciously choose to
participate in an activity that is life threatening in exchange for their
survival. Recounting the true incident of Pramila Vaghela, a professional surrogate mother, Kishwar Desai seeks to expose the dark side of
postcolonial surrogacy in India. She writes:

> Dr Manish Banker, from the Pulse Women's Hospital, is reported to
> have said that Premila had come for a check-up. "She suddenly had a
> convulsion and fell on the floor," he said. "We immediately took her
> for treatment. Since she was showing signs of distress, we conducted an
> emergency caesarean section delivery." The child, who was born a month
> premature, was admitted to the intensive care unit. Premila was moved
> to another hospital, which claims she was in a highly critical condition,
> having suffered a cardiac arrest. Although there's no suggestion that this
> was the case with Premila, sadly, in many cases the surrogate's life is

secondary. It is the baby, for whose birth the hospital is being paid, that is paramount. Most mothers sign contracts agreeing that even if they are seriously injured during the later stages of pregnancy, or suffer any life-threatening illness, they will be "sustained with life-support equipment" to protect the foetus. Further, they usually agree to assume all medical, financial and psychological risks—releasing the genetic parents, their lawyers, the doctors and all other professionals from all liabilities.[48]

As marginalized women, Rahab and the Indian surrogate mother are pushed to perform their agency under dire circumstances in the hope that participation in a "risky operation" will eventually lead to the betterment of themselves and their families. While in the case of Rahab, her risky behavior pays off because she and her family are saved from the Israelite invaders, Pramila Vaghela, the Indian surrogate mother, is not quite as lucky and pays with her own life for her desire to provide a secure future for her family. As a result, Rahab and the Indian surrogate mother are not just symbols of faith or empowerment, but marginalized women who not only seize the opportunity to create a better life for themselves and their families, but will also go to any lengths to achieve that security.

Ruth

The third mother to be mentioned by Matthew in his genealogy is Ruth. Amy-Jill Levine introduces her reader to the story of Ruth in her *Women's Bible Commentary Essay*:

> In this deceptively simple narrative a poor, widowed foreigner becomes the wife of a respected man from Bethlehem and the great grandmother of King David. Ruth is depicted as the ideal daughter-in-law, wife, and Gentile. For Naomi, she offers the loyalty and support associated less with daughters-in-law than with husbands, and her worth is proclaimed by the women of Bethlehem as being greater than that of seven sons. In motivating Boaz to action and in bearing his child, Ruth proves herself a worthy wife.[49]

The pattern of the poor, childless, widow, marginalized by society, continues with the story of Ruth. However, there is one more layer added to the marginalization of Ruth, that is not found in any of the other narratives. Ruth 1:22 reads: "So Naomi returned together with Ruth the Moabite, her daughter-in-law, who came back with her from the country of Moab. They came to Bethlehem at the beginning of the barley harvest." As the text tells us, Ruth is not only a foreigner (an outsider by race) but also follows her mother-in-law to a foreign country. In other words, Ruth, a childless widow, is doubly marginalized as both a woman within a patriarchal culture and as a Moabite (read: foreigner), living in a foreign land. It is interesting to note that while Tamar's controversial decision begins and ends with her participation in a sex act that falls outside the traditional boundaries of marriage, the controversy in Ruth's life begins at a much earlier stage. In her book *God and the Rhetoric of Sexuality*, Phyllis Trible states:

> Not only has Ruth broken with family, country, and faith, but she has also reversed sexual allegiance. A young woman has committed herself to the life of an old woman rather than to the search for a husband, and she made this commitment not "until death us do part" but beyond death. One female has chosen another female in a world where life depends on men. There is no more radical decision in all the memories of Israel.[50]

It is important to note that Trible's interpretation also implies that by clinging to her mother-in-law Naomi, Ruth commits herself to a lesbian relationship.[51] Although Ruth's decision to follow her mother-in-law would have been considered a bold choice, such an action puts her in charge of an old woman as she now becomes responsible for two lives, Naomi and hers. Thus it appears to be something that even Naomi realizes. Ruth 3:1–5 states:

> Naomi her mother-in-law said to her, "My daughter, I need to seek some security for you, so that it may be well with you. Now here is our kinsman Boaz, with whose young women you have been working. See, he is winnowing barley tonight at the threshing floor. Now wash and anoint yourself, and put on your best clothes and go down to the threshing floor; but do not make yourself known to the man until he has finished eating and drinking. When he lies down, observe the place where he lies; then, go and uncover his feet and lie down; and he will tell you what to do." She said to her, "All that you tell me I will do."

Naomi expresses to Ruth that she needs to provide some security for herself. However, as the text has already illustrated to its readers, the character of Ruth is depicted as a loyal woman who will not leave her mother-in-law under any circumstances. Ruth 1:14–16: "Then they wept aloud again. Orpah kissed her mother-in-law, but Ruth clung to her. So she said, 'See your sister-in-law has gone back to her people and to her gods; return after your sister-in law.' But Ruth said, 'Do not press me to leave you or to turn back from following you! Where you go, I will go; where you lodge, I will lodge; your people shall be my people, and your God my God.' " Naomi, similar to Ruth, has lost not only her husband, but also her sons (Ruth 1. 2–5), and, furthermore, she has aged and this means the chances of her starting a new family are probably slim. As a result, the only way for Naomi to reinsert herself into her community and ensure her security is through her younger, child-bearing daughter-in-law, Ruth.[52] Furthermore, given Ruth's loyalty toward her mother-in-law, Naomi would have surely realized that security for her daughter-in-law could very well mean security for herself.

Palattiyil, Blyth, Sidhva, and Balakrishnan note, "Uneducated and disadvantaged women, with limited alternative opportunities to generate comparable levels of income and having limited autonomy in patriarchal familial contexts, may experience economic and family pressure to participate in surrogacy."[53] Once again, the Indian surrogate mother and the character of Ruth may not be exactly alike; after all, one is a mother who participates in conception for monetary compensation and is already a mother, while the other is a childless widow whose conception guarantees the insertion of her body into the patriarchal system of her society. However, the point that connects both these women is that they not only participate in an *irregular conception* that could be termed illegal/illegitimate by their respective societies, but they are also coaxed/coerced to participate in such a conception by their own families. In other words, while Ruth is coaxed by Naomi to participate in a conception that by all means would be considered illegal,[54] the Indian surrogate mother, plagued by her poverty, is often times pressured by her family to participate in commercial surrogacy. Supporters such as Dr. Patel, the doctor at Akankasha Infertility clinic in Gujarat, would argue against this notion of exploitation of the Indian surrogate mother at the hands of her family, saying:

> The people she [Dr. Patel] does feel good about helping are the local women—the surrogates—so long as they're not being coerced by their husbands or in-laws eager for a paycheck. "I must be certain it's a woman's own decision," she explains. "If there's any sign of tension or unwillingness, I spot it straightaway." Patel also helps to ensure each woman keeps control over her fee. "For example, if she wants to buy a house, we'll hold her money for her until she's ready. Or if she wants to put it in an account for her children, we'll go with her to the bank to set up the account in her name." The money gives many women their first taste of empowerment.[55]

Although Patel insists that her clinic works hard to protect the Indian surrogate mother from being exploited by her husband or her in-laws, the reality as many surrogates have explained in their own words, time and again, is quite the opposite. Usha Rengachary Smerdon questions this "free choice" emphasized by Dr. Patelwhen she argues:

> As attorney, Susan Crockin noted, "to the extent that people are looking to India because of the less expensive arrangement they can make, if you do the math, they're making ten times their husband's, then, that's the equivalent of paying somebody here probably $150,000 to $200,000 for being a gestational surrogate. When the 'choices' can be so dire, it is possible that Indian women may be pressurized by their families, brokers, and personal circumstances to lend their bodies for cash."[56]

One is already aware that the marginalization of Ruth and the Indian surrogate mother occurs because of their social circumstances, in that both these women have no economic security to fend for themselves. This means that both Ruth and the Indian surrogate mother, having grim choices and not much to lose, are coerced by their families into using the only one weapon that can help them overcome their poverty, and ensure their security—their bodies, more specifically their wombs. Thus, the text of Ruth, read through the lived realities of the Indian surrogate mothersheds new light on her *willing obedience* and her participation in an irregular conception. In that, in the case of Ruth, it is the marginalized family member, that is, Naomi, who persuades her to participate in a reproduction that, while illegitimate, provides them with the hope to lead a legitimate life. Yet the only way to achieve this security for both Ruth and the Indian surrogate mother is to use their bodies as a tool that must be exploited in order that they can exploit the societies that exploit them.

Bathsheba: 2 Samuel 11

The fourth woman to be mentioned in Matthew's genealogy is not named, but instead, is introduced simply as the *wife of Uriah*. The character of Bathsheba stands in complete contrast to the three women discussed above. This is because she is not a widow and is married. And as the text tells us, her husband Uriah, the Hitite, was a soldier in the army of king David. In addition to these two main differences, Bathsheba, especially in comparison with the other women, is depicted as passive and meek. She rarely speaks, negotiates, and does not aggressively insert herself into society. Schaberg points out:

> In many ways the story of Bathsheba is the most horrifying of the four Old Testament stories. She is not mentioned by name in Matthew's genealogy, probably because identification of her as the wife of Uriah stresses her adultery and not her subsequent marriage to David, or because even as married to David she was still in some way the wife of Uriah. In her appearance in 2 Samuel 11, she is so colorless, passive, and pathetic a figure that she is nearly anonymous there also.[57]

In addition to her submissiveness, the character of Bathsheba participates in a conception that is not only illegitimate, but also devoid of any choice on her part in the matter. As the text of 2 Samuel 11:4–5 says:

> It happened, late one afternoon, when David rose from his couch and was walking about on the roof of the king's house, that he saw from the roof a woman bathing; the woman was very beautiful. David sent someone to inquire about the woman. It was reported, "This is Bathsheba daughter of Eliam, the wife of Uriah the Hittite." So David sent messengers to get her, and she came to him, and he lay with her. (Now she was purifying herself after her period) Then she returned to her house. The woman conceived; and she sent and told David, "I am pregnant."

Although the character of Bathsheba is not marginalized or placed outside the patriarchal framework in exactly the same way as Tamar, Ruth, or Rahab, she still finds herself standing in the margins. This is because, while the three women before her are ostracized because of their status as widows or prostitutes and the only way for them to insert their bodies back into society is through an irregular/illegal conception or action, the body of Bathsheba, in contrast is removed from the patriarchal structure precisely because of her sex act, her adultery. The marginalization of Bathsheba occurs on two levels. First, this woman is placed in a position of complete powerlessness before an authoritative and powerful king,[58] and, second, compounding this already subjugated position, the text deprives her of any space for her voice that would be illustrative of her choice in the manner of her participation. But the question remains, what does the ancient character of Bathsheba have in common with the Indian surrogate mother living and working in a postcolonial India?

The exploitation and the insertion of Bathsheba into the patriarchal framework, similar to the Indian surrogate mother and the other mothers presented before her, occurs through her womb. According to 2 Sam. 12:24: "Then David consoled his wife Bathsheba, and went to her, and lay with her; and she bore a son, and he named him Solomon."[59] Not only is Bathsheba inserted into the patriarchal royal lineage by David through marriage, but her status as a queen is further solidified when she bears a son.The wife of a soldier is transformed into a queen and finally into the mother of a baby boy, who, incidentally is also the heir to the throne. Wainwright, illustrating this journey of Bathsheba, notes, "Although, the text of 2 Samuel lays the fault very clearly at the feet of David (11:27) and Bathsheba is presented as passive throughout the story, the manner of referring to her points to the anomalous situation in which David's action places her. She is a danger to the patriarchal family structure, a danger which David removed by murdering Uriah and making Bathsheba his wife legally, thus incorporating her into that structure."[60]

In some sense similar to Bathsheba, but not quite the same, is the Indian surrogate mother whose incorporation into a capitalistic economy is illustrated by her irregular conception. Having been incorporated into the system, the lives of such women is expected to become better. However, the incident of their exploitation continues to haunt them and restricts them from reaching their potential as human beings. Elizabeth Anderson states, "Most surrogate mothers experience grief upon giving up their children—in 10 percent cases, seriously enough to require therapy. Their grief is not compensated by the $10,000 fee they receive. Grief is not an intelligible response to a successful deal, but rather, reflects the subject's judgment that she has suffered grave and personal loss."[61] The Indian surrogate mother uses her womb as a commodity that is exchanged to fulfill her economic needs, but she is unable to completely extricate herself from the bond that ties her to the child. Thus, for a successful surrogacy to take place not only must the bond between the surrogate mother and the child be under constant scrutiny, but also the motherly love that the Indian surrogate mother feels toward the child must be repressed as she must maintain her image as a professional mother. Palattiyyil, Blyth, Sidhva, and Balakrishnan observe the tension between the monetary and the emotional aspect of this business:

> Anecdotal evidence indicates that at least some surrogates suffer from postpartum depression and a sense of emptiness as a result of being unable to breastfeed their baby. But the surrogate is often encouraged to focus on the altruistic basis for her action. This notion of unselfishness,

along with other notions of "good karma" or positive actions that will yield other beneficial effects encourage the surrogate to emphasize the immediate monetary benefits and disregard the potential health and social consequences of surrogacy, assuming she was aware of the latter in the first place.[62]

In the process of repressing her love toward the child she is being paid to carry, the Indian surrogate mother may receive a better life, monetarily speaking, but she continues to be haunted by the feelings of guilt, thus preventing her from reaching her full potential as a human being and as a mother.

Schaberg, quoting J. A. Wharton writes, "'The figure of Bathsheba haunts the whole narrative with extraordinary ambiguity....One is forced to guess, without being able to conclude, what meaning these events had for her, whether she was victim, or accomplice, or somehow both at once.' The author may intend to portray not her shallowness but her entrapment, a total entrapment, in a situation where her feelings, right, plans, perhaps love all counted for nothing."[63] It is interesting to note that the feelings of Bathsheba, while not repressed by her, are definitely suppressed by the author of the text. While 2 Samuel 11:26 tells us that Bathsheba expresses her grief openly for her husband Uriah's death, the very same text remains silent in 2 Sam. 12:18 when her first child by David dies. Jo Ann Hackett states: "The narrative does not seem to hold her responsible for her actions with David, and the punishment that is meted out, that their child should die, is aimed by Yahweh and Nathan at David, not Bathsheba. Her feelings are not ignored completely; it is said that David comforted her in her grief (though it is David's grief and not Bathsheba's that the narrator describes at length. Further, she and David have another son, Solomon, to replace the dead child."[64] Similar to the Indian surrogate mother who is expected to forget the grief of giving up one child because she has another child waiting for her, the text does not allow any space for Bathsheba's grief, and instead tries to replace her grief with the joy of another child. Pande writes:

Naseem, a thirty-year-old surrogate and mother of a three-year-old boy heard about surrogacy from the nurses when she went to have her second child aborted: "When Jayati [a nurse at the clinic and an informal broker] heard that I am getting the cutting [abortion] done because I can't afford to feed another child, she told me about surrogacy. She told me there is nothing immoral about it, so I agreed." It is indeed poignant that Naseem, who cannot afford to have her own second child or even feed the first, is instead having a child for someone else to keep.[65]

It is ironic to note that both Bathsheba and Naseem were never given the chance to express the loss of their dead child, but instead directed to focus on the happiness that the second child, legitimated by the power of Yahweh/the surrogacy industry, would bring to their lives.

However, if the modern context of Indian surrogacy has highlighted any aspect of this business, it is that the feeling of losing a child, either through death or surrogacy, is never erased, repressed maybe, but never forgotten, and so it continues to haunt the mother. Schaberg argues: "She [Bathsheba] personifies tragic passivity, unlike Tamar, Rahab, and Ruth who stood up against the fates offered them by society, took matters into their own hands, and bettered their positions within the patriarchal framework. Bathsheba who survives as a queen, never emerges as a person."[66] It is true that Bathsheba does not aggressively seek to better her position in society. As a woman unprotected by her husband, she becomes vulnerable to exploitation at the hands of a powerful man (David). However, in the end, Bathsheba does become a part of the powerful and elite structure of her society. Her insertion into patrilineage, similar to the other mothers preceding her and the Indian surrogate mother following her, is completed through two steps: her exploitation at the hands of the patriarchy, which leads to a conception that is legitimated by patriarchy. A passive Bathsheba, exploited at the hands of a patriarchal power, secures her position by becoming a queen and, more importantly, exploits her new identity as a mother by producing the future heir to the throne of David. In other words, the exploited wife of another man, seduced/raped by the ultimate patriarchal power (the king), transforms her subjectivity and secures her position by becoming an exploiter of the patriarchal structure.

Mary, the Mother of Jesus: Matt. 1:16

The fifth and the last mother to be mentioned in Matthew's genealogy is Mary. There are a few differences between the mothers of the Hebrew Bible and Mary. The first obvious difference is found in the text itself. The mothers of the Hebrew Bible are all mentioned over a span of three verses (1: 3–6), which accentuates the connection between them, while Mary is mentioned after a long gap of ten or so verses. This increases the challenge for the readers of finding creative ways to connect the character of Mary to the four mothers who came before her. In addition to this spatial difference, Mary, the mother of Jesus, is quite different from the four mothers of the Hebrew Bible in another way. While Ruth, Rahab, Tamar, and Bathsheba are all women who were either married, widowed, or had a scandalous history with men, the character of Mary, as the author of Matthew tells us, is unmarried and a virgin. Matt. 1:18 reads: "Now the birth of Jesus the Messiah took place in this way. When his mother Mary had been engaged to Joseph, but before they lived together, she was found to be with child from the Holy Spirit." In spite of this glaring difference, however, many scholars would argue that a connection exists between Mary and the other four women in the Matthean genealogy.

Raymond Brown, in his essay "The Annunciation to Joseph (Matt. 1:18–25)," tries to construct a connection between all five mothers in the Matthean genealogy. He argues:

> Anomalously for genealogies, among Matthew's forty-two fathers (his count) were listed four Old Testament women, all of them with a history before marriage or childbirth that made their situation either strange or scandalous. In particular, Tamar, the widow of Judah's son, was found to be pregnant indecently long after her husband's death; Judah denounced her till he realized that he was the father. Bathsheba, the wife of Uriah, became pregnant not by her husband but by David. Yet in all these instances the woman was God's instrument in preserving Israel and/or the lineage of the Messiah. So also, the fifth woman of the genealogy, Mary, is in a seemingly scandalous pregnancy.[67]

Raymond Brown is only one of a number of scholars who note that the one thing all five mothers share is that they all conceive in highly irregular manners that fall outside conventional patriarchal relationships. But why? It may be, as Schaberg has supposed, that these four female precursors groom the reader to interpret Mary as one in a line of scandalized women, whose atypical paths to motherhood end up restoring Israelite society's integrity. Their sons are all recognized as legitimate, in a move that Schaberg considers to be not divine intervention but God allowing for, or even sanctioning, the chaos of humans whose actions are not foreordained.[68] Although Schaberg and Brown fundamentally disagree, in that Schaberg interprets Mary's birth through the lens of illegitimacy, and Brown sees Mary's birth as irregular and unconventional, the one thing they both agree upon (to some extent) is that this irregular conception is righted by the God of Israel. Another twist on God's active role in Mary's story comes from Wainwright, who says that God's maneuver with Mary is so atypical, so nonpatriarchal, that women may have been the ones who recognized the pattern and influenced Matthew's presentation of Jesus's genealogy.[69] Dismantling androcentric interpretations of the narrative is a goal I share with Schaberg and Wainwright, but I see that such a commitment can lead to constructing the mothers in Matthew's genealogy and infancy narrative in one of two ways: as victims of patriarchy or heroes of empowerment. If our hermeneutic considers what is not being said in the text as well as what is being said, we can agree with Wainwright that the presence of these four women (five, including Mary) exposes the lie of a water-tight Israelite patriarchy, and we might further suppose that countless women brushed up against the androcentric kinship system and there-fore affected the eventual birth of Jesus.[70] There is a shadow history that accompanies the dominant account—even the first evangelist couldn't suppress it entirely. And therein lies the potential for gender liberation.

Both Schaberg and Wainwright consciously choose to direct their interpretations toward a place of liberation, and this is what leads them to read the mothers in Matthew as symbols of female empowerment.[71] Such interpretations, while extremely important, nevertheless fail to fully accommodate the complexity that surrounds the participation of these mothers in an irregular conception. In other words, because of their desire to liberate the women in Matthew's text, feminist scholars overlook the fact that the only way these mothers are able to achieve empowerment is through the insertion of their bodies into the patri-lineage—that is, through submitting to exploitation. This raises the question of whether, as a feminist, one can truly label the mothers in Matthew's genealogy as symbols of empowerment or "shapers of an alternative tradition," when the only path to agency for any of these mothers is through their willingness to accept oppression? Keeping this question in the forefront, I now turn to the last mother in the Matthean genealogy, Mary, the mother of Jesus.

Mary is markedly different from the other women included in Matthew's genealogy; she is even more exceptional. Tamar, Rahab, Ruth, and Bathsheba propelled Jesus's ancestry along, but they each had the help of a male partner. The Indian surrogate mother is similar to the character of Mary found in Matthew's genealogy in this regard. Both Mary and the Indian surrogate mother not only participate in a controversial conception, but are also, able to conceive without physical intercourse. Nirmala, a broker and matron of a surrogacy hostel, tells Pande: "To convince the women I often explain to them that it's like renting a house for a year. We want to rent your womb for a year, and Doctor Madam will get you money in return. I tell them surrogacy is not immoral. It is much better than a woman going from one man's bed to the next to make money. Prostitution will not pay her much and can also lead to diseases."[72] Comparing surrogacy with prostitution high-lights the nature of the scandal that the Indian surrogate mothers face in the surrogacy industry. The remnants of a scandalous conception are also found in the ancient infancy narrative of Matthew. Matt. 1:20 tells readers: "Her husband Joseph, being a righteous man and unwilling to expose her to public disgrace, planned to dismiss her quietly." Mary's place in society is threatened on two counts. First, as a young betrothed virgin she participates in a conception that falls outside the patriarchal norms of her time, thus, potentially exposing her and her family to shame. And second, her position is further compromised when the nar-rator tells his audience that Joseph is planning to divorce her because of her shameful pregnancy. In contrast to the four mothers whom we previously discussed, who all use their illegitimate conception as a way to insert themselves back into their patriarchal society, it is Mary's scan-dalous pregnancy that pushes her into the margins of society.

The gravity of Mary's decision is further amplified when the nar-rator tells his audience, "Now after they had left, an angel of the Lord appeared to Joseph in a dream and said 'Get up, take the child and his mother, and flee to Egypt, and remain there until I tell you; for Herod is about to search for the child, to destroy him.' Then Joseph got up, took the child and his mother by night and went to Egypt and remained there until the death of Herod" (Matt 2:13). Scholars have often read this part in Matthew's narrative through the lens of Exodus. As Wainwright rightly observes: "It is the Exodus and especially the Mosaic tradition in its biblical and popular Jewish expositions that is reread to interpret Jesus in Matthew 2."[73] While one cannot deny the influence of Exodus on the narrative, to me, as a contextual hermeneutic, Matt. 2:13 also strongly evokes the neocolonial context of surrogacy in India. Palattiyil, Blyth, Sidhva, and Balakrishnan observe: "A surrogate may experience conflicting pressures over the social mores of pregnancy. She may be subject to the strain of having to live in secrecy, concoct stories about her pregnancy, or move away from home so as to conceal her pregnancy if it cannot be construed as legitimate in her social setting."[74] I am not, of course, suggesting that the situations of Mary and the Indian sur-rogate mother are exactly alike. Rather, by placing the contextual and textual bodies of both these women alongside one another, I would like to highlight some of the similarities that connects these mothers, and in making these associations, shed light on the ambivalences that are present in their irregular conceptions.

Similar to Mary, who is forced to hide her conception from society and is depicted by the author as an endangered woman, the Indian surrogate mother (while not in any danger for her life) is also forced to cover up her pregnancy. In many cases, the Indian surrogate mother is forced go into hiding and many a times has to relocate to a new town. Pande mentions the degree of secrecy and scandal that often plagues the Indian surrogate mother: "In India...the surrogates face a [high] degree of stigma. As a consequence, almost all the surrogates in this study decided to keep their surrogacy a secret from their community and very often from their parents."[75] Matt. 1:24–25 reads: "When Joseph awoke from sleep, he did as the angel of the Lord commanded him; he took her as his wife, but had no marital relations with her until she had borne a son and he named him Jesus."[76] As the author of Matthew tells his readers, the illegitimate conception of Mary is legitimated (or rather covered up) by Joseph when he decides to bring her into the honorable patriarchal structure of society through marriage. It is not just Mary or the Indian surrogate mother, therefore, who are forced to live a secret life; Joseph and the husband of the Indian surrogate also become co-conspirators in this process. Reporting on a surrogate named Reshma and her husband, Vinod, Anuj Chopra notes:

> Reshma's husband Vinod—not his real name—says his paltry $50 monthly pay as a painter would not be enough to educate his two children. He says the extra money will allow him to invest in his children's education and to buy a new home. But surrogacy is yet to be widely accepted here. For the past six months, Reshma and Vinod have been living in a neighboring village to keep the pregnancy a secret. "Otherwise, we'll be treated like social pariahs," he says. "This isn't a respectable thing to do in our society."[77]

Although the stigma of an irregular conception is dealt with differently by Mary and the Indian surrogate, in that the former conceals her secret under the deception of traditional marriage, while the latter lies about the death of the infant as an excuse to hide her scandal,[78] the fact remains that both these mothers, haunted by their conception, are forced to live a life of secrecy and deceit.

Mary as a Patriarchal Construct

The voice of Raymond Brown has unequivocally been one of the most important contributions to Marian scholarship within the field of New Testament studies. His early article titled "The Problem of the Virginal Conception of Jesus," focused on the virginity of Mary and the birth of

Jesus conceived as occurring without any human intervention. However, Brown clarifies his definition of the term "virginal conception," arguing that his discussion of the infancy narratives is limited only to the conception of Jesus. He writes, "I am concerned with the belief that Jesus was conceived in the womb of a virgin without the intervention of a human father, that is, without male seed; and every time I use the expression 'virginal conception,' I use it in that sense."[79] Separating himself from the works of Karl Rahner, who argues for Mary's postpartum virginity, Brown argues that the interpretation of Mary's postpartum virginity is dependent upon the way one reads the textual passages that references the familial relationship between Jesus and his brothers (and sisters) found in Mark 6:3, Matt. 13:55, John 2:12 and 7:5.[80] While Rahner, in common with most theologians, begins his interpretation of the infancy narratives by taking them at face value and without questioning their historical veracity, Brown begins his interrogation of the virgin birth by questioning its actuality. Brown's problem with the conception of Jesus is precisely its lack of historical evidence. He argues that while: "Matthew and Luke accepted the virginal conception as historical, we cannot be certain where they got their information on this point."[81] In an attempt to answer the historical question, Brown follows the comparative method. He reads the Christian birth narratives in parallel with stories of non-Christian miraculous births. And in doing so, Brown interprets the lack of sexual intercourse in the Christian narratives not only as being different, but, implicitly, as signaling Mary's moral and sexual superiority to her competitors.[82]

Brown's argument to preserve "Mary's virginity" in the Matthean gospel is built on four main pillars. First, he argues that the intention of the virginal conception is "clearly implied" through the Holy Spirit.[83] Second, he argues that Matthew uses Isaiah 7:14, in its Septuagintal form, to interpret the birth of Jesus. He writes: "*Hellenistic Judaism* has seemed a more fertile field for search because Matthew makes reference to the Greek (LXX) text Isa 7:14, 'The virgin shall conceive.'"[84] For Brown, Matthew's insertion of Isaiah into his infancy narrative was an attempt to accommodate Jesus to the lineage of David. His third reason focuses on the women present in Matthew's genealogy. Brown argues that the women are not sinners, but play an active role in furthering God's plan. He writes: "The women showed initiative or played an important role in God's plan and so came to be considered the instrument of God's providence or of His Spirit."[85] Brown suggests that Mary be read in this genealogy as God's intervention, that is far greater than in the case of the other women: "This intervention . . . was even more dramatic than the OT instances; there God had overcome the moral or biological irregularity of the human parents, while here He overcomes the total absence of the father's begetting."[86] Brown's depiction of the women in Matthew's genealogy poses two problems: (a) the female characters are depicted as using their agency or power to help further the male agenda of the text, thus allowing themselves to be constructed as mere pawns in the bigger plan of the male God; and (b) by highlighting Mary's virginity as a greater obstacle that needed to be overcome by God, Brown constructs a hierarchy that seeks to divide women against themselves. The fourth reason, according to Brown, is this: "to preserve the motif that a virgin would give birth to a son (Isa 7:14), Matthew added the assurance that Joseph did not have sexual relations with Mary before she gave birth to Jesus (1:25)."[87] In other words, Brown argues that the case to preserve Mary's virginity also rests on the simple assurance of the text.

The Lucan infancy narrative as read by Brown also makes the case for virginal conception. In constructing his argument, Brown once again offers four reasons for his defense. The first he calls *step-parallelism*, in which the greatness of Jesus over John is consistent within the text. In his article titled "The Virginal Conception of Jesus in the New Testament," Joseph Fitzmyer argued that when the Lucan narrative is read in isolation, without the influence of Matthew, the birth of Jesus appears to be quite an ordinary and usual event. Fitzmyer wrote:

> When this account is read in and for itself—without the overtones of the Matthean annunciation to Joseph—every detail in it could be understood of a child to be born of Mary in the usual human way, a child endowed with God's special favor, born at the intervention of the Spirit of God, and destined to be acknowledged as the heir to David's throne as God's Messiah and Son.[88]

However, Brown replying to Fitzmyer counters this argument by suggesting that the author of Luke inserts the virginal conception in his narrative with the intention to prove that the birth of Jesus is greater than that of John.[89] The second objection that Brown raises has to do with Mary's objection to the angel.[90] His third reason focuses on the answer given to Mary by the angel. He notes:

> [T]he angel's answer (1:35) speaks of a realistic but nonsexual begetting. The terms *eperchesthai*, "come upon" and *episkiazein*, "overshadow" which some have considered sexual, approximate language of Pentecost

and the transfiguration, but in a literal rather than figurative way, with a connotation of creation rather than of adoption or of cooperation with any human activity. This child is totally the work of God.[91]

Once again, Brown relies on the use of the Holy Spirit in the text to help bolster his argument to maintain the virginal conception of Jesus, but this time he links the work of the Spirit to Genesis.[92] The final reason for Brown's preservation of Mary's virginity is demonstrated in Elizabeth's response to Mary in Luke 1:42–45. Brown argues: "It is to the virginal conception rather than a natural conception that Elizabeth refers when she says of Mary: 'Fortunate is she who believed that the Lord's words to her would find fulfillment' (1:45). No belief would really be required if Mary was to conceive as any other young girl would conceive."[93]

In looking at his arguments, it becomes apparent that Brown's defense of Mary's virginity is entrenched in his own subjectivity as formed through his Roman Catholicism. Reilly notes, regarding the influence of Catholicism on Brown's scholarship: "[I]n 1981, he wrote that he 'personally' did not think that the meaning intended by the biblical writer could be contradictory to that intended by the church; and he rejected as 'modernism in the classic sense'—as a denial of any real content to doctrine—any openness to a historical-critical judgment 'that Jesus was conceived normally.' "[94] However, Brown's insistence on Mary's virginity is more about the reflection of Jesus (the man) than about the woman's subjectivity in the text, as when he asks "how a seduction tradition could be squared with early Christian 'insistence on the sinlessness of Jesus,' or a rape tradition with Mark's portrayed presumptions of family claims (Mark 3:31–35) and of family normality."[95] Thus, for Brown, Mary's virginity is inextricably intertwined with Jesus's sinless subjectivity as the Son of God. Such a reading not only displaces the female character in the text, but it also exposes the objectification of women's bodies by patriarchal societies (both ancient and modern). The female body, as a result, serves as a mere reflection to captures and preserve the fantasy of Christian purity. Mary is never allowed to catch a glimpse of her own subjectivity in the midst of her-story.

Janice Capel Anderson, in her article "Mary's Difference: Gender and Patriarchy in the Birth Narratives,"[96] acknowledges the importance of gender in biblical studies. She writes, "The chief contribution, as in many other areas of study, has been to indicate the significance of gender as a primary analytic category. Thus, feminist criticism has exposed the significance of gender in the production of biblical texts, the texts themselves and the interpretation and use of the texts over the years."[97]

The use of gender as a *primary analytic category* exposes the androcentric presuppositions that are already present among both the authors and readers of the texts. Acknowledging the works of peers such as Brown's *The Birth of the Messiah,* and joint efforts by Roman Catholic and Protestant scholars such as Brown, Karl P. Donfried, Joseph Fitzmyer and John Reumann, editors of *Mary in the New Testament,* Anderson notes that even though these works addressed "some nascent feminist concerns" in that "[t]heir emphasis on Mary as the first Christian believer, disciple, and model of faith for men and women, recognizes issues raised by modern women,"[98] they still fail to use gender as an interpretive lens to highlight some of the androcentric and patriarchal presuppositions in the Matthean and Lukan birth narratives.

Anderson argues that at the heart of Matthew's and Luke's infancy narratives lies a male fantasy of female gender, and it is this fantasy that leads to a narrative involving "a human mother, the creative action of God as progenitor, and a human legal father."[99] She notes that constructing such a plot forecloses the idea of illegitimacy or scandal surrounding the birth of Jesus. She argues: "They [the Matthean and Lukan infancy narratives] eliminate any possibility of biological human fatherhood and/or illegitimacy with a virgin conception prior to full marriage relations between the human mother and legal father."[100] Anderson also acknowledges that the virginal conception of Mary creates a tension in the text. Looking in detail at the four women in the Matthean genealogy, Anderson observes:

> Thus, Mary's female difference and her extraordinary conception are incorporated into a patriarchal framework as were those of her four predecessors in the genealogy. Her remarkable conception of Jesus without a male partner is highlighted—Jesus is Son of God through Mary—but the genealogy and the first episode of the birth story place this in context of the legal paternity of the Davidic descent. Tensions remain, however. Mary conceives in an anomalous state outside of marriage. God rather than a human male, "fathers" Jesus through a nonsexual creative act.[101]

While Mary is similar to Tamar (1:3), Rahab (1:5a), Ruth (1:5b) and the wife of Uriah (Bathsheba, 1:6) in that "The women foreshadow Mary and prepare the implied reader for a woman's irregular production of the Messiah outside of ordinary patriarchal norms yet within God's overarching plans and an overall patriarchal framework,"[102] her difference lies in her ability to conceive without a male partner—something that not only sets her apart from the other women, but also constructs her female body as uncontrollable by the patriarchal structures that seek to domesticate her.[103] Furthermore, Anderson compares the slippery virginal body of Mary by contrasting her with the dry barren bodies of Elizabeth and Hannah. In her reading of the Lukan infancy narrative, she observes:

> Virginity is not the locus of Mary's lowliness. The barrenness of Hannah, Elizabeth and other married women may be presented as a matter of reproach and pain, but the virginity of someone betrothed is not. Virginity is a unique status for the heroine. Mary's virginity is an obstacle overcome by God, as is barrenness, but it is not the source of humiliation. It exalts what God has done and both Mary and Jesus.[104]

Mary's virginal conception is the slippery trope that escapes the control of man and allows her to be different from the other women preceding her, and it is in her difference that her liberation from patriarchy occurs. Thus, the stake in maintaining Mary's virginity plants the seed of liberation in the minds of women who come after her. Anderson writes: "The way in which the birth narratives project and undermine versions of a male ideology of female difference also helps us understand how women in later church history achieved partial independence and exercised leadership through vows of virginity despite pervasive androcentrism and patriarchy."[105] Thus, Mary's virginal conception, in deconstructing and escaping the patriarchal frameworks, exalts her status and constructs her as a hero who paves the way for other women in the Christian tradition. This exaltation of Mary formed through her virginity not only illustrates her liberation from patriarchy, but also constructs her as a hero whose virginal body is used as a tool to dismantle the patriarchal text.

It is interesting to note that, given their differences, neither Brown nor Anderson question the virginity of Mary. Their agendas, nonetheless, are strikingly different. The stake for Brown in Mary's virginity arises from his Roman Catholic context: "The problem of virginal conception; as he [Brown] understood it, included its status as 'a doctrine infallibly taught by the ordinary magisterium,' that is, as a constant and universal teaching of the Catholic hierarchy."[106] As such, Brown's preservation of Mary's virginity is linked with the preservation of hierarchy and the keeping of male authority within the church. In contrast, Anderson's construal of Mary's virginity is an act of defiance designed to promote women's control of their own bodies, making Mary an instrument of agency in the history of the church. For Anderson, the preservation of Mary's virginity emerges from her feminist conscious-ness, which resists androcentric and patriarchal views. However, it seems to me that Anderson's attempt to liberate Mary from patriarchy remains partial, because while the use of gender liberates the virginal body of Mary by exposing her difference from other textual women and deems her uncontrollable, Mary is never fully free, because in celebrat-ing her difference, her commonality with other women is denied.

Elisabeth Schüssler Fiorenza, in her pioneering study *In Memory of Her: A Feminist Theological Reconstruction of Christian Origins*, had noted that the problem with using gender binaries is that these opposi-tions are rooted in naturalized meanings of sexes and, therefore, unable to fully expose the multiple levels of oppression.[107] Exposing the miracle of Mary's virginal conception by contrasting her with barren women such as Elizabeth and Hannah in the Lukan infancy narrative, and the women who produce a child using a physical male body in Matthew's genealogy, Anderson not only exposes patriarchy present in the infancy narratives, but also draws a line of difference between the textual women. This line produces a hierarchy, in which Mary's virginity is elevated only by distancing and exposing the sexual/barren bodies of other women. Schüssler Fiorenza, however, complicated oppression by acknowledg-ing its multiplicity. She wrote: "Such a reconceptualization allows one to explore the multiplicative structures of oppression and exploitation upon which cultural and historical texts operate. It provides a more adequate model that can uphold women's agency, while, at the same time unsettling the kyriarchal notion of historical agency."[108] Schüssler Fiorenza replaced the word patriarchy with kyriarchy, because, as she noted, patriarchy formed in a dualistic understanding exposes only the domination of men over women. However, the term kyriarchy refers to "socio-political system of domination and subordination that is based on the power and rule of the lord/master/father. Such a socio-historic analytic model allows one to relate the cultural-religious discourses of kyriocentricism and kyriarchy differently."[109] The question arises, how-ever, as to whether Anderson is implicitly positing a kyriarchal superior-ity of Mary over the other women in the Matthean infancy narrative. While Anderson provides a compelling reading of Mary's virginal body as uncontrollable and ambiguous, she is able to access this image of an empowered virginal mother only by setting her against and above the failures of the other women. In other words, the liberated, virginal, and virile body of Mary involuntarily oppresses the dry and sexual bodies of other women, both in text and society.

Jane Schaberg's book *The Illegitimacy of Jesus: A Feminist Theological Interpretation of the Infancy Narratives* plays an important role in the discussion of Mary's virginal conception as found in the infancy narratives. The struggle between Schaberg and Brown is the ultimate conflict between patriarchy and feminism. Frank Reilly writes:

> Theirs [Brown and Schaberg] is a classic conflict between teacher and student. It also is a defining confrontation between patriarchal and feminist biblical scholarship. For Brown, seeing himself as a faithful and obedient Roman Catholic was the most important thing. For Schaberg, also a Roman Catholic, "reading as a woman"—which a few years later she called "reading with a feminist consciousness"—was the most important thing.[110]

In her book, Schaberg discusses the four approaches commonly used by feminist biblical scholars to read a text. The first approach exposes the androcentric views and the sexism that is present in both the text and its interpretation.[111] The second approach, as Schaberg illustrates, "counters biblical sexism by reinterpreting texts that have been distorted, revisioning previous androcentric exegesis, or by highlighting counter cultural texts positive to women, ones that challenge patriarchal structures, attitudes, images and presuppositions."[112] The third approach focuses on retelling the narrative in ways sympathetic to the women present in the narrative. She writes: "Sometimes the critic interprets against the narrator, plot, other characters and the biblical tradition; at other times forgotten or neglected nuances in the text are discovered."[113] The fourth approach centers on the reconstruction of biblical history, and is an "attempt to show that the actual situations of the Israelite and Christian religions allowed a greater or a different role for women than the canonical writings suggest."[114] Elisabeth Schüssler Fiorenza in her book, *In Memory of Her* argues that a

> commonplace premise of scholars tends to assume that women were only peripheral or not at all present in the past, if historical sources either do not mention or refer to them only occasionally. I argue to the contrary, that women were not marginal in the earliest beginnings of Christianity; rather, biblical texts and historical sources produce the marginality of women. Hence, texts must be interrogated not only as to *what they say* about women but also *how they construct what they say* or do not say.[115]

In addition to these four approaches, Schaberg lays out a fifth approach in which, rather than focusing on individual texts, she reads the Bible as a whole, in the "hope of finding a theological perspective, such as the prophetic insistence that God sides with and liberates the oppressed."[116] Schaberg argues that her reading engages in a revisionist reading of the infancy narratives and overlaps with the four approaches mentioned above.

At base, however. Schaberg characterizes her interpretive strategy as reading as a woman. She writes: "Primarily this exegesis is an exercise in 'reading as a woman.' "[117] Nevertheless, she is quick to point out that her reading is quite different from other feminist scholars whose "feminist hermeneutics always attempts to ground its analysis in the experience of women's oppression and power."[118] Schaberg argues that reading as a woman does not necessarily lead to a *feminist reading* of the text because women, too, "have been trained to read as men, to identify themselves with a masculine perspective and experience, which is presented as the human and universal one."[119] Thus, she observes that to become a feminist reader of a text is to become "a resistant reader rather than assenting reader, and by this refusal to assent, to begin the process of exorcising the male mind that has been implanted in us."[120] This resistance, then, becomes the starting point that leads to her interpretation of the illegitimacy of Jesus's birth.

Refusing to take the virginal conception of Mary at face value, Schaberg resists the dominant reading presented in the text and argues that both the authors of Matthew and Luke were aware of the illegitimacy of Jesus. She writes that they had, in fact, "inherited a historical tradition of illegitimate conception; intend their readers to understand that the conception of Jesus followed the seduction or, more probably, the rape of Mary; and communicate the theological message that God, siding with the wronged woman, has made her child the Son of God."[121] Tracing this historical tradition to the pre-gospel stage, Schaberg argues that both evangelists took the illegitimacy of Jesus for granted and believed that this detail was known to their audiences. This explains why their narratives highlight the absence of Jesus's biological father. Additionally, the evangelists were convinced that in spite of Jesus's human origins, he is still considered to be the Son of God.[122] In her essay "The Foremothers and the Mother of Jesus," Schaberg writes: "Both evangelists express faith conviction that in spite of his human origins, the child will be God's, since the Holy Spirit is ultimately responsible for this conception. In both Gospels this conviction is presented by depicting an angelic announcement that the pregnancy is divinely ordained."[123] In her reading of the Matthean infancy narrative, Schaberg highlights four elements that help her formulate this argument. She begins by focusing on the women found in his genealogy and argues that a "careful look at the stories of the four in the Hebrew Bible shows that their sociological situations are comparable."[124] According to Schaberg, four points connect the stories of these women: first, all four women stand outside the patriarchal family structures; second, all four are "wronged by the male world; third, their sexuality risks causing damage to the social order in which they lived; and, finally, their situations are righted by the actions of men, who 'acknowledge guilt and/or accept responsibility for them.'"[125] Schaberg argues that these points link the body of Mary to the other women in the genealogy. She writes: "The mention of the four women is intended to lead Matthew's reader to expect another story of a woman who becomes a social misfit in some way, is wronged or thwarted; is party to a sexual act which places her in great danger; and whose story has an outcome which repairs the social fabric and ensures the birth of a child who is legitimate or legitimated."[126] This observation not only cements Schaberg's position as rejecting Mary's virginity in the Matthean text, but it also distances her from other feminist scholars.

Elaine Wainwright, using feminist redaction criticism to read the Gospel of Matthew, notes that up until now, Matthean scholars have been deaf to certain aspects in the narrative because "of the particular set of presuppositions they have brought to their task, one of which is an androcentricism that considers men central to history and women's participation an anomaly."[127] Wainwright notes that this point is best illustrated in the past descriptions of the women present in the genealogy of the Matthew infancy narrative. She writes: "The foremothers of Jesus are rendered invisible by virtue of the patriarchal construct which considers women merely vehicles of reproduction and hence insignificant historical subjects."[128] She argues that it is when this narrative is heard with a critical ear for gender, that a new perspective emerges.

Wainwright and Schaberg both agree that the foremothers in Matthew's Gospel stand outside the patriarchal system. Wainwright observes: "Each is a woman who at some point in her story is in a situation that renders her dangerous to the patriarchal system, an anomaly, because she is not properly related to man either in marriage or as a daughter."[129] Both agree that God does not intervene on behalf of these women as it often happens in the case of male heroes. Schaberg writes: "The stories show a significant lack of miraculous, direct intervention on the part of God, to right the wrongs, or remove the shame, or illuminate the consciousness, or shatter the structures."[130] However, when it comes to connecting these women with Mary, Schaberg and Wainwright make two separate claims. Schaberg argues that Mary's link to the four women is based on the notion that she participates in an illegitimate birth, and her wronged action is righted by Joseph. Wainwright argues that "the implication in v.19 that the child is not 'of Joseph' provides for the reader an account of Mary's conception of Jesus without reference to male begetting. A woman who is named *virgin* is with child, and the child is holy. The reproductive power of woman and her role in the birth of the Messiah are affirmed outside the patriarchal structure."[131]

It is interesting to note that both Wainwright and Janice Capel Anderson come to similar conclusions in that they link Mary's virginal conception to the reproductive power of women that falls outside the patriarchy. Anderson writes:

> Mary as woman and mother is different but can be normalized and sanctified as wife. However, conception prior to marriage without a male partner renders her different in an unprecedented way. She is already sanctified through a direct relationship to God. God's nonsexual creation of Jesus in her exacerbates tensions already present in the earlier scriptural traditions where God ultimately controls reproduction.[132]

Therefore, for both Anderson and Wainwright, the ultimate control of Mary's womb lies with God, and this is what differentiates her from the other women whose reproductive power, while anomalous, is formed in relation to the males in their society. The absent male motif in the Matthean narrative also sets Mary apart from other women and, in turn, creates a false hierarchy between them. To explain further, by maintaining Mary's virginity, both Anderson and Wainwright are able to successfully demonstrate her subversion of the patriarchal structures that surround her. Wainwright argues: "Such a reading functions to deconstruct the androcentric perspective of the genealogy and birth narrative which symbolized woman as vehicles of reproduction."[133] However, the preservation of Mary's virginity, as directly linked to her liberation, depends on contrasting her with the other women present in the genealogy of Matthew. Specifically speaking, the absent male in Mary's conception as a point of difference from the other women not only illustrates her as subverting the patriarchal structures that define her reproductive capabilities, but also constructs a hierarchy among the women, where Mary as the virgin mother stands above the rest.

The reading proposed by Schaberg, in contrast, tackles this hierarchy by suggesting that all these women share a common experience in that they are misfits of society. However, Schaberg's reading is also engaged in the task of liberating Mary from the patriarchal values that surround her. Schaberg observes: "Reading as a woman, aware that all women live with male violence, I found myself deeply interested in how seduction or rape would be legally determined, what would be the fate of the woman involved and, in a case involving pregnancy and birth, what would be the fate or status of the child."[134] For Schaberg, refuting Mary's virginity demonstrates God siding with the oppressed and the wronged women. She notes: "This God, as I have argued, is shown by the story to be one who sides with the outcast, endangered woman and child. God 'acts' in a radically new way, outside the patriarchal norm but within the natural event of a human conception."[135] Rejecting Mary's virginity is an attempt to expose the violence done to women's bodies by men. Schaberg's interpretation of Mary as a raped or seduced woman, depicts her as a victim of patriarchy who is vindicated when God stands by her side. It is interesting to note that the preservation or rejection of Mary's virginity is intimately tied to her ability to stand apart from other women or to be identified with them. While refusing to be defined by the reproductive powers of patriarchy constructs Mary as a hero, interpreting Mary as a raped or seduced woman depicts her as a victim. In the process of liberating the body of Mary from androcentricism and patricarchy, feminist scholars split her character into dichotomous categories of hero or victim.

In her second major argument, Schaberg shifts her attention to the situation of Mary's pregnancy. She notes that marriage in first century Palestine took place in two stages, where betrothal came first and "was a formal exchange in the presence of witnesses of the agreement to marry, and the paying of the bride price."[136] The betrothal served as a public recognition in society and confirmed the act of marriage. However, as Matt. 1:18–25 depicts, the pregnancy of Mary occurs between the betrothal and the formal marriage between Mary and Joseph. Schaberg writes: "Mary is described as having been found pregnant in the period between the betrothal and the completed marriage, before she and Joseph 'came together,' probably meaning before Mary was brought to Joseph's home."[137] This liminal stage of Mary's pregnancy leads Joseph to come to two conclusions: Mary was either raped or she was seduced. This situation is handled in the Hebrew Bible only in Deut. 22:23–27. Schaberg observes: "It is important that we try to determine as far as possible how this law was applied in Matthew's time, and the range of options that would be presented in such a case as he described involving pregnancy."[138] Thus, for Joseph the options to deal with Mary's pregnancy ranged from a formal hearing before the judges, to divorce. Schaberg notes:

> Concerning the fate of children of an adulteress, Sir. 23:22–26 contains harsh words: her cursed memory and disgrace live on in them, and punishment falls on them (perhaps the assembly's decision that they are illegitimate, and the husband's rejection of them as heirs). They are piously wished premature deaths and sterile unions. We can suspect that the children of raped women or women only suspected of adultery were also such social misfits.[139]

In addition to these repercussions, Schaberg also mentions a humane provision which involved, "regulations concerning adoption: the ruling principle was that any male child accepted under the rule of the head of a family was considered his son in all respects."[140] Given all these options, Schaberg argues that Joseph takes the more humane approach by "accepting the pregnant Mary into his home, accepts responsibility for the child she is carrying. The words to Joseph in 1:21, 'You will call his name Jesus,' are equivalent to a formula of adoption. Joseph, by exercising the father's right to name the child, acknowledges Jesus and thus becomes his adoptive and legal father."[141] Thus, for Schaberg, Joseph's act of adopting and naming the child when in fact he had other choices strengthens her case for an illegitimate birth of Jesus.

The third major argument deals with the act of virginal conception. Schaberg argues that this act must be understood as a figurative symbol, rather than a literal act of penetration leading to conception. She writes:

> Since pagan myths consistently involve a type of *hieros gamos* or divine marriage, with pregnancy resulting from sexual penetration of some sort-since nothing in the context of Matthew 1 requires us to read the phrases in terms of a virginal conception, they should be read against the Jewish and Christian background. This means they should be read in a figurative or symbolic sense.[142]

Brown argues that this reading presented by Schaberg, leads to the exclusion of God from the Matthean infancy narrative. Reilly writes: "Brown's criticism of Schaberg's suggestion that 'begotten from the Holy Spirit' should be understood in 'a figurative or symbolic, rather than a literal sense' has merit as a comment on one phrase. The wording seems to mean that God was not really involved in the conception of Jesus."[143]

However, for Schaberg, "Mt 1:18, 20 can be read to mean that the Holy Spirit empowers this birth as all births are divinely empowered, that this child's existence is willed by God, that God is the ultimate power of life behind and in this as in all conceptions."[144] Thus for Schaberg, the ability to locate the divine will of God in the raped conception of Mary, not only leads to the emancipation of Mary, but also brings to the fore all the bodies of those women who are violated and marginalized by the masculine powers in their societies.

Schaberg's final argument for rejecting Mary's virginity suggests that the author of Matthew was not thinking of Isaiah 7:14 in his infancy narrative, but rather was intending the use of the law found in Deut. 22:23–27. She argues, "The Greek translation of Isaiah's Hebrew 'alma (young woman) by parthenos (virgin) does not indicate a miraculous conception. Rather, the Greek translator simply meant that one who is now a virgin will conceive by natural means."[145] Therefore, for Schaberg, the word parthenos played an important role in Matthew's narrative because "Matthew was not thinking of a virgin conceiving miraculously, but of the law in Deut. 22:23–27 concerning the seduction or rape of a betrothed virgin, the law he presupposes in his presentation of the dilemma of Joseph."[146] Hence, as Schaberg points out, the problem that lay before the author of Matthew was to make sense of the illegitimate pregnancy of Mary in the text. It is at this point that we shift to Schaberg's interpretation of the virginal conception found in the Lucan infancy narrative.

Schaberg argued for the illegitimacy of Jesus in Luke by presenting four arguments. They are as follows: The introduction and response of Mary to Gabriel, the law of Deuteronomy 22:23–27, the Magnificat, and the step-parallelism between John and Jesus. Schaberg, similar to Brown, tackles the translation of Mary's question in Luke. However, unlike Brown, who translated Mary's question as "How can this be,?" Schaberg moves to translate Mary's question as "How will this be?" This move, she concurs, "does not prejudice the reader to think immediately of an event that is considered physically impossible."[147] At the same time, Brown's need to translate Mary's question as "can" rather than "will" evokes a feeling of familiarity within the mind of the reader. Reilly writes: "Brown translated 'How can this be?' rather than as 'How will this be?' because in Matthew, the story follows the structure of the Hebrew scriptures annunciation-of-birth pattern. Mary presents her virginity as an obstacle to the angel's announcement."[148] This argument is also shared by Bea Wyler. In her essay titled, "Mary's Call," Wyler points out that call narratives found in the Hebrew text have six components: The divine confrontation, introductory word, commission, objection, reassurance, and sign. Wyler argues that this pattern is "used in a most impressive way in Lk. 1:26–38, in the annunciation to Mary. The person called is not the main protagonist, but his future mother."[149] Wyler argues that such a pattern is followed in Luke so as to evoke feelings of familiarity among the readers. She writes: "The text of 'Mary's call' follows the pattern established in the Hebrew Bible (the 'Old Testament') in such pure and clear ways that an audience familiar with the text of the Hebrew Bible must have noticed the similarity at once."[150] For both Wyler and Brown, the use of Hebrew Scriptures in the gospels serves as a way to set up the miraculous conception of Mary.

Schaberg translates the phrase *epei andra ou ginôskô* (Lk. 1:34) in the present tense, "I have had no relations with a man." In contrast, Brown translates this phrase as, "because I do not know a man."[151] Similar to Brown, Wyler translates it as, "since I have no husband." However, Wyler argues that this question posed in 1:34 ("How shall this be, since.") must be read in connection with the corresponding Hebrew narratives. She observes:

> This echoes a number of objections. Sarah basically says, "How can this be? I (with my husband) am too old" (Gen 18:11–12), Moses responds with who am I? (Exod 3:11)...Mary is a combination of those variants. She points to her state of being unmarried, hence her inability to meet the task; but, since she is betrothed, conceiving will soon be in the realm of her possibilities. Her objection, in other words, is not very convincing.[152]

Schaberg, similar to Wyler, detects an ironical tone in Mary's objection. She writes: "Mary's words have nothing to do with being unmarried, since in the Lucan text as it stands she is betrothed, in the first stage of her marriage. (The RSV translation, 'since I have no husband' ignores or obscures this fact.) But would a betrothed woman or girl object to the announcement that she will become pregnant?"[153] Brown, it appears, is unable to detect the irony in Mary's question and prefers to understand her objection as a literary motif that helps highlight her virginity. In contrast, Wyler illuminates Mary's question in light of the Hebrew Scriptures and highlights its prophetical nature. She argues that Mary's question must not be read as a "sign of the prophet's innate humility or sense of adequacy, but rather a part of his office as servant, mediator and agent of Yahweh."[154] Wyler's interpretation of Mary's question is not only tied to the preservation of Mary's virginity, but also exalts Mary as a prophetess. Meanwhile, Schaberg tries to resolve the tension in the question posed by Luke's Mary, arguing that "the present tense of the verb does not indicate a present state based on past behavior. It focuses on Mary's objection in the present; it tells the reader that Mary expects her pregnancy to come about in the near future, before she goes to live with Joseph."[155] The interpretations of Mary's virginity presented by Wyler and Schaberg expose their stake in defending or rejecting Mary's virginity. In other words, for Wyler, preserving Mary's virginity is intimately tied into her understanding of Mary as a prophet or an agent of Yahweh. However, for Schaberg, rejecting Mary's virginity is tied into her reading of Mary as an oppressed woman whose side is taken by God, since she is victimized by the patriarchal structures that surround her. Mary is a hero for Wyler, a victim for Schaberg.

The next point is the most critical and crucial aspect of Schaberg's argument. She writes: "There is a verbal closeness between Luke's description of Mary in 1:27...and Deut 22:23 LXX. The phrase in Luke seems to be derived from the LXX of Deut 22:23."[156] Drawing a distinction between Matthew and Luke's usage of Deuteronomy, Schaberg argues that "Luke, however, does not narrate or have the angel refer to seduction or rape, and unlike Matthew he does not depict Joseph wrestling with the application of this law."[157] However, she notes the passage of Deuteronomy runs throughout the narrative of Luke and the first inkling of its existence is seen in the Magnificat. This narrative, also knows as Mary's song or hymn, is a "song of liberation, personal and social. It praises God's liberating actions on behalf of the speaker, actions that are paradigmatic of all God's actions on behalf of the lowly, the oppressed, the suffering."[158] Schaberg poses the question, "Why would the author of Luke insert such a song in his narrative?" She asks, "What has happened to Mary that would elicit such a hymn?"[159]

The tone of this song, Schaberg argues, is battle-like and has traces of violence and revenge. This song has often been called Mary's song of victory; however, her victory is most often understood as spiritual and "Luke's meaning is unexamined."[160] The word *tapeinôsis* (1:48) has been translated by Fitzmyer and others to refer here to Mary's humble state. It expresses "her unworthiness to be the mother of the Davidic Messiah and Son of God."[161] However, Schaberg argues that this word actually means humiliation. Reilly, elucidating her argument, writes: "It has this meaning in [the LXX of] Deuteronomy 22:24 describing the humiliation of the betrothed virgin, and in Genesis 34:2; Judges 19:24 and 20:5; 2 Kings 13:12, 12, 22 and 32; and Lamentations 5:11. These passages describe the rape of Dinah; the rape of the Levite's concubine; the rape of David's daughter, Tamar; and the rape of the virgins of Judah."[162] Therefore, translating *tapenôsis* in light of Deut. 22:24, Schaberg posits Mary's humiliation as emerging from rape, rather than an obstacle that is overcome by God.[163] Continuing her point further, Schaberg argues that "In her Magnificat, Mary preaches as the prophet of the poor. She represents the hope of the poor, but she represents that hope *as a woman* who has suffered and been vindicated as a woman."[164] For both Anderson and Schaberg, the humility or humiliation of Mary's virginal or illegitimate conception showcases her heroism, thereby making her the liberated/vindicated role model for others. However, the difference is that Anderson's Mary arrives at her special status as a virgin woman who escapes patriarchy, while Schaberg's Mary arrives there as a raped or seduced woman who is a victim of patriarchy. Although Schaberg's Mary is a hero, like Anderson's Mary, her heroism is embedded in her victimization.

Schaberg's final point refers to the step-parallelism between Jesus and John. She writes: "Luke has constructed a step-parallelism, designed to show point by point the superior greatness of Jesus over John the Baptist."[165] In her essay titled "Elizabeth and Mary-Naomi and Ruth: Gender-Response Criticism in Luke 1–2," Arie Troost notes that the superiority of Jesus over John grows as the narrative proceeds. She observes: "The analogy between John and Jesus does not mean that the two children are equal in status. On the contrary, as the narrative proceeds, Jesus' importance appears to grow at the expense of John's, until-in Lk. 3:16-John is not even worthy of unfastening the straps of Jesus' sandals."[166] Troost argues that this narrative, read in light of the Genesis conflict narratives where "the latter-born takes over the first born position,"[167] offers a new insight. John Dominic Crossan makes a similar observation when he writes, "You can see clearly from the parallelism of John and Jesus in Luke 1–2 that the virginal conception of Jesus is intended to exalt it over the *miraculous* conception of John and thereby over the entire biblical tradition summarized in the Baptist's aged and infertile parents."[168]

However, while all three scholars (Schaberg, Troost, and Crossan) agree that the birth of Jesus is represented as higher than John's, their argument for making such a case comes from three separate places. Schaberg notes: "In my opinion, step-parallelism is indeed present in the two questions and in Luke's understanding of God's role in each of the conceptions. But what is 'greater' in the case of Jesus is not a miraculous manner of his conception, but God's overcoming of the deeper humiliation of his mother."[169] Thus, for Schaberg, overcoming rape is a harder and bigger obstacle for God than barrenness, and this is what makes Jesus greater than John. She elaborates: "[T]he humiliation of a betrothed virgin who was seduced or raped, and who became pregnant by someone other than her husband, was far worse. In contrast to the humiliation of the barren woman (see Isa. 54:1–3; Sam. 2:5), this kind of humiliation was never explicitly promised reversal."[170] In contrast, Troost's interpretation hones in on a different facet of Jewish scripture as she reads the relationship between Mary and Elizabeth in light of that of Ruth and Naomi. She argues that these female pairs help each other to face awkward situations. "Naomi and Ruth, Elizabeth and Mary work together in facing their awkward position in society. Both in the book of Ruth, and in Luke we find the cooperation between the two women, to the extent that their narrative roles merge."[171]

Troost declines to tackle directly the tensions and suspicions attaching to virginal conception in the narrative, arguing instead, that specific interpretations of texts are intrinsic to the experiences and social locations of readers. She illustrates this point with reference to Schaberg's work. She writes: "As Schaberg herself lives in one of the larger cities of the USA, a city with enormous social problems, her concern is with the many, often very young, women in the larger cities of the world who have so-called illegitimate children, and with the struggle for life these women and their children have to face."[172] Troost, however, omits to reflect on the aspects of her own social location or personal experience that, by her own logic, shaped her interpretation of the Lukan infancy narrative. Nevertheless, highlighting the importance of women's social locations and personal experience, in their interpretations is a common point for Schaberg and Troost. Their decision to approach the text as women is foundational for their methodology as feminist critics of the text. Therefore, it seems that for both Schaberg and Troost, their immediate connection to Mary as a woman, and their desire to not only read the text in its historicity but also move it into the reality of contemporary women's lives exposes their stake in rejecting or resisting the urge to take Mary's apparently miraculous virginity at face value.

Meanwhile, John Dominic Crossan's depiction of Mary's virginity emerges from historical slander that was leveled against the legitimacy of Jesus. He notes: "I will be specifically concerned...with slander against Christian Jews by non-Christian Jews, that is, with those who countered claims of Mary's virginity with the obvious rebuttal of Jesus' bastardy."[173] He writes: "A child born of an aged and/or infertile mother is visibly known, empirically evident, legally provable and socially undeniable while one born of a virginal mother can be believed only at that mother's positive statement and the father's negative one."[174] Unlike Schaberg, Crossan's discussion of Mary's virginity is not intimately tied to her victimization by patriarchy, and unlike Troost, he expresses no interest in the situations of real women interpreters and their stakes in maintaining or rejecting Mary's virginity. Crossan's interpretation of Mary's virginity remains within its historical confines, and does not attempt to move beyond these borders into the lives of real women. It is important to note, however, that Crossan introduces into the discussion something that has so far been overlooked by other scholars: the issue of empire. He notes: "Divinity and virginity were dangerous claims for Jesus' conception, but they were also one way to oppose and transcend imperial claims for divinity and non-virginity."[175] For Crossan, the virginal conception of the Lukan narrative is an instance of Lukan anti imperial rhetoric. He writes: "[I]t placed Judaism within the Roman Empire and among those Jews who opposed Rome's ideological ascendancy and theological eschatology. But to do that it had to also somehow ground that un-Jewish idea in biblical precedent and once it looked for that, and probably only when it looked for that, Isa. 7.14 was a very appropriate choice."[176] Schaberg and Crossan have different stakes in rejecting or preserving Mary's virginity. While the rejection of Mary's virginity, for Schaberg, is bound up with her feminist convictions, Crossan's preservation of Mary's virginity (not as supernatural event but as literary trope) is bound up with his empire-critical convictions.

In her book titled *Her Image of Salvation*, Gail Paterson Corrington argues that both Matthew and Luke may have been aware of Jesus's illegitimacy; however, they choose to ignore this tradition, unlike their predecessor Mark. Paterson Corrington notes that Mark's gospel provides a rather negative image of Mary, while Matthew and Luke present a more positive image of her by "emphasizing her virginal conception of Jesus and her relationship to him as a disciple, both at the expense of depicting her reality as his mother."[177] She argues that the reason the illegitimacy tradition is ignored by both Matthew and Luke is the way they both read the Jewish Scriptures. Matthew, in particular, is driven by a "messianic teleology," to use the languae of Paula Fredriksen. Patterson Corrington goes on to say that: "Matthew begins with the given that Jesus is the messiah. He also knows the tradition that a woman named Mary is his mother and that there is something 'irregular' connected with that birth."[178] A couple of differences between Schaberg and Paterson Corrington may be noted. First, while Schaberg argues that Matthew's understanding of the virginal rape/seduction is embedded in his interpretation of the law found in Deut. 22:20–21, Paterson Corrington argues that Matthew used the text of Isaiah 7:14 to construct the virginal conception in his narrative. Additionally, both Schaberg and Paterson Corrington argue for pre-gospel traditions. However, unlike Schaberg who suggests that previous traditions about the birth of Jesus highlight his illegitimacy, Paterson Corrington argues that the pre-gospel tradition suggests a virginal conception of Jesus. She notes: "The authors of *Mary in the New Testament* suggest that, even prior to the composition of the Gospel, there was a tradition of the virginal conception of Jesus, which Matthew uniquely made part of his portrayal of the messianic nature of Jesus, a portrayal supported throughout his Gospel by constant references to prophecy."[179] Although the preservation of Mary's virginity by Paterson Corrington, and the rejection of it by Schaberg begin from different starting points, they lead to one common goal: God sides with the oppressed.[180] Both scholars argue for a reading in which God sides with the oppressed/humiliated woman and this ultimately leads to her emancipation because the cycle of power is subverted. However, I would argue, for reasons that I stated earlier, that such a reading entrenched in Mary's oppression/victimization can never realize the full potential of her emancipation.

In her essay "Proud Mary: Contextual Constructions of a Divine Diva," Cheryl A. Kirk-Duggan pioneers a womanist reading of Mary. Womanist theory, Kirk-Duggan notes, "is interdisciplinary and multifaceted, building on the lives, oral traditions, and writings of African-American women. Womanist theory is a strategy for naming, exposing, interrogating, and helping to transform the oppression of all people, especially those affected by gender, race, and class discrimination."[181] Interpreting the infancy narratives of Matthew and Luke from a womanist perspective, Kirk-Duggan argues that a "womanist reading presses us to explore the paradoxical, the less romantic, the experiences that smack of oppression."[182] Similar to other feminist theological scholars, Kirk-Duggan keeps her interaction with both the text and other biblical scholars to a minimum. While she does refer to Schaberg's work on Luke and women, her reference still remains at a general level. She notes that "Jane Schaberg warns the reader . . . of the danger of reading the Gospel of Luke as though it is unambiguously pro-woman."[183] At the same time, it seems that this warning is not completely heeded by Kirk-Duggan because she still holds onto the untainted virgin image of Mary, and in so doing, "foster[s] . . . an elision of possible sexual violence suffered by Mary," a possibility that evokes "the specific danger of sexual violence against women in occupied territories."[184] Or in male-dominated communities anywhere. In other words, while Kirk-Duggan's womanist reading of Mary suggests her survivor status, the problem of her pregnancy is never addressed head-on. Kirk-Duggan argues that her womanist interpretation of Mary is "embodied in the lives of African American women. She is womanist: she not only survives but transcends. She makes out of rags quilts that get hung in the Smithsonian. She makes soul food that becomes haute cuisine. Admired by some, and feared by others, Proud Mary is who she is without apology."[185] To her credit, however, and unlike other feminist scholars, Kirk-Duggan introduces race into her interpretation of Mary when she argues that Mary can be seen as prototypical of African- American women.

Similar to Kirk-Duggan, South African theologian and biblical scholar Itumeleng J. Mosala argues for an understanding of Mary as "a single mother from the ghettos of colonized Galilee."[186] Feminist interpretations of Mary focus on gender, patriarchy, and the effect of Mary on the lives of real women. However, these discussions seem to exclude the racialization of Mary by the West and its effects on people of color. Mosala argues that "[t]he way the birth narratives have functioned in the churches of Western Christianity, including those geographically situated in the Third World, is an eloquent witness to the success of Luke in his ideological suppression of the social revolutionary-class origins of Mary, the mother of Jesus."[187] Therefore, for Mosala, the interpretation of Mary as a single mother from a colonized territory serves a twofold purpose, in that it not only introduces race as a valid category for interpreting Mary, but also argues that this reading makes her "a key symbol of a revolutionary movement to overthrow the dominant oppressive structures of church and society."[188] It is interesting to note that though Kirk-Duggan and Mosala make two separate claims for Mary's virginity, in that Kirk-Duggan wants Mary to maintain her virginity while Mosala does not, the stakes for their interpretations emerge from the same place. In other words, for both Kirk-Duggan and Mosala, Mary is an underclass hero whose actions not only lead to her own liberation, but also enable her to serve as an emblem for the liberation of oppressed and marginalized people.

CHAPTER 4

Surrogacy as Performance of Violent Love: Reading Luke's Magnificat alongside the Bodies of Indian Surrogate Mothers

> The individual is interpellated as a (free) subject in order that he shall submit freely to the commandments of the Subject, i.e. in order that he shall (freely) accept his subjection.
> —Louis Althusser, *Lenin and Philosophy and Other Essays*[1]

In a predominantly traditional society such as India, infertility has been, and, in some circles, continues to be considered a curse. The desire to have a male child, combined with the role of a woman as a mother, makes the surrogate industry in India a successful business venture. The stigma of infertility not only plagues the wombs of Indian women, but is also a matter of grave concern for their Western female counterparts. However, one of the major differences between Indian women and western women is that the former deal with this condition in isolation because infertility, overshadowed by religious connotations, continues to stigmatize women's bodies. Sadie Stein points out: "Surrogacy, in America, is normalized. No one blinked an eye when a surrogate gave birth to twins for Sarah Jessica Parker and Matthew Broderick; the inevitable class tensions were gently lampooned—and conveniently resolved—by Tina Fey and Amy Poehler. And while nothing involving maternity can ever be treated with the rakish dash recent rom-coms have shown the sperm donor, more pop-cultural mainstreaming seems both inevitable and in some wise desirable, too."[2] In contrast to India, discussions about infertility in western societies are more open and sometimes even glamorized and celebritized in popular culture.

Therefore, in a world driven by consumerism and capitalism, countries like India provide fertile ground for entrepreneurs, even in the realm of infertility. Raywat Deonandan highlights this point in his article, "The Ethics of Surrogacy":

> The existence of a global infertility epidemic is clearly at odds with our conception of the world as being overpopulated. But, primarily in wealthier, developed nations, the provision of medical reproductive services to people deemed infertile is now a billion- dollar global industry, spurred on both by advances in technology and the emergence of a globalized economy. Unsurprisingly, India is one of the world's most popular providers of reproductive services, leveraging her medical depth, advantageous currency exchange, and pervasive poverty. But when human reproduction meets commerce, gender inequality, and wealth disparity, the potential for ethical transgression becomes great indeed.[3]

The success of surrogacy in India relies on two important aspects. First, the cost of surrogacy in India is quite low. In addition to this, laws/regulations relating to this industry are lax, especially when compared to the developed and advanced countries in the West.[4] Second, the use of medical intervention leading to a successful conception, plays on the sentiment that the women struggling with infertility are finally able to achieve their true essence of womanhood through motherhood. Nancy Chodorow writes: "In all cases, the implication is that the mode of reproduction of mothering is unchanging, and retains the form of its earliest origins. These accounts argue that women's mothering is, or has been, functional—that children, after all, have been reared—and often imply that what is and has been ought to be—that women ought to mother."[5] Therefore, the dreams of wealthier couples are implanted in the wombs of poor and low caste Indian women. These women, who were once reproducing solely for domestic purposes, are groomed and transformed into professional surrogate mothers in a capitalistic economy.

Such hybrid moments captured, brought to light, and maybe even acknowledged by the vocal voices discussing the ethical implications of surrogacy in India, could lead to a fuller picture of a maternal identity rooted in an ambivalent love, obscuring the barriers between being an unselfish mother to a genetically different child and becoming a professional mother, selfishly daring to dream about a better future for her own children. The divided body of the Indian surrogate mother never fully fits into the dichotomous categories preordained either by Indian or Western societies, thereby constructing her motherhood through an ambiguous light oscillating between points of love/violence, liberation/ oppression, and her subjectivity as a hero or a victim. The Indian surrogate mother performs a motherhood that encapsulates her ambivalence as her maternal subjectivity erupts between categories of violence and love promising a liberation that is contingent upon her oppression.

This form of motherhood is not particular to the modern context of surrogacy and can also be found within ancient literature. One such example is the textual character of Mary, constructed in the Lukan infancy narrative. In this text, the literary body of Mary is often read through the binary lens of victim vs. hero. While the character of Mary is described by some as being active, having agency and playing an important role in the conception of Jesus, others read her as a victim who passively receives the seed of God, has no agency, and is exploited by this God for the betterment of her people. While I find both these interpretations compelling, I would argue that though similar to the Indian surrogate, the character of Mary is much more complicated and deserves a new way of reading. My own reading, therefore, resists the interpretation of Mary as a monolithic character who falls into the category of either a victim or a hero. Instead, I prefer to read her textual body as a site of contradiction that fluctuates between the points of violence and love, thereby constructing her motherhood as an act that is performative of a *violent love* that never fully fashions her as a subject or as an object and, in the end, leaves her in a space of ambivalence and uncertainty. Additionally, by attempting to read the figure of Mary through, and alongside the body of the Indian surrogate, I hope to bring to the surface the complexities present in the bodies of both these women who are never fully free or fully enslaved. I will argue that both Mary and the Indian surrogate stand as victimized heroes who "almost but not quite" (to adapt Bhabha's terminology) become subjects or objects, but ultimately stand in ambivalence.

Connections between the ancient infancy narratives of Matthew or Luke and the modern postcolonial context of surrogacy in India are yet to be drawn by scholars from either side of the aisle. In her article titled "No Country for Young Women" Ratna Kapur states: "Sex and intimacy are cast as negative, degrading and indecent, something from which the good, decent Indian woman ought to be protected. The protectionism combines with a sex phobia that ensures sex remains in the closet. And any claims for sexual rights become bizarrely associated with something Western, decadent, hedonistic or deviant."[6] Thus, in a country where sex is expected to be practiced only within the confines of a traditional marriage, the reproductive tourism industry in India fashions itself not only as a legal business, but a moral and ethical operation that promises to protect the social and sexual dignity of Indian women. In other words, it is acceptable for the Indian woman to transgress her marital boundaries and cross her cultural and traditional values, as long as her body is clinically penetrated by a needle, rather than a physical penis. As will emerge in my argument, the patriarchal double standard also connects the contextual body of the Indian surrogate mother with the textual body of Mary in the Lukan infancy narrative.

Of course, there are also significant differences between the Lukan Mary and the Indian surrogate mother. For example, Mary is a virgin, while the Indian surrogate mother is not.[7] It seems to me, however, that these women are connected by similarities that run deeper than this superficial and obvious textual membrane of separation. Both Mary and the Indian surrogate mother choose to walk the fine line between morality and immorality by participating in a conception that pushes the sexual boundaries of tradition and culture, but at the same time protects their sexual honor in a patriarchal society. Additionally, the unselfish *choice* to carry a child for another is directly intertwined with their selfish motivations for an economic or a salvific hope for a better future for their people and/or their families. Finally, interpretations and discussions surrounding the contextual and the textual bodies of both these mothers characterize these women into categories of hero/victim, oppressed/liberated and as a result, fail to depict their maternal subjectivity that erupts between points of violence and love.

Motherhood as the Performance of a Violent Love

The theme of the absent male in the modern context of surrogacy appears to be a common one. In most of the interviews available, the voices of both the Indian surrogate and the Western woman play a dominant role, while the husbands of these women never seem to be mentioned or appear only in passing in the text. The absence of the Indian male is uncharacteristic for the Indian context, where invisible/visible masculine anxiety is often unloaded onto women's bodies, especially when the woman's sexual honor is at stake. Thus, in such a context, it is surprising that the Indian women not only appear as willing participants, ready to perform the act of surrogacy for the other, but are also married (or so it seems) to extremely cooperative husbands. The first sign of support is illustrated in the written consent of the husband of the Indian surrogate. Usha Rengachary Smerdon writes: "The consent forms are, in general, startlingly short. The sample consent form for a potential surrogate mother must be signed by her husband."[8] Some would term the quiet participation and cooperation of the Indian males as a sign of their passivity or weakness. However, it seems to me that the willing consent of the Indian husband in the business of surrogacy must be explored more deeply and the double standard patriarchal sentiment, disguised in the written consent brought to light. Highlighting the hypocrisy in her novel, Desai describes the surrogacy industry as not only capitalizing on traditional patriarchal values of the Indian society, but also seducing men into allowing their wives to participate in an act that ensures the protection of their sexual honor in the community. She writes:

> "This one is Shobha." He [Sharma, the middleman/broker supplying surrogates to the clinic] nodded at the more confident woman. "Like Preeti, she is from Uttar Pradesh, from a village near the Nepal border. Her husband stays in the village. She has one child but needs the money because they want to build a house." "I hope she knows there is very little money upfront and she may have to stay here for nine months before she gets the entire amount? Who will look after her child while she's here?" "Her husband." Subash remembered the last fracas. "But what about the community? What if they find out she's pregnant, it's not her child—and that she can't keep it?" "They won't know, sir. Her relatives are all in the village. Her husband couldn't come but we have explained it to him. No physical *ghapla*, you know—he knows it will be all done in a tube, and then an injection.[9]

The ability to recreate a virginal conception that can at once fulfill the patriarchal requirements of protecting a woman's sexual honor and, at the same time, allow her to transgress marital boundaries by opening her body up to foreign penetration, illustrates the delicate balance between capitalism and patriarchy, an invaluable formula that helps drive the success of commercial surrogacy in India.

Such a hypocrisy buttressed by financial motivation permits the Indian surrogate mother, if only temporarily, to cross her sexual and marital boundaries and experience a partial freedom within a patriarchal-capitalistic society. As one surrogate mother, Mansi, told Amrita Pande:

> The hostels constitute a gendered place, one that generates emotional links and sisterhood among the women. Mansi, a surrogate, talks about

her relationship with other surrogates in the hostel: "We are seven surrogates in this room—seven sisters pregnant at the same time! Our villages are not very far—I am sure we will be able to meet each other even after we leave this place. We have convinced Raveena *didi* [the matron] to train us in the beauty business. I don't think English and computer will get us a job, but we may be able to work in a beauty parlor. Once we are done here I want to start a beauty parlor with surrogate Diksha."[10]

Though the pregnant body of the Indian surrogate mother is placed under constant surveillance and disciplined by the medical staff, doctors, and brokers working for the fertilization clinics, the access to form a surrogate sisterhood permits the Indian surrogate mother to experience a moment of temporary emancipation as her swollen body sheltered away from the male gaze is briefly able to escape the patriarchal and capitalistic control levied upon her. Pande observes: "For Mansi, the ties with other surrogates serve as resources and networks for future employment. These ties and coalitions also serve as a powerful tool against the brokers."[11] Continuing further, Pande notes that some of the surrogate mothers seem angered by the middlemen/middlewomen (or, as they call them, brokers) who take big commissions from both the clinics and the surrogates. A surrogate named Regina compares her situation to fishes living in a dirty pond and paying off the crocodile (the broker) a commission for simply finding volunteer surrogates. She notes:

We all are like fishes in a dirty pond. Why let the crocodile take control? I am going to tell her [the researcher] everything. This Nirmala, she takes Rs 10,000 [$200] from us for getting us to the clinic. We take all the pain, and she earns so much money. See, we come here because we are desperate, but she has made a business out of this. This shouldn't be allowed to happen. We have complained to Raveena *didi*. We want it written in the contract that the couple hiring us will pay for people like Nirmala. This money means a lot to us. Why should we have to give it to someone else?[12]

It is important to note that the surrogate hostels, constructed as a place to impose capitalistic control over the working womb of the surrogate mother, fail to capture completely moments of resistance that erupt in between the cracks of scrutinized control of the surrogacy clinics and their staff, thereby offering these women exploited by the powers of patriarchy and capitalism to vocalize their single moment of agency illustrated in their resistance. And yet this shared resistance to express power and control over their own bodies while constructive is experienced only in their consent to exploitation exemplified through the capitalization of their reproductive services.

Scholars note that one of the main differences between the infancy narratives in Matthew and Luke is the relative prominence of the role of Joseph. Jane Schaberg writes:

> Some of the most obvious differences pertain to our investigation. Luke begins his Gospel not with a genealogy of Jesus (although he does indeed have a genealogy placed later, after the baptism of Jesus), but with a formal prologue (1:1–4), stating his intention as an Evangelist, that his reader may be assured about the instruction received. His narrative begins with an angelic annunciation to the aged priest Zechariah telling him that his barren wife Elizabeth will bear him a son of greatness. Then, coordinated with this announcement in careful fashion, there is an angelic annunciation to Mary (not to Joseph) that she will conceive a son of superior greatness.[13]

It is surprising that the author of Luke chooses to ignore the character of Joseph in his narrative and focuses only on Mary, especially in a world where males were socially prominent. The active appearance of Joseph occurs only in 2:4ff. (cf. 1:27), which deals with the birth of Jesus. Turid Karlsen Seim argues that the "later appearance of Joseph in the text signals the presence of his character within the tradition of the gospels and later helps with the adoption of Jesus into the lineage of David."[14] While I agree with Karlsen Seim, it appears that the absence of Joseph in the Lukan narrative may signal a more important motif. In my opinion, the author of Luke pushes Joseph into the shadows to create space within the text so that the ominous and fantastic miracle can begin to form within the body of Mary. Paradoxically, the phenomenon of surrogacy in modern India may shed further light on the absence of the physical male in this text.

Reading the Lukan narrative alongside the context of surrogacy helps the reader see the character of Joseph in a different light. In the Greco-Roman world of the New Testament, gender was interpreted through binary lenses of active/passive, public/private. Ancient authors depicted males as public figures who are active, and who possess powers of sexual penetratation. Tat Siong Benny Liew, citing David Halperin, writes: "Sexual aggression, sexual prowess, and sexual promiscuity were all characteristics of a 'manly man' in the ancient Mediterranean world. For sex, in that world, was not perceived as an activity people jointly engaged in but as an action performed by an 'active penetrator' upon a 'passive penetrator' "[15] The characterization of active/passive can be applied to the male characters present in both the Lukan and surrogacy texts. Schaberg points out:

> Luke has with greater sophistication integrated Matthew's fulfill-ment citations (especially Isa. 7:14) into a narrative; created a dialogue between the angel (now named) and Mary; developed in different ways the Matthean motifs of journey and visitors to the child; omitted for literary, theological, and political reasons Matthean material such as the characters of the Magi and the massacre of children by Herod; and reversed Matthew's priorities by pushing Joseph into the background and Mary into the foreground.[16]

To push Schaberg's analysis even further, the author of Luke not only pushes Joseph into the background, but also constructs him as a passive male devoid of the power to penetrate or speak. Schaberg continues: "A careful reading shows that Luke agrees with Matthew on many points. They both report that the parents of Jesus were Mary and Joseph, and that the pregnancy occurred when Mary was betrothed to Joseph (Matt 1:16, 18; Luke 1:27), who was of Davidic descent (Matt 1:16, 20; Luke 1:27). They agree also that Joseph was not the biological father of Jesus (Matt 1:18–19, 25; Luke 3:23)."[17] Thus, in a world where the power to penetrate was a constitutive masculine trait, Joseph's inability to penetrate the body of Mary calls his masculinity into question. Pande argues that Indian women already having children are most vulnerable to the highly manipulative and exploitative practices of the surrogacy business. She writes: "Recruitment tactics often tapped into women's anxiety about being bad mothers—mothers who were unable to provide for their children or, especially, mothers who could not get their daugh-ters married on time. In India, although fathers are expected to play the breadwinner role, mothers are often castigated by the community for not getting their daughters married."[18] Thus one could argue that in a predominantly male-dominated society such as India where the task of providing for the family is limited to the male gender, the inability of the Indian husband to perform this task and having to rely on his wife's reproductive skills, constructs the husband of the Indian surrogate as a passive male in society. Similar to the Indian husband of the contem-porary surrogate, Joseph too is, by implication, a passive male. Both men stand aside while the powerful Other penetrates the bodies of their women. At the same time, while this passivity calls the masculinity of these men into question, it nevertheless frees up the women and creates a space for them to perform their agency by allowing them to reproduce with the Other.

Dr. Nayna Patel tells Abigail Haworth that

the "surrogacy business" has taken off beyond her imagination. She says that she has about 150 "foreign couples" who are currently on the waiting list, and every day at least three new Indian women sign up to be "potential surrogates." However, Dr. Patel is quick to explain that unlike other doctors who are interested in exploiting women, she is interested in the welfare of the Indian surrogates. She explains that most women who apply to her clinic hail from lower middle class, poor and low caste families. Patel says that she feels good about helping these women, as long as she is aware that these women are not being coerced into this act by their husbands or their in-laws.[19]

Chandra Talpade Mohanty writes: "We see how Western feminists alone become the true 'subjects' of this counter history. Third World women, on the other hand, never rise above their debilitating generality of their 'object' status."[20] Even though Mohanty is speaking of white Western feminism and its interaction with Third World women, her words are pertinent to the Third World context of Indian surrogacy, in that, we often see educated women like Patel use homogenizing discourses to represent the uneducated women of their own country. This universalization of the Indian surrogates as poor women, with no agency not only constructs their bodies as objects and deprives them of agency, but it also pushes them into the shadows, and counters their subjectivity with educated individuals like Patel who, through their Western education, construe themselves as Subjects and use their agency to ensure a better life not only for their objectified sisters, but also for themselves.

One common aspect that stands out in the discussion of surrogacy in the Indian context is the notion of will or agency of the Indian surrogate. Patel explicitly notes that it is the consent of the Indian woman that makes her a willing participant in this act of motherhood. An article in the *New York Times* titled "India Nurtures Business of Surrogate Motherhood" notes: "Under the guidelines issued by the Indian Council of Medical Research, surrogate mothers sign away their rights to any children. A surrogate's name is not even on the birth certificate."[21] The gesture of signing away the rights to the child works as a way to protect the rights of the couple that uses the services of the surrogate woman. In almost all of the interviews, the reader is told explicitly by the doctor and the surrogate that this act is not an act of exploitation, and the women participating in it are agents of their own free will. However, scholars such as Rengachary Smerdon question the notion of "free consent" asking:

> Free choice must also be questioned in terms of what is meant by informed consent and the extent to which surrogates are adequately counseled about the physical risks of surrogacy. The physical hazards of gamete transfer, embryo implantation, pregnancy, and birth are multifold and include perforation of organs, increased risk of ectopic pregnancy, complications from multiple pregnancies, fetal reduction, and cesarean sections. Some posit that "the relative biological strangeness of the fetus to the gestational mother, as compared to a woman carrying a child conceived through sexual intercourse," carries with it an "even greater biological investment from her during pregnancy." As such, the gestational mother may face even greater risks of developing severe pregnancy complications. Are surrogates truly counseled thoroughly about these risks?[22]

It remains to be seen whether this act of willingness can be seen as a gesture that is truly liberating to the Indian surrogate because it depicts her ability to use her agency, or whether it is an act that camouflages a sinister oppression, that manipulates a woman to use her agency and enslaves her body as a receptacle for the Other. In other words, the question we must ask ourselves is whether a *verbal or written consent* truly encapsulates a mother's altruism to become a surrogate to another.

Feminist biblical and theological scholars who choose to read Mary as an active character focus on her willingness to serve God. In Luke 1:38, Mary says to God, "Here am I, the servant of the Lord; let it be with me according to your word." In her book *A Virgin Conceived: Mary and Classical Representations of Virginity,* Mary Foskett reads this response of Mary as follows: "The narration of her response, unparalleled in biblical birth narratives, serves to convey a sense of agency that counters the representation of Mary as vulnerable object. Although, no response is sought by the angel, Mary makes a choice in a situation where none is demanded. By offering her consent, the virgin asserts her own voice into the scene."[23] In addition to this, it can also be argued that with the absence of Joseph in the text, the voice of Mary at least to some extent does not get filtered through male authority. Similar to Foskett, Karlsen Seim reads Mary's sacred readiness as a sign of her agency. She writes: "The obedient and responsive attitude is not a particularly female requirement encouraging passivity. Mary is rather the prototype of the Lord's servant, and this role is signaled by her obedient relationship to the word of God."[24] Though I agree with both Foskett and Karlsen Seim that Mary illustrates her own agency within the Lukan text, I am tempted to ask the question, does the agency of Mary truly counter a characterization of her as a victim of passivity/oppression? In fact, it seems to me that the agency of Mary points to a more complex understanding of obedience or willingness.

My conjecture is that both Karlsen Seim and Foskett miss the bigger picture when they depict Mary purely as a woman who uses her agency to serve God. I would argue that the bodies of the Indian surrogate and Mary seen through the economic lens of demand and supply problematize the notion of agency. Deborah L. Spar points out:

> Even if these women had chosen surrogacy over other alternatives; if they had decided on their own that carrying a stranger's child was preferable to sewing shirts or stitching sneakers, one could still argue that their choice was skewed by the inequities of the global trading system. Is it free choice, after all, if a mother of three becomes a surrogate in order to feed her children? When she signs the formal contract, is this woman exercising free will or providing evidence of the desperation caused by inequality? Most critics of surrogacy would insist strongly on the latter. Or as Oliver writes, "in the case of surrogacy, freedom is an illusion."[25]

Najima tells the journalist that the money she will receive as a surrogate will be used to educate her daughter and fulfill her dreams of becoming a school teacher.[26] The angel tells Mary, "He will be great, and will be called the Son of the Most high, and the Lord God will give to him the throne of his ancestor David. He will reign over the house of Jacob forever and of his kingdom there will be no end" (Luke 1:32–33). Though, one can argue that Mary and the Indian surrogate are different in that one receives monetary compensation and the other does not, I want to point out that what actually connects these women is the promise of the material hope realized before their eyes by the powerful Other. In Luke 1:38, Mary explicitly states her willingness. However, this nod of approval happens only after she hears that her son will be great and become the recipient of the throne of David. Thus, one could say that both Mary and the Indian surrogate state their willingness overtly only when they realize that their future and the future of their children/people can be transformed through their decisions. This draws me to read Mary's eagerness to please God and her open obedience with caution. Furthermore, while the agency/willingness of Mary and the Indian surrogate depicts the liberation and independence of women at one and the same time, it also demonstrates the way power (be it economic or divine) inflicts violence and exploits bodies of economically inferior women by seducing them with hopes of a better future. Mary and the Indian surrogate are contradictory sites on which an agency of violence is performed, one that promises them freedom but only at the cost of their violated bodies.

Interpretations surrounding Mary's consent in the Lucan text are twofold. While one group of scholars (as we saw earlier) depict Mary's consent in an active light, highlighting her agency and empowerment,[27] others argue that Mary's construction of herself as God's slave hinders any efforts of liberation or agency.[28] However, as Schaberg has demonstrated, Luke's presentation of Mary's consent and her reference to herself as *doulē* must be read within the larger context of Deut. 22:23–27, which deals with a betrothed virgin's rape or seduction—both issues of a woman's lack of consent for sexual contact.[29] When Mary says in Luke 1:38, "Here am I, the servant of the Lord; let it be with me according to your word," Schaberg detects a nuance: Mary will carry and bear the child, but she is not saying that the conception was on her terms.[30] This particular master/slave relationship must be understood as mutual dependence illustrated in the performance of service. Mary's reference to herself as a *doulē* must be read within Judaism and the mystery religions, where human dependence upon and service to God are understood as a kind of slavery.[31] Paradoxically, this enslaving God holds the door to humans' freedom: "the real 'ruler' is one who frees the oppressed and yet is a servant."[32]

Schaberg continues: "The language of slavery and servanthood to God was appropriated to convey belief in the spiritual freedom of Jesus and the Christian from the powers of the world. Luke's choice of the term *doulē* in 1:38 and 1:48 (cf. 2:29) surely is intended to have a positive dimension."[33]

It is important to note that unlike biblical and theological scholars who depict Mary's consent as indicative of her status as an active subject of empowerment and agency, Schaberg's interpretation of Mary's empowerment, depicted in her consent, stems from her subjectivity as a victimized woman wronged by patriarchy. She argues:

> Mary's consent is read as consent to the miracle that will preserve her "purity," her sexual innocence and inexperience. This is seen to have religious value, in that her virginity is "void" in which God's new creation is brought into existence; her consent provides the opportunity for this

"action" of God and is a response to the grace of God. Mary's description of herself as a slave of the Lord would express the "vessel's" sense of powerlessness and nothingness. But within the context of the interpretation offered here, Mary's consent is to a conception whose origin, she has protested, can or will not be marital relations with Joseph—She consents, in other words, in ignorance of her specific fate, but in trust that she will be empowered and protected by God.[34]

Thus, according to Schaberg, Mary's consent and the reference to herself as a slave of God is indicative of her freedom that she experiences in her enslavement to the Lord. In other words, Mary enslaves herself willingly to a God/master who himself humbly submits to humanity. Although such an interpretation makes a conscious attempt to reconstruct Mary's consent within a predominantly patriarchal tradition with the hope that such a move would lead to liberation both within and outside the biblical narrative, it seems to me that the only way to achieve this goal is by dichotomizing Mary's subjectivity and limiting her role to that of a powerless woman victimized by patriarchy but, at the same time, empowered by a male God.

Commenting on Homi Bhabha's critique of the logic of liberation, Hardt and Negri state: "Power or forces of social oppression, function by imposing binary structures and totalizing logics on social subjectivities, repressing their difference. These oppressive structures, however, are never total, and differences are always in some way expressed (through mimicry, ambivalence, hybridization, fractured identities, and so forth)."[35] Hence, while splitting Mary's textual subjectivity into either an active subject of empowerment or a victimized object liberated by a male God may help identify structures of patriarchal power and allow feminist biblical and theological scholars to create strategies of resistance that can counter androcentric bias and biblical sexism dominating our religious texts and our society, such strategies miss the moments of ambivalence within the text often suppressed by the totalizing narratives put forth by Marian scholars. It seems to me that Mary's consent, read through the lived realities of the womb-mothers in the surrogacy industry, complicates the binaries that seek to restrict her subjectivity into categories of victim or hero.

Discussing the ethical effects of surrogacy in India, Nilanjana S. Roy writes:

Manju, 29, a domestic helper [commonly known in India as a domestic servant] in Delhi, who asked that her full name not be used, said she thought about surrogacy ever since her sister-in-law gave birth to a surrogate baby two years ago. "She went off to Gujarat and the family kept it very quiet." Said Manju alluding to the stigma that sometimes attaches to surrogate mothers in India, "But she made a lot of cash, much more than my income for a year."[36]

Luke 1:38 reads: "Then Mary said, 'Here am I, the servant of the Lord, let it be with me according to your word.' " While Mary figuratively characterizes herself as a *doulē* or a servant of God, Manju, the Indian surrogate mother tells reporter Roy that her primary real life occupation in Delhi is being a domestic servant. The depiction of both these women as servants/slaves in predominantly patriarchal societies is often understood as expressive of an exploitative, victimized lens. Although such a characterization is accurate, the opportunity to demonstrate their agency, performed as a result of their marginalization, is often foreclosed. It is important to add that I am in no way suggesting that being a slave in the ancient world and being a domestic worker/servant in postcolonial India are similar in every aspect. In her essay titled "Early Christianity, Slavery, and Women's Bodies," Jennifer Glancy draws a strict line of difference even between slavery in the Roman Empire and slavery in United States of America. She writes:

> Roman slavery was different in significant respects from the images of plantation slavery familiar to most Americans. Roman slavery was not based on race, for example, and Romans ultimately freed a higher percentage of their slaves than Americans. Nonetheless, Roman slavery was brutal, vicious, and dehumanizing—a system of corporeal or bodily control sustained by violence and the threat thereof. One dehumanizing practice common in the Roman Empire as well as the Americas was the treatment of slaves as sexual property of their owners.[37]

In addition to these main differences, slaves in the ancient world had no rights and were often seen as occupying the lowest rung of the human ladder in society. Schaberg observes: "The slave was commonly believed to exist on a lower level of humanity and was unable to own property or have a family or a genealogy in the proper sense. A slave had no rights at law, and was regarded as ethically inferior, was subject to cultic obligations and the law only to a limited extent. Slavery is a service that is not a matter of choice but subjection to the alien will of an owner."[38] While being a servant in India is not based on race, in parts of India this occupation is often based on caste and gender. Commenting on the real-life struggles of servants and domestic helpers in India, Sister Josephine Amala Valarmathi points out:

> Domestic workers in India, similar to their counterparts in other parts of Asia and the Middle East, face harsh working conditions. Nearly 90% of domestic workers are women, girls or children, ranging from ages 12 to 75. These women have typically left their own homes to look after other people's homes. The majority of domestic workers are illiterate. Domestic workers are engaged in such tasks as cooking, washing, and cleaning, which are traditionally seen as women's work and therefore undervalued. In India, the stigma for domestic work is heightened by the caste system, as tasks such as cleaning and sweeping are associated with low castes.[39]

It is important to note that similar to the ancient world, differences in gender continue to play an important role in the marginalization and exploitation of female servants living in the postcolonial context of India. Schaberg observes: "The term *doulē* (feminine) always and everywhere carries associations that *doulos* (masculine) does not: associations of sexual use and abuse. Slavery (whether a literal socioeconomic, historical reality or a religious metaphor) means something different for women and for men. A male slave in a man's world has a different experience in any age, from a female slave in a man's world. She sinks lower, and the very boundaries of her personhood and her bodily/physic safety are more endangered."[40] Thus, given the social implications of slavery in the ancient world, it is ironic that the character of Mary, a free woman, willingly constructs herself as a slave of God. Although Mary's reference to herself as a slave illustrates her passivity and provides her with no agency, it seems to me that it is precisely her designation as a slave that allows Mary to transgress boundaries of class and gender and create a new identity for herself through this act of transgression.

In her article titled "Gender, Slavery, and Technology: The Shaping of the Early Christian Moral Imagination," Shiela Briggs points to the transformation of the slave body in the ancient world into an economic resource. She notes:

> The link between slavery and technology appears in one of the most influential discussions of slavery in the ancient world. Aristotle defined the slave as a "living tool" who could use inanimate tools to create the material fabric of human society. Slaves who were prostitutes had their bodies used as a tool like the loom, the mill, or the dyeing vat to produce

income for their owners. A slave's sexual labor was as morally acceptable as any other form of labor. In Roman society, prostitutes and gladiators were either slaves or lower-class persons considered no better than slaves.[41]

Though Briggs connects prostitution and slavery in the ancient world and highlights the conversion of the ancient slave body from a liability into an income-producing asset, her observations allow us to view Mary's characterization of herself as a slave of God in a different light. Roy writes about Manju, the domestic servant from Delhi: "A month ago Manju was approached by the representative of an unlicensed surrogacy clinic in the northern state of Haryana looking for surrogate mothers. She said she might take them up on their offer. 'It's good money,' she said. 'Risks, what risks? Any fool can have a baby, it takes a smart woman to get paid for it.' "[42] Both Mary and Manju opt to willingly enslave their bodies to the powerful Other with the hope that such a decision will finally liberate them and liberate others as a result.

Catherine Belsey, using Louis Althusser's work to understand the construction of the subject, writes:

> Ideology suppresses the role of language in the construction of the subject. As a result, people "recognize" (misrecognize) themselves in the ways in which ideology "interpellates" them, or in other words, addresses them as subjects, calls them by their names, and in turn "recognizes" their autonomy. As a result, they "work by themselves," they "willingly" adopt the subject-positions necessary to their participation in the social formation. In capitalism they "freely" exchange their labour-power for wages and they "voluntarily" purchase the commodities produced.[43]

Luke 1:30–31 reads: "The angel said to her, 'Do not be afraid Mary, for you have found favor with God. And now you will conceive in your womb and bear a son, and you will name him Jesus.' " The angel of the Lord addressing Mary by her name not only demonstrates the subject status of Mary in the narrative, but also provides her with the autonomy to make a decision about her body in a predominantly patriarchal context. Furthermore, recognizing their independence allows female subjects like Mary and the Indian surrogate mother to recognize their exchange value and turn their bodies, more specifically their wombs, into commodities that are exchanged for a price. In other words, the characterization of both these mothers as servants or slaves may very well determine their objectified, exploited status in society; however, their ability to identify their bodies as sites of production and use this skill to negotiate the terms of their social and economic freedom for both themselves and their people highlights their subject status. In short, Mary's status as a *doulē* in the Lukan text, read through the lived realities of the Indian surrogate mother, constructs her maternal body as a hybrid site whose subjecthood, achieved only through the objectification of her womb, leaves her in a state of perpetual ambivalence.

Mary's motherhood constructed in an ambivalent light also creates opportunity within the text for her to transgress her boundaries, as her uncontained, hard to label body slips between dichotomous categories of victim/hero, subject/object, etc. Referring to Thomas Lacquer, Colleen Conway writes: "The perfect man was featured at the top with other less complete or perfect versions of masculine identity falling at various points on the axis. In this view, a woman was understood not as the biologically opposite sex of man but as an imperfect, incomplete version of man."[44] In the one-body gender model common in the Greco-Roman world, bodies of both women and slaves stood in complete contrast to the perfect male body, as they represented bodies that lacked self-control. In such a context, where women find themselves already at the bottom of the gender gradient, the author of Luke, by constructing Mary as a slave, designates her as a victim who is doubly oppressed. Karlsen Seim writes: "For Luke, it is decisively important that Jesus's birth is from God and is accomplished by the Spirit, and that Mary states her willing acceptance....[T]he Spirit acts in such a way that social boundaries, concepts of decency and appropriate objections are overcome."[45] One cannot help but notice that the transgression of boundaries is an important theme within the Lukan infancy narrative. In other words, not only is God transgressing the divine boundaries and inserting himself into the earthly realm, but Mary is also transcending her gender and her status, by participating in a birth that falls outside the traditional role of reproduction within marriage. Thus, one could say that the encounter between Mary and God is representative of an infiltration, where both God and Mary insert themselves into the other's realm. And while this penetration helps Mary cross her boundary from being a passive slave of God to an active mother consenting to conceive the son of God, the price of this penetration falls more heavily on the shoulders of Mary, than on the divine shoulders of God.

The Lukan text demonstrates God breaking human barriers, and it also depicts a woman willing to transgress her own boundaries pertaining to her gender, status, and desire. This crossing over could be translated through the lens of an active desire that begins to take form in the Holy Spirit and Mary. In other words, while God actively works to penetrate Mary, the character of Mary, by expressing her desire aggressively and stating her intent, also penetrates the realm of the divine. The active/passive binary was used to illustrate male and female behavior within the Greco-Roman context. Hence, the active intent performed by Mary in the text makes her dangerously masculine, threatening her subjectivity as a passive woman. In addition, the interpenetration between the two is expressive of the desire of each for the other. As a result, the Lukan narrative shifts back and forth between categories of receiving and giving. While God gives his seed to Mary and Mary receives it, Mary also gives her womb to God and God receives it. Furthermore, while God expresses his desire for a child through the body of Mary, the character Mary also expresses her own desire for freedom for both herself and her people as demonstrated in the Magnificat. Luke 1:46–48 reads: "And Mary said, 'My soul magnifies the Lord, and my spirit rejoices in God my Savior for he has looked with favor on the lowliness of his servant. Surely, from now on all generations will call me blessed.' " Gayatri Chakravorty Spivak writes: "Stanadayini's [the breast-giver's] lesson may be simply this: when the economics as such (here shown in terms of a woman's body) enters in, mothers are divided, women can exploit, not merely dominate. Ideology sustains and interpenetrates this operation of exploitation."[46] Thus, once Mary and the Indian surrogate become aware of their appreciated bodies, they aggressively seek to become reproductive grounds for the Other, openly stating their willingness and constructing their services to the powerful Other through the medium of servanthood. However, this willingness not only causes them to penetrate the realm of the Other, searching for an acceptance through the use of their bodies, but also constructs them as objects willing to exploit themselves in order that the others around them may benefit. Najima Vohra, for example, explains to Abigail Haworth that "[s]he plans to divide her surrogacy windfall three ways: buying a brick house, investing in her husband's business, and paying for her children's education. 'My daughter wants to be a teacher,' she says. 'I'll do anything to give her that opportunity.' "[47] The need to transform the lives of their people/families pushes both the Indian surrogate and Mary to become objects that serve as a means to an end.

In addition to manipulating the minds and bodies of the Indian surrogates and Mary, society also finds ways to idolize these women and turn them into Divine Objects. Jessica Ordenes hugs Vohra, her surrogate, as she cries, "You're my angel, you're my angel."[48] In India, the status of a woman is not only complete through her ability to reproduce; her ability to become a mother pushes her from an earthly into a divine realm. Karlsen Seim, meanwhile, writes: "Over against the metaphorical, symbolic usage, there is no talk in Mary's case of a spiritual birth, even if it is a birth from the Spirit. The child is real enough."[49] One cannot help but notice that the fantastic miracle of the virgin birth is quickly glossed over and the focus is immediately placed on the child: Jesus. But in the process, Mary, the peasant woman, is transformed into the mother of "the Son of God" (Luke 1:35), herself becoming divine through association. Mahasweta Devi writes: "Such is the power of the Indian soil that all women turn into mothers here and all men remain immersed in the spirit of holy childhood. Each man the Holy Child and each woman the Divine Mother."[50]

The characterization of the mother as a divine being, however, must not be seen as an indication of her power to attain freedom. My assertion is that both Mary's and the Indian surrogate's divinity lasts as long as their productivity. Devi writes: "Jashoda's good fortune was her ability to bear children. All this misfortune happened to her as soon as that vanished. Now is the downward time for Jashoda the milk-filled faithful wife who was the object of reverence of the local houses devoted to the Holy Mother."[51] Unlike the "holy child" Jesus whose divinity comes with a lifetime warranty, the divinity of Mary and the Indian surrogate comes with expiration dates. Whatever is Mary's fate in the subsequent history of Christianity, she is a disposable figure for Luke, barely featuring in the two-volume narrative after her cameo performance in the infancy narrative. The divinity of the Lukan Mary and the Indian surrogate mother expires as soon as their ability to reproduce begins to recede into history. Therefore, this need to feel idolized, that is already socially constructed and imposed upon the bodies of these women, drives them to engage in a motherhood, resulting in their bodies being exploited in order that the other may live.

Devi writes:

> After keeping the fast of Shiva's night by watching all night picture shows they are no longer obliged to breast feed their babies. All this was possible because of Jashoda. As a result Jashoda became vocal and, constantly suckling the infants, she opined as she sat in the Mistress' room, "A woman breeds, so here medicine, there blood-peshur, here doctor visits. Showoffs! Look at me! I've become a year-breeder! So is my body failing, or is my milk drying?"[52]

One cannot help but notice the pride in Jashoda's voice that is the direct result of her status as the "Divine Mother." Mary, for her part, sings: "My soul magnifies the Lord, and my spirit rejoices in God my Savior, for he has looked with favor on the lowliness of his servant. Surely, from now on, all generations will call me blessed; for the Mighty One has done great things for me, and holy is his name" (Luke 1:46–49). In the Magnificat, Mary refers to herself explicitly as a lowly servant; however, at the same time she also immediately sets herself apart by noting her exceptional state of blessedness. One could read this sentence of exclusivity not only as a statement of happiness and surprise, but also as a statement of pride, one that illustrates her status as the chosen one.

The Indian surrogate and Mary both participate in a motherhood that takes place without the physical presence of a male. They are both penetrated by a powerful Other that is almost, but not quite, a part of the Empire. They participate in a motherhood that promises them a better future for their children/people. Finally they are both women who take pride in their ability to become mothers. This pride stands dangerously on the brink of arrogance as each woman voices her choseness to become the Milk Mother, the Surrogate Mother, or the Holy Mother. This pride in becoming a mother to an Other sets them up on altars as objects of worship where the violent gaze of their devotees pierces their bodies and shatters their subjectivity. Their desire for Divine Motherhood promises them unity. In the end, however, even the Divine Mother is unable to escape the violence that love inflicts on her body. As a result, her motherhood is born from a "violent love" that lives on in the ambiguity and uncertainty of her body.

Karlsen Seim writes: "Through the transference of Mary's maternal relationship from the physical family to the fictive family of God, the possibility of an alternative motherhood is opened up, and it is no longer limited to her, but is given to all women who hear God's word and do it."[53] It is interesting to note that the definition of family also changes within the context of the Indian surrogate, where relationship is no longer defined through DNA but by mere association:

> Mondal, a clerk in a bank [Mondal's job description exposes the myth that surrogacy is performed by only uneducated women] has just given birth for a couple in California. The couple Karen and Thomas send Mondal pictures of their son Brady every couple of weeks and Karen tells the journalist that she plans to bring Mondal to the United States to celebrate the first birthday of her son. Karen feels that it is important that her son have a "relationship" with Mondal.[54]

One can see that just as the brown body of Mondal gets absorbed into the higher white, Western family, so also the character of Mary is absorbed into the divine family of the Hebrew God. However, while I agree with Karlsen Seim that the character of Mary symbolizes a new form of motherhood, I would also point out that reading Mary through the lens of the Indian surrogate woman highlights the formation of a new kind of family. This family transgresses physical distinctions such as race, class, caste, and economy. But while both these women are accepted lovingly into their new families, they are still never allowed to claim ownership over their children, reminding them subtly but strongly that in this new family these women stand purely as gestation sites. " 'Why were you searching for me?' the Lukan Jesus reproves his 'mother.' 'Did you not know that I must be in my Father's house (or: about my Father's business—*en tois tou patros mou* [2:49]).' "

For a reader of the gospel of Luke, the character of Mary takes on a prominent role in the narrative during her conception. During this period Mary is presented in the text as being an active, autonomous woman with an authoritative voice. Luke 2:15–19 reads:

> When the angels had left them and gone into heaven, the shepherds said to one another, "Let us go now to Bethlehem and see this thing that has taken place, which the Lord has made known to us." So they went with haste and found Mary and Joseph, and the child lying in the manger. When they saw this, they made known what had been told them about this child; and all who had heard it were amazed at what the shepherd told them. But Mary treasured all these words and pondered them in her heart.

It is interesting to note that the minute Mary gives birth to Jesus, her voice in the text is muted and she transforms from an extrovert virgin into an introvert mother. Desai writes: "Not that surrogacy was easy anyway. There were so many physical issues to overcome—and then there were emotional problems as well. Many of them really did get attached to the child after they gave birth. Sometimes it was a huge wrench for them to promise never to see the baby again."[55] In order to control the maternal bond, that threatens to form between the surrogate mother and the child she is being paid to carry, the swollen belly of the Indian surrogate is constantly supervised, placed in isolation, and not allowed to have any contact with either the outside world or the commissioning parents. Gail Sexton Anderson notes:

> For the Indian surrogate, it is a one-sided, isolating experience and in most cases, the surrogate will never meet the intended parents she has helped. In fact, the surrogates are discouraged from having any interaction with the intended parents. Not only is the surrogate separated from

her family and society in a dormitory with other surrogates, she never gets to experience the joy of handing over the couple's baby and seeing their faces when they see their child for the first time. American surrogates, and even the husbands of American surrogates, have told me that this is what being a surrogate is all about: sharing that moment of joy and knowing you have given life to this couple's dream. The relationship between surrogates and intended parents in the U.S. is interactive throughout the whole process.[56]

Yet, with all the precautionary measures taken to control the maternal bond between the surrogate mother and the child she is being paid to carry, the moments of love between the womb-mother and child continue to slip constantly between the violent lines of capitalism and patriarchy. Surrogate Vohra tells Haworth, "'If I do feel sad after the birth, I won't show it. I can understand how much Jessica wants this baby.' In India, she explains, infertility is considered a curse."[57] Similarly, Manishaben Ramabai Parmar, a surrogate for Steve and Jennifer Benito Kowalski says: "I will be sad about it... But I know my responsibility, and I'm doing it for the money and they're doing it for the baby, so I can understand it."[58] Similar to Mary in the Lukan text whose true feelings about the child she was chosen to carry are narratively silenced, the Indian surrogate mothers only express their true feelings after much persuasion from the reporters as they acknowledge the sadness they will feel at parting with the child they are being paid to carry. Aware of their temporality as *mothers to an other*, both Mary and the Indian surrogate are forced to mask their inner thoughts as they mentally prepare themselves to hand the child over to its true family. Thus, even though Mary and the Indian surrogate mother are able to transgress the physical boundaries of race, economy, class, and/or caste and are "absorbed" into a new family in which their role as *mothers to an other* is redefined, they never fully belong to this new family, nor are they allowed to claim full ownership over the child they are hired to carry. "My mother and my brothers," says the Lukan Jesus, "are those who hear the word of God and do it" (8:21).

The Magnificat as a Song of Oppressive Liberation

The Magnificat, or Mary's song of praise, found in Luke 1:46–56 plays an important role in constructing Mary's character as an active woman, unafraid to use her voice to express how she feels. While feminist biblical and theological scholars tend to see the Magnificat as an expression of a woman's liberation from patriarchy, male commentators, have, in the past, commented on the anomalous tone of this song. Schaberg writes: "Commentators have often remarked on the seeming inappropriateness of the tone and sentiments expressed in the Magnificat, as attributed to Mary."[59] While feminist scholars make a conscious attempt to reclaim the voice of Mary in order that they may be able to expose the androcentric and patriarchal interpretations that have dominated, silenced, or dismissed a strong female character, they in turn have dichotomized Mary's voice into a plea for revenge or a song of liberation. Although these interpretations variously construct Mary as a liberated woman, none of them, I would argue, take into account the complexity surrounding Mary's new subjectivity as a liberated woman. It is for this reason that the Magnificat, read through the lives of the Indian surrogate mothers, complicates our definition of liberation, constructing it as an emancipation that *does not quite* promise freedom and is contingent upon Mary's acceptance of enslavement to the other. This leads me to ask the question: Can one adequately read Mary's Song of Praise/Victory simply as an expression of her liberation? Or is it rather a statement of ambivalent hope embedded in a motherhood that is an expression of violent-love?

Feminist interpretations of Mary's Magnificat are based in an understanding and interpretation of the virginal conception of Mary. This is because feminist biblical and theological scholars reading the Lukan infancy narrative regularly, approach the text with the clear intention to liberate the character of Mary from the clutches of patriarchy, in order that they may begin to construct a *Woman's Mary,* relevant to the lives of everyday women. However, as women readers, sometimes we gloss over or unconsciously ignore the hesitant ambivalences that often slip through the cracks of our own liberation discourses. While biblical scholars like Schaberg argue that this song shows God siding with the oppressed, wronged mother in the narrative, theologians like Rosemary Radford Ruether and others suggest that as a song of liberation, this hymn bears testimony to a woman's liberation from the powers of patriarchy. However, interpretations such as these, while helpful in resisting patriarchal attempts to silence women's voices, are able to function only by limiting Mary's voice to binary categories of victim, on the one hand, or hero, on the other.

Schaberg argues that the author of Luke knew of the illegitimacy tradition that surrounded the birth of Jesus, and it was this tradition that he was trying to communicate to his readers in his version of the infancy narrative. She remarks: "Luke's point is not that the girl who utters the Magnificat is lowly, humble, unimportant, insignificant, in comparison to the mighty God. It is rather that she, who was humiliated and degraded, and the child whose origin is in humiliation and degradation, were helped by God (v. 54)."[60] Her argument relies on the notion that Mary's humiliation must be understood through the text of Deut. 22:23–27. In making her argument she is also taking on male biblical scholars like Fitzmyer and others who argue that Mary's humiliation must be understood from an economic perspective. She notes: "As Fitzmyer remarks, usually the term *tapeinosis means 'humiliation,'* but he and others understand it to refer here to Mary's 'humble station.' It expresses her 'unworthiness to be the mother of the Davidic Messiah and the Son of God.'"[61] By understanding Mary's humiliation to refer to her poverty, commentators like Fitzmyer foreclose the possibility that Mary's humiliation could refer to sexual humiliation. As a result, Mary's virginal body demarcated from the rest of womankind, becomes an ideal for all women, a symbol of perfection, purity, and humility.

Brown also argues that the word *tapeinosis* means economic humiliation. Significant here is Luke 2:21–24:

> After eight days had passed, it was time to circumcise the child; and he was called Jesus, the name given by the angel before he was conceived in the womb. When the time came for their purification according to the law of Moses, they brought him up to Jerusalem to present him to the Lord (as it is written in the law of the Lord, "Every firstborn male shall be designated as holy to the Lord"), and they offered a sacrifice according to what is stated in the law of the Lord, "a pair of turtledoves or two young pigeons."

Brown notes that the use of turtledoves as sacrifice, rather than a lamb and a bird, could be a textual sign that depicts the poverty of Jesus's parents.[62] Schaberg points out that even though one could read the sacrifice of two young pigeons as a sign of Mary and Joseph's poverty, the textual evidence does not fully support this argument. She argues: "In any case, there is no special emphasis by Luke on Mary's poverty. For what it was worth, her betrothal has incorporated her legally into the Davidic lineage, perhaps into the one of the nonaristocratic, lateral branches."[63] Another way scholars have tried to make sense of Mary's *tapeinosis* in the Magnificat is by linking her humiliation to that of Elizabeth. Schaberg points out: "Mary's statement that God 'has regarded the *tapeinosis* of his servant' (1:48) is linked to the preceding Lucan narrative in yet another way. The line is reminiscent thematically of Elizabeth's statement in 1:25."[64]

However, as Schaberg accurately notes, Mary's humiliation cannot be linked to Elizabeth because she is not a woman who is barren. In other words, Mary's humiliation, unlike that of Elizabeth and Hannah, does not stem from her barrenness, thereby suggesting that her *tapeinosis* is the result of something far more serious. She contends: "My argument is that Luke alludes again to the law in Deut 22:23–27 with his insertion of 1:48 into the Magnificat. He achieved here, then a double allusion: to Hannah and to the law. The virgin betrothed to a man (1:27) was sexually humiliated. But her humiliation, like the barrenness of Hannah (and Elizabeth) was 'looked upon' and reversed by God."[65] Thus, by interpreting Mary's *tapeinosis* to mean sexual humiliation, a humiliation she experiences through the violation of her body, Schaberg hopes to dismantle the patriarchal barriers that construct and place the virginal body of Mary above those of all other women. She writes:

> The Virgin Mary is also a great contrast to real human women. Mary establishes the child as the destiny of woman, but does not experience the sexual intercourse necessary for all other women to fulfil this destiny. Defined as wholly unique, she is set up as a model of womanhood that is unattainable. As the male projection of idealized femininity, a patriarchal construction, she is the good woman, stripped of all dangerous elements: she receives worship, not equality. Man exalts Mary for virtues he would like woman to exhibit, and projects onto her all that he does resolve to be.[66]

By rejecting a literal reading of Mary's virginal conception, Schaberg makes a conscious attempt to blur the boundaries separating Mary from the rest of womankind. However, in her eagerness to construct a narrative of Mary that will aid in the liberation of everyday women, caught in the clutches of patriarchy, she creates a victimized, sexually violated mother, whose only hope for salvation comes at the hands of a male God. Hence, although, Schaberg's interpretation is inspirational, her reading fails to recognize the ambivalence present in Mary's liberation as a vindicated woman. In other words, even if Mary had suffered sexual humiliation and was vindicated by God, her liberation, tainted by her sexual humiliation, results in an emancipation which is partial and incomplete because it continues to be burdened by her enslavement to patriarchal power, here embodied in the person of the patriarchal God.

Similar to Schaberg, feminist theologian Rosemary Radford Ruether also understands the Magnificat as a song of liberation. She writes: "In contrast to the patriarchal theories of divine grace, exemplified in

Augustine and Calvin, Lucan Mariology suggests a real co-creatorship between God and humanity, or, in this case, woman. The free act of faith is possible only when we can recognize the genuine unity between response to God and our own liberation."[67] Another vocal feminist voice pushing for a reading of Mary through the lens of liberation is Elizabeth Johnson. In her article titled "The Marian Tradition and the Reality of Women," Johnson argues the following of the Mary of the Magnificat:

> Proclaiming words of praise and prophecy, she is a symbol of tremendous power as the singer of the song of justice in the new age of redemption. Liberation theologies of all types have claimed Mary under this aspect, recognizing that her proclamation of the greatness of God who puts down the mighty and exalts the humble, fills the hungry with good things but sends the rich away empty, fits well with the understanding of the importance of engagement for justice and peace. Feminist theologians find particular meaning in this symbol. It is noted that the Lukan community found such a proclamation a fitting expression for Mary, with its focus on the social and political rather than on the maternal and private.[68]

Although Schaberg, Ruether, and Johnson agree that the Mary of the Magnificat in the Lukan infancy narrative is an expression of God's liberation of the oppressed, Schaberg is one of the few scholars who chooses to insert the discussion of a sexual humiliation into her reading of Mary as a vindicated woman.[69] Both Ruether and Johnson read the character of Mary in the Magnificat as the new Church, symbolizing a new humanity liberated by God. Ruether argues: "The key text for the Lucan identification of Mary with the Church, the New Israel, is the Magnificat (Luke 1:46–55)."[70] In addition, both Ruether and Johnson also highlight Mary's poverty.[71]

The impulse to liberate Mary from the textual and social patriarchy of her time, for both Ruether and Johnson, appears to stem directly from their own felt need to liberate women from contemporary patriarchy and androcentricism. This leads to both these scholars characterizing Mary as a heroic woman whose voice is elevated to represent the voice of all oppressed people everywhere, especially oppressed women. Johnson argues:

> With the Magnificat Mary appears as an active agent in salvation rather than the passive handmaiden, an image also countered by the idea of Mary as disciple. She is highly exalted because through her God is given

order of things in which victims will be justified. It is a revolution in which she finds great joy. And Mary does not just proclaim this. In her own person she embodies the humble and the hungry, the oppressed who are being liberated by God's action.[72]

It is interesting to note that while Schaberg seeks to dismantle the mythological patriarchal construct of Mary by reading her as a victimized woman whose sexual humiliation is avenged by God, Ruether and Johnson, employing a similar tactic, attempt to blur the boundaries between this goddess mother and ordinary women by constructing her motherhood as an embodiment of poverty and economic humiliation so that she may become relevant to the lives of oppressed people everywhere. Ruether argues that Mary "herself is both subject and object of this liberating action. She makes it possible through her act of faith, but the liberating action of God in history liberates her. She herself embodies and personifies the oppressed and subjugated people who are being liberated and exalted through God's redemptive power. She is the humiliated ones who have been lifted up, the hungry ones who have been filled with good things."[73]

Although Ruether acknowledges the dual subjectivity that Mary possesses as subject and object, she does not delve deeper into this ambivalence but quickly moves past it and, in a manner similar to Johnson, elevates Mary into a heroic woman whose voice offers empowerment to the oppressed. And although these attempts to deconstruct a patriarchal, mythological Mary are relevant and helpful in both exposing and resisting the forces that hinder women from reaching their full potential, they nevertheless fail to address or even articulate the complex ambivalences that drive the lives of everyday women, not least in postcolonial India and other regions of the global South. This leads me to ask the question, when the lives of everyday women filled with complexities, ambivalences, and hesitancies lead them to make choices that cannot be strictly dichotomized into right/wrong, liberation/oppression, victim/hero, why then, do we, as women readers, compel textual women such as the Lukan Mary to live out such black and white lives in our interpretations? I am arguing that reading the Magnificat and the rest of the Lukan infancy narrative alongsided the contextual lives of Indian surrogate women—obviously, other differently situated women engaged in different forms of struggle might also have been chosen for this reading experiment—provokes not just a more realistic interpretation of the textual Mary, but also an interpretation that begins to expand our own definition of liberation.

Ruether's understanding of liberation focuses on a reversal of binaries whereby the one-time oppressors now become the oppressed. Ruether argues: "Luke's liberation language is explicitly economic and political. The mighty are put down from their thrones; the rich are sent away empty. This theme grates unpleasantly on the ears of most affluent Christians."[74] Johnson similarly argues: "Luke's sensitivity to women as members of the poor and despised classes adds this dimension to the image of Mary singing of justice; she herself represents the subjugated who will be lifted up and filled with the good things in the messianic revolution."[75] Hardt and Negri remark: "One of the primary and constant objects of Bhabha's attack are *binary divisions*. In fact, the entire postcolonial project as he presents it is defined by its refusal of the binary divisions on which the colonialist worldview is predicated. The world is not divided in two and segmented in opposing camps (center versus periphery, First versus Third World), but rather it is and has always been defined by innumerable partial and mobile differences."[76] I am in no way suggesting that Ruether's, Johnson's, and Schaberg's interpretations constitute a colonizing discourse. Instead, my goal is to merely highlight some of the ambivalences that are often subsumed under totalizing narratives that use binary divisions to address issues of liberation and oppression. On the surface, the verses sung by Mary appear to fit neatly into categories of liberation vs. oppression. However, it is when the voice of Mary is placed next to the voice of the Indian surrogate mother that the definitions of liberation, oppression, and humility begin to be altered subtly.

Luke 1:46–48 reads: "And Mary said, 'My soul magnifies the Lord and my spirit rejoices in God, my Savior, for he has looked with favor on the lowliness of his servant. Surely, from now all generations will call me blessed.'" One surrogate mother named Vidya defends her decision to become a surrogate as follows: "I am doing this basically for my children's education and my daughter's marriage. I am not greedy for the money. This surrogacy is like God has blessed me and given me the opportunity to do something for them [meaning the commissioning parents]."[77] Mary's reference to herself as a "blessed" woman is often understood by scholars to refer either to her elevated status among women, her empowerment symbolizing hope for the oppressed, or her vindication by God as a woman who has been sexually violated by the powers of patriarchy. And while all these interpretations are relevant and important, none of them considers the idea that Mary's reference to herself as "blessed" could stem from her eagerness to become a mother to the Other in order that she might rise above her straitened circumstances. In other words, both Mary and surrogate Vidya explicitly state that they are "blessed" women because they have been chosen by the powerful Other to become a womb-mother to that Other's child.

Luke 1:49–55 reads:

> For the Mighty One has done great things for me, and holy is his name. His mercy is for those who fear him from generation to generation. He has shown strength with his arm; he has scattered the proud in the thoughts of their hearts. He has brought down the powerful from their thrones, and lifted up the lowly; he has filled the hungry with good things, and sent the rich away empty. He has helped his servant Israel, in remembrance of his mercy, according to the promise he made to our ancestors.

Once again, these verses are often understood as a cry of liberation placed upon the lips of a lowly, yet strong woman. Johnson writes that Mary "is the personification of those who, having nothing, are gifted by the action of God and charged to continue the liberating action of God in the world. It is precisely in her femaleness that she is the sign of the new redeemed humanity, the powerless who are empowered in the reign of God. Pray the Magnificat from a feminist perspective, and whole new meanings are declared."[78] Pande reports the story of Pushpa, a surrogate mother in one of the clinics. She writes:

> While Pushpa was undergoing treatment for her second client from the United States, she spoke about her dream to go abroad: "I built one house with the money I got the first time. I want to do this again and again. You know, I've always wanted to be an air hostess and visit America. Maybe now I can.... But don't think I am being selfish. This is only for my children. If I go abroad I can send money back home for them." Even Pushpa, labeled a greedy surrogate by the medical staff, is reluctant to talk about surrogacy in purely business terms and instead reiterates her higher motivations.[79]

For Puspha, but also for Mary, the dreams of liberation and a better life stem from the exact same place as their oppression. For Pushpa, the United States of America is both the place that chooses to exploit her poverty and capitalize on her cheap labor as an Indian surrogate, and it is also the place that symbolizes for her economic prosperity and freedom, a place she eagerly desires to become a part of. Similarly, Mary is willing to surrender herself as a slave to the male God while also looking to the same God to liberate her and her people from bondage and oppression. In short, the exploited mothers willingly consent to their exploitation with the hope that their victimization will eventually lead to a better life for their children or their nation. These mothers thereby dismantle the binary divisions between liberation and oppression and perform a motherhood that depicts an oppressive-liberation as they realize that the path to liberation of themselves, their families, and their people, can only be achieved through their *willing consent* to being exploited, victimized, and used by the patriarchal and powers of their respective cultures. Hence, I would argue that the Magnificat, read through the contextual lives of the Indian surrogate mother, must not simply be read as a "call for liberation" that depicts the empowerment or avenging of a woman or women in general, but rather as being illustrative of an ambivalent liberation that promises a freedom contingent upon one's enslavement to another. Such a liberation, I would argue, never fully frees nor fully enslaves Mary or the Indian surrogate, but leaves them pining in an ambivalent hope for something that was promised to them, but never quite seems to arrive.

Focusing on the Magnificat in Luke, Ruether interprets Mary as the new Israel: A symbol of liberation,[80] perhaps; but assimilating Mary with the liberated Israel not only has a woman's body stand in for a land or nation—a common colonial trope from antiquity down to modernity—but it also intimately connects a woman's body with her ability to reproduce.[81] Ruether's attempt to read Mary as "a woman from . . . the poor classes of a colonized people under the mighty empire of Rome"[82] makes a genuine effort to transform Mary for all women, but Ruether's Mary is liberated through her ability to reproduce: A child, a nation, and a community. As such, her Mary discriminates against those women who are unable to perform the reproductive function.[83] Ruether's interpretation of a liberated Mary begins with her consent, her free choice is "an expression of her faith."[84] Mary's consent, as a result, can be interpreted by feminist scholars in two ways.

While Ruether is the most prominent among a number of feminist interpreters who see Mary's consent as a free choice, others see her consent as passive receptivity at best. Mary Daly, perhaps the paragon of a second-wave radical feminist theologian, agrees with Schaberg that Mary is a victim of rape. In her book *Gyn/ecology: The Metaethics of Radical Feminism*, Daly writes: "The catholic Mary is not the Goddess creating parthenogenetically on her own, but rather, she is portrayed/betrayed as Total Rape Victim—a pale derivative symbol disguising the conquered Goddess."[85] While Schaberg argues for the rape *or seduction* of Mary, Daly forecloses the textual opportunity for Mary to emerge as anything other than a victim. The rape of Mary is illustrated in her response to God, which, Daly claims, moves beyond her consent and demonstrates an attitude of nonresistance: "The rape of the rarefied remains of the Goddess in the Christian myth is mind/spirit rape— the angel Gabriel appears to the terrified young girl, announcing that she has been chosen to become the mother of god."[86] This mind/spirit rape is a form of religious violation by which Mary is impregnated with the "Supreme seminal idea, who becomes the 'Word made flesh.' "[87] For Daly, the Virgin Birth is a patriarchal myth that was designed to eliminate female presence from the text. Although Daly begins with the *intention* to liberate Mary from the patriarchal myth of the Christian birth narrative, she inadvertently dichotomizes Mary's textual character and slots her into the category of a rape victim. This interpretation of Mary strips her of any textual agency, and so her emancipation must remain partial.

Elizabeth Johnson's concern with Mariology is its dissociation from women's lived experience.[88] She proposes that reclaiming the historical Mary allows her to become familiar to all women: "Her life's context was an economically poor, politically oppressed, Jewish peasant culture marked by exploitation and publicly violent events."[89] In another proposal, Johnson focuses on the Magnificat and sees Mary's song of praise as "representing the subjugated who will be lifted up and filled with good things in the messianic revolution."[90] Mary's virginity symbolizes her autonomy and power, especially in a time where women were subject to patriarchal control.[91] Her untouched body marks her active independence, in that she refuses to let the patriarchal structures confine her to the traditional role of motherhood. In this way, preserving Mary's virginity becomes intimately tied to Mary's liberation and intrinsic to Johnson's interpretation of Mary as a hero.

More recent critics Tina Beattie and Anne Elvey have brought Mariological study in line with critical theory, and each focuses on a particular symbolically rich part of the female anatomy. Using psychoanalytic theory, Beattie draws from Derrida, who conceptualized the hymen as a permeable boundary that could be seen to challenge binarism.[92] Although the unruptured hymen has traditionally been seen as signifying the unspoiled body of a daughter officially passed to a husband by her father, this membrane also stands for "the space between" and challenges the dominant symbolic order.[93] The ruptured hymen being a traditional, if unreliable, mark of male interference means that Mary is reproducing outside phallocentric regulation.[94] The hymen may preserve the in-betweenness of Mary, but the same membrane separates her body from other women. It not only enables her to escape the phallic constrictions of patriarchy but also demarcates her body from the rest of womankind.

For her part, Elvey focuses on the placenta—and its agency.[95] In *An Ecological Feminist Reading of the Gospel of Luke: A Gestational Paradigm,* Elvey reads the Lucan infancy narrative in conjunction with a wide range of critical theorists, including the French feminist theorists Julia Kristeva and Luce Irigaray.[96] In the Magnificat, Elvey says, "Mary *assents* to Gabriel's announcement in 1:34, 38, and 47–55, but she does not *consent*—nor does Gabriel ask for her consent:[97] The Lukan divine purpose, while inviting and requiring human response, is characterized by a kind of necessity."[98] Mary's assent makes her at best an equal of God, entering into an agreement with him. Were she to actually consent, to give her permission, *that* might indicate that she is in a position of agency. In a predominantly patriarchal world, women assent all the time; consent is something else. In fact, Elvey postulates, the subject Mary is not in control of her impregnated body. This does allow Elvey to agree with Capel Anderson and Beattie in that Mary's virginal or pregnant body slips through the cracks of patriarchy and does something basically inhuman—but her body is not at Mary's bidding. The virginal or pregnant body of Mary exhibits a heroic uncontrollability that transcends the patriarchal structures that surround her. For the poststructuralist-inflected Elvey, Mary's maternal body even seems to elude Mary's own control.

Deborah Sawyer in her article "Hidden Subjects: Rereading Eve and Mary," engages in reading the textual figures of Eve and Mary using psychoanalytic and gender criticism. Sawyer suggests ways in which the figures of Mary and Eve can be refigured "as the true subjects of the foundational narratives they inhabit."[99] She argues that "[a]s Eve emerged as the seductress who introduced sexual lust into the world by offering the forbidden fruit to Adam, so Mary's virginal state, her sexual purity, became the most significant feature of her life."[100] Sawyer notes that the figures of Mary and Eve have often been highlighted for their difference; however, their commonalities are never dwelt upon.[101] Sawyer highlights the common characteristics between the two female archetypes: "Both Eve and Mary said 'yes' to being truly human; both lived through the death of a child, experiencing being human at its expense."[102] The archetypes of Eve and Mary, Sawyer argues, must not be discarded "because they were appropriated and rewritten for us by patriarchal hands. Instead, focusing on their essence, they can be understood to embody and confirm the hopes and fears of what it means to be human, and most significantly how 'becoming woman' can be lived."[103] The purpose for revisiting archetypes such as Eve and Mary, for Sawyer, is also intimately tied into their redemption so that their common experiences can lead to positive experiences for all women. However, in the process of reclaiming these women as role models for the everyday woman, it seems to me, we begin to sharpen the blurry edges that help us truly construct these female characters as being human.

CHAPTER 5

The Synoptic Marys and the Synoptic Hierarchies

> Private and public, past and present, the psyche and the social develop
> an interstitial intimacy. It is an intimacy that questions binary divi-
> sions through which such spheres of social experience are often spatially
> opposed.
>
> —Homi Bhabha, *Location of Culture*

The mothers in Matthew's genealogy and the infancy narrative
are often depicted through binary lenses of hero or victim, and
although these interpretations are relevant, they fail to capture
the maternal ambivalence performed by each of these women within
their respective patriarchal contexts. It seems to me that the Matthean
mothers and the postcolonial Indian surrogate mothers are connected
through this performance of an ambivalent motherhood, one that permits them both to be exploited by the patriarchal structures, and, at
the same time, to use their bodies as tools that enable them in turn
to exploit these structures of powers. In short, these mothers participate in an *exploiter-exploited motherhood* in which their maternal bodies
slip between the either/or binary lines, constructing their subjectivities
both, as marginalized women and empowered mothers.

Legitimate Fathers of an Illegitimate Conception: The Matthean Joseph

Dominating the Matthean infancy narrative, in a significant manner,
is the character of Joseph. Scholars observe that the Matthean Joseph
is an active, righteous, and obedient earthly father. However, the common perception of the Matthean Joseph as an active character arises

mainly from reading the Matthean infancy narrative in juxtaposition with the Lukan infancy narrative. Yolanda Dreyer illustrates this well. She writes:

> A marked difference between the gospels is that Joseph, the patriarch, plays the leading role in the Gospel of Matthew—God speaks to *him*. Luke gives the leading role to Mary—God speaks to *her*. In Matthew, Mary quickly recedes into the background. She does not sing the *Magnificat* (Lk 1:46–55) and she is not a character in the story of the 12 year old whose wisdom supersedes that of the learned men in the temple (Lk 2:4–52). In the story of the flight to Egypt, which is told only in Matthew (2:13–18), Joseph is mentioned (Mt 2:13), but not Mary. Mary is also not present amongst the women who witness Jesus' death on the cross (Mt 27: 55–56).[1]

While this interpretation is perceptive and relevant, it, too, fails to accommodate some of the ambivalences that the character of Joseph demonstrates in the text. Some of the cracks in the patriarchal armor of the Matthean Joseph appear when his character is interpreted alongside the contextual body of the Indian surrogate's husband. Such a reading dismantles Joseph's image as an active man, whose righteousness is reflected in his obedience to God, and, understands his decision to accept Mary's miraculous conception as one that exposes his desire for wanting a better life both for himself and his people.

There is no doubt that the character of Joseph in Matthew, when read through the text of Luke appears to have a more substantial role, is more active, and most importantly, is transformed into a hero, whose righteousness is illustrated in his *willingness* to accept his already pregnant fiancé. As Jack Dean Kingsbury states: "[I]t is Joseph to whom Mary is betrothed. It is Joseph who must wrestle with the problem of Mary's unanticipated pregnancy. It is Joseph, who, because of his righteousness and compassion, decides he must divorce Mary but determines to do so as leniently as possible."[2] Furthermore, the author of Matthew claims that the reason why Joseph decides to divorce Mary quietly is because of his righteousness (1:19). Surprisingly, this claim is never questioned or interrogated by biblical scholars. Willhelmus Weren, for example, argues that the nobility of Joseph is accentuated in his action to divorce Mary quietly, in spite of her transgression: "Joseph is a righteous man (Matt 1:19). He wants the law to be observed. He is willing to have disciplinary measures taken because his wife has conceived without his involvement. His law-abiding nature acquires special dimension when

he refuses to denounce Mary publicly."[3] Although Joseph's righteousness is highlighted in his action to "quietly divorce" Mary, the text
remains mysteriously silent after Joseph finally accepts Mary knowing
fully well that she has conceived in a fashion that does not fit the standards of a respectable society.

Joseph's *willingness/consent* has never been interrogated, and in fact
most scholars would argue that his *consent* to accept Mary's unplanned
pregnancy is a direct result of his Jewish righteousness and his obedience to God's command, as mediated through the angel. As Elaine
Wainwright puts it: "Jesus's birth is legitimized through the righteous
man, whom the law protects and whose obedience to divine command
establishes him as the legal father of the child, thus giving closure to the
patrilineage."[4] While such scholarly interpretations of Joseph's consent
may be relevant, they fail to illustrate the way patriarchy plays a role
in influencing Joseph's decision to accept his betrothed's miraculous
conception for a higher cause.

Modern surrogacy helps recreate a conception that is not only immaculate, and legitimate, but also fits within the patriarchal mindset. As a
result, the success of surrogacy in a male dominated society such as
India lies in its ability to reproduce a conception that not only ensures
the protection of the sexual chastity of the Indian surrogate mother, but
also assures the Indian husband that his social honor remains unviolated and intact within his community. Consider, again, Matthew 1:
20: "But just when he had resolved to do this, an angel of the Lord
appeared to him in a dream and said, 'Joseph son of David, do not be
afraid to take Mary as your wife, for the child conceived in her is from
the Holy Spirit.'" Similar to the husband of the Indian surrogate who is
counseled by the doctors and the medical staff of the surrogate industry,
the angel assures Joseph that the chastity of his fiancée is intact and,
therefore, he must not hesitate to claim her as his wife.[5] It does seem
ironic, however, that Joseph's *consent* to accept Mary occurs only after
his "patriarchal self" is convinced that his betrothed has not been physically penetrated by a penis and her chastity is intact. This leads one to
question his image as a righteous and obedient man, and subject his
character to a more human, if not a more ambivalent, interpretation—
even if this entails reading against the grain of probable Matthean
intention. In other words, the character of Joseph might be read as a
man who accepts his already pregnant fiancée not out of a sense of duty,
obedience, or righteousness, but out of a *patriarchal relief* that her body
has not been—physically penetrated—by another man, and her virginity remains intact and ready to be claimed by her husband, Joseph.

The recreation of a virginal conception in the surrogacy industry is the perfect tool that promises to safeguard the honour of the Indian surrogate's husband. Matthew. 1:21 reads: "She will bear a son, and you are to name him Jesus, for he will save his people from their sins. All this took place to fulfil what had been spoken by the Lord through the prophet: 'Look, the virgin shall conceive and bear a son and they shall name him Emmanuel,' which means, God is with us." However, as Amy Jill Levine has shown us in her work, the Hebrew version of Isaiah simply states that "a young woman" has conceived. The author of Matthew, translating from Septuagint, uses the word "parthenos" or virgin when he writes down his account of the narrative.[6] The concept of conception without intercourse ingeniously provides a way for the Indian wife to cross the traditional boundaries of marriage and yet, at the same time, protect her sexual honor completely. In her article titled "Rent-A-Womb: Surrogacy in India on the Rise," Deepali Gaur describes how surrogacy takes on the air of the miraculous:

How can one fully protect a poor, uneducated woman who has spent her life in a patriarchal set-up, fed on those patriarchal beliefs even when laws have failed to give her any relief? What stops the middle men here (clinics/doctors) from exploiting her, let alone her own family? Added to this, in traditional rural, largely uneducated societies where people understand little about medical technology surrogacy comes with its own set of moral complications. For many there is no comprehension of conception without sex, which places the surrogate in a twilight zone of legality and immorality. Hence, many families during the course of the surrogacy actually have to abandon their communities to keep the situation under wraps.[7]

Both Mary and the Indian surrogate mother tow the line between morality and immorality, as their vulnerability is exploited by the powers of patriarchy and the capitalistic society of a globalized India, and their bodies are targeted by their husbands who seize the opportunity to use participation in a conception that falls outside the traditional bounds of marriage to create a better life for themselves and their community. One woman, Neetu Sangar, lost the 300,000 rupees that she earned from her first surrogate pregnancy on a failed business venture of her husband and has become a surrogate for a second time for the sake of her children and her husband.[8]

Like Joseph, these husbands consent to their wives' participation, because they believe that such a conception will promise them hope for a better future. Sangar, signing up to become a surrogate for the second time, hopes that the money earned from this operation will help her husband get back on his feet. Meanwhile, Joseph accepts a pregnant Mary only after he learns that the child she is carrying will "save his people from their sins."

Between the genealogy and the infancy narrative, the character of Joseph is mentioned nine times by name, while Mary, the mother of Jesus is mentioned only three times by name. This alone suggests to the reader that the protagonist driving this narrative is Joseph, and yet, the reader never once hears his voice in the text. Joseph is depicted as a righteous man who must respond to his fiancée's untimely and unconventional pregnancy, and so he takes the decision to divorce her privately.[9] The internal struggle illustrated in Matthew. 1:19 is the only time that the reader comes close to hearing the voice of Joseph, but even then it is not his direct voice but the internal voice of his conscience. The only voice heard in the text is that of the angel of the Lord, who speaks to Joseph directly in three dream sequences. Joseph's dominance in the infancy narrative of Matthew is further eclipsed when the textual body of Joseph is read in tandem with the contextual body of the husband of the Indian surrogate mother. Pande, for example, claims that her research "has included in-depth open format interviews with forty-two surrogates, their husbands and in-laws, eight intending parents, two doctors, and two surrogacy brokers."[10] It is interesting, though, that even though Pande notes that she has interviewed husbands of Indian surrogate mothers, the readers never get to hear them speak. Similarly, most articles or interviews about commercial surrogacy in India focus on the Indian surrogate mother, the client, or even the doctor, but never the Indian husband. This does not mean that the husband of the Indian surrogate mother is absent from the whole process. His presence in many cases is the driving factor that pushes the Indian woman to become a surrogate mother.[11]

While it is pertinent to note that the decision to become a surrogate mother is often a family affair, it is ironic that in many cases the voice of the husband is never heard in the interviews. Most surrogate mothers admit openly that poverty is the only reason they are participating in such an operation. Similar to the character of Joseph in the Matthean infancy narrative, who is a partially fleshed-out presence due to his lack of a voice, the invisible presence of the Indian surrogate's husband is felt throughout the interviews; but, like Joseph, his voice never reaches the ears of the readers. In this regard, Joseph is a peculiarly "feminized" character, despite being the protagonist of Matthew's infancy narrative, to the extent that lack of voice/lack of lines is a recurrent condition for female characters in biblical narrative.

As Lacan theorized, speech is a necessary trait for a person to obtain a subject position in any symbolic world, and the ability to speak, along with the ability to penetrate, were consummately definitive of men in the ancient world. Because Jesus is generated through the Holy Spirit, and not through the procreative activity and penetration of Joseph, Joseph in this genealogy comes off as passive, even weak. Thus, if penetration was not just the marker of masculinity, but was the symbol of active masculinity in the ancient world, one can further make the case that the character of Joseph in Matthew's infancy narrative is depicted as passive.

In addition to being deprived of the act of generation, Matthew's Joseph is also deprived of speech. In the ancient world speech was also a marker of masculinity, as Jerome Neyrey notes: "According to gender stereotypes, males in 'private' space outside the household have voice but females do not, a distinction all the more true of the 'public'-political world."[12] Thus, in a symbolic world where speech constructs a person's subjecthood and is illustrative of his/her power in society, the husband of the Indian surrogate mother and the character of Joseph are both feminized by a lack of speech and a lack of an act of generation that would account for their wife's pregnancy. As phallic symbols, the tongue and the penis pave the path through which males can *enter* (both physically and symbolically) into the symbolic order and set themselves up as subjects. Thus, Joseph's inability to speak in the Matthean narrative prevents him from becoming a full and active male member of his culture. Instead, he is a passive male denied of both sexual and oral penetration. Although the character of Joseph in Matthew may seem to have a more active role than his female counterpart, Mary, especially when compared to the Lukan Jospeh, it seems to me, his *lack of voice* symbolizes his passive subjectivity. Like the husband of the Indian surrogate, Joseph is a passive subject and hence also a passive object who can be manipulated and exploited by the higher power.

Ultimately, then, the positionality of Joseph within the Matthean infancy narrative is not markedly different from the positionality of Mary within it. The wedge that Matthean scholars, most of all feminist scholars, have tended to drive between active Joseph and passive Mary has revealed an important aspect of the narrative, but it has concealed another aspect of it that may be even more important. Joseph and Mary are both passive pawns moved around by a higher power in this narrative, and, as such, both are exploited figures. It is for this reason, that the consent of both Mary and Josephe must be read through an ambivalent light because their willingness to serve the divine is embedded in their powerlessness and their material greed for a hope.

As Michael Hardt and Antonio Negri observe of slavery: "Capital's relationship to colonial slavery...is...intimate and complex. First of all, even though capitalism's ideology is indeed antithetical to slavery, in practice capital nonetheless not only subsumed and reinforced existing slave productive systems throughout the world but also *created new systems of slavery* on an unprecedented scale."[13] Pushed to the fringes of society, and having nothing to lose, and dire choices before them, the mothers we have been considering seek to participate in a freedom or a liberation that is contingent upon their enslavement; a new form of slavery, if you will. In the struggle to reinsert themselves back into society, these mothers, exploited by patriarchy, in turn, exploit the systems of power for a chance to lead a better life. However, as we have seen with each of these narratives, when read through and alongside the Indian surrogate mother, this transaction proves costly for these women. The long-term scars of exploitation continue to haunt the bodies of all these mothers, ancient and modern.

Surrogacy, Race, and Language

Although it has been more than 60 years since India received its independence from the British Empire, the remnants of a colonial identity continues to influence the construction of the Indian subject in postcolonial India. As a result, discussions surrounding the reproductive tourism industry in India would remain incomplete and inaccurate without the insertion of race into the issue of surrogacy. Discourses on race, especially when dealing with the surrogacy industry, are often based on rudimentary attention to stringent dichotomies between white and brown. Deborah L. Spar evokes this racial codification when she notes:

> The price for surrogacy is essentially flat, and traits of the surrogate (aside from compliance) are increasingly irrelevant to the conception process. Economically there is no reason why poor Asian women should not carry children for rich western couples, why young impoverished Africans should not be in the business of bearing babies. Today, these women populate the lower ranks of the international labor market: they sew shirts in Cambodia; assemble sneakers in China; and eke out a living making handicrafts in Mexico. Purely on economic grounds, there

is no reason why these same women could not instead provide the labor of birth.[14]

In this narrative, the success of surrogacy in countries like India rests on a racial binary, in which women of color become breeding instruments for white couples and mothers hailing from the West. Such a dichotomizing, while accurate, is also troubling because it reduces the bodies of these colored mothers to objects that are exchanged in the global market for a suitable price. The experience of the Indian surrogate, subsumed under the blanket narrative of exploitation and victimization, forecloses the acknowledgement of her maternal agency and denies her human dignity. Constructing a rigid narrative, however well-intentioned, that seeks to label the Indian surrogate mother as powerless, colored, and poor, inadvertently cooperates with globalized forces that seek to control and exploit her body for economic gain. As Nelson M. Rodriguez writes: "[T]he fear of not being able to control other bodies, those bodies whose exploitation is so fundamental to capitalist economy, [is] at the heart of whiteness."[15]

The transient, dehumanized, instrumental role, attributed to the Indian surrogate mother, is apparent in the reaction of this white British couple Octavia and Dominic Orchard. Octavia, the commissioning mother, tells reporters Helen Roberts and Francis Hardy:

Our baby has no biological connection to the surrogate.... Her womb is just the receptacle in which it is being carried. Perhaps it sounds cold and rather clinical, but this is a business transaction. There is no altruism involved on the surrogate's part: she is being paid to have our baby. It's a contractual agreement. Her function is to sustain the foetus we have created. Her blood is pumping around its body and she is feeding it through her placenta, but she is just a vessel. The baby she gives birth to on our behalf will carry none of her genes and bear no physical resemblance to her. He or she will have white skin and, in all probability, red hair like my husband. Of course I want her to do her best to have a successful pregnancy, and I'll be very upset—quite devastated, in fact—if it doesn't go full-term. But we do not want to get emotionally involved with our surrogate's story. I'm not interested in her background. I don't want to be part of her life. She speaks a different language. She lives in a world culturally, economically and socially so remote from ours that the distance between us is unbridgeable."[16]

Here the commissioning Western mother uses a rigid narrative to not only describe the cultural gap that separates her from the Indian surrogate mother, whose services she is employing, but also to construct her as a *visibly different* who is at once the *other* and yet *knowable* in her position in the neocolonial economy even while remaining *unknowable* in her sociocultural location.[17] As Bhabha has repeatedly pointed out in his work, the problem with stringent binaries or rigid narratives that seem to fix colonized subjects into stereotypes that visibly identify them as the Other is that such discourses are subverted by the moments of ambivalence or hybridity that slip through the cracks of (neo)colonial power. But as Hardt and Negri remark: "Hybridity itself is a realized politics of difference, setting difference to play across boundaries. This is where the postcolonial and the postmodern most powerfully meet: in the united attack on the dialectics of modern sovereignty and the proposition of liberation as a politics of difference."[18] Therefore, while for most commissioning parents the bond between themselves and the Indian surrogate mother is rooted in a fundamental economic relationship of demand and supply, the maternal dependency performed in surrogacy slips through the dialectics of race, caste, class, and culture, and constructs a hybrid maternal subjectivity whose *love for the other* erupts from a place of ambivalence and ambiguity.

The Indian surrogate mother gazes at the white child who has gestated in and emerged from her own brown body. This is the first site/sight of visual difference. The white child—the master-signifier of racial difference—has violently separated itself from the brown maternal body of the Indian mother. But the infant also signifies to her the promise of success, opportunity, and the possibility for a brighter future for her own family. In her novel, Desai notes the reaction of the Indian surrogate mothers when they give birth to a child genetically different from them: "It was all the more difficult when a beautiful white baby emerged from between their dusky thighs, as though they had given birth to a god or a goddess. It was a miracle they would remember for the rest of their lives—and their excitement was palpable."[19]

Although Desai's novel is a fictionalized account that critiques the reproductive tourism industry in India, her comments and observations about the Indian surrogate mother's reaction to the white child begs for a deeper exploration. Commenting on the visibility of whiteness and its connection to success, Kalpana Seshadri-Crooks argues: "Whiteness, which founds the logic of racial difference, promises wholeness. (This is what it means to desire Whiteness: not a desire to become Caucasian!, but, to put it redundantly, it is an 'insatiable desire' on the part of all raced subjects to overcome difference.) Whiteness attempts to signify being, or that aspect of the subject which escapes language."[20] The excitement that the Indian surrogate mother feels for the white child, the master signifier emerging inbetween her dark brown thighs, is itself produced by a desire to become a part of the white success that symbolizes hope and prosperity. However, Whiteness as the master signifier within the Indian context, attaches itself not only to success, fame, and marital bliss, but also to the divine—or at least to western divinity. Desai narrates an exchange between Nazar Ali and Diwan Mehta, characters in her novel who work in the Customs and Excise Department at the international airport in Mumbai:

> "Boss, these are only embryos—not yet a human being." "I say they are human beings. *Saala, . . . banjo,*[21] do they think they can bring in little American babies and make us into a white-white *gora* nation?" "*Gora English* babies, boss, not American," Mehta started to say, though he quickly regretted it. Suddenly Ali went very still, and a glow of understanding dawned in his eyes. He snapped his fingers under a startled Mehta's chin. "Perhaps not even just *gora* babies—but Christian babies! That must be it. *Saala*, these *goras* are always thinking how to grab us by our balls." Mehta protectively grabbed his own groin, and was reassured that everything was as it should be.[22]

In a country like India where the majority of the religious population is Hindu or Muslim, stereotypes attached to Christians are often based in popular culture. As a result, Christians are often depicted as English-speaking, Western-attire-wearing individuals who pray to a milky white God (Jesus) who flaunts an effeminate physique and features. So it does not come as a surprise that Nazar Ali, the character in Desai's novel, draws a strong correlation between being white and being Christian.

In addition to whiteness producing a visual difference, and being closely associated with Christianity, western identity, and success, whiteness as a master signifier also produces within the colonial subject the drive to attain an ideal of perfection and success.[23] The need, then, to achieve this perfection embedded in the history of whiteness also produces within the colonial subject a feeling of unworthiness. Desai points to this feeling of unworthiness in her novel: "One woman was convinced that the baby would never drink milk from her dark breasts and was astonished when the child happily clung on with a hungry, rosebud-red mouth. She forgot the pain of the delivery and kept gazing at the child in wonderment—till the weary moment when he was taken."[24] The wonderment expressed by Desai's character underscores her own insecurity that she feels as a dark-skinned woman living in a culture that clearly prefers fair-skinned brides, mothers, and daughters. As Amrit Dhillon reports, "The Indian obsession with fair skin has always been a distasteful phenomenon. The fairness cream industry is gigantic, with men as well as women lathering these silly potions on their faces to make their skin a few shades lighter. Pregnant women in rural areas believe they will give birth to light-skinned babies if they consume lots of 'white' dairy products such as milk, cream, yoghurt, and butter. Dark models and actresses struggle for work as their skin isn't regarded as desirable."[25] Thus, the sight of her brown nipple in the pink mouth of the white child hungrily sucking the milk from her body creates a temporary moment of emancipation that allows the Indian surrogate mother to feel a sense of acceptance. The white child desiring the brown breast of its surrogate mother in turn produces in her the desire to accept her own brown body, as she views her own desirability through the eyes of the white child to whom she has become a womb-mother.

Language plays an important role in aiding the postcolonial subject to become like the Other. As Lopez argues: "[T]he cultural memory of the moment and circumstances of colonization and the memory of a precolonial cultural history are suppressed, for the sake of submission to the colonizer—or more to the point, success or even survival within the colonial context."[26] In a postcolonial context such as India, the colonizer's language, English, has not only become the language of success and economic prosperity, but has, in fact, been transformed into a language of survival. The ability to speak what was once defined as the "white man's language" has become a matter of pride and a sign of upward economic mobility for the postcolonial Indian subject. As most Indian surrogates tell reporters, the money they will earn from being surrogates will help them provide their children with an education (read: English education).The use of English within a globalized India, of course, becomes an important way in which the Indian subject can insert himself or herself into the capitalist system.

How might all of this be related to the Lukan infancy narrative? Language, coupled with the desire to be (like) the Other, are the bridging elements between the text of the infancy narrative and the context of the Indian surrogate mother. In the infancy narrative, the angelic emissary of the Hebrew God speaks Greek, one of the two official languages of the Roman Empire, to the Palestinian peasant woman. She responds in Greek rather than in Aramaic, and her womb is infiltrated by the child of the divine Other. In the contemporary postcolonial Indian context, the Indian doctor, speaking English, the language of the former colonizer, infiltrates the womb of the Indian woman and plants the fertilized egg of the racial Other—the white western couple—in her, an Otherness that itself carries associations of divinity, as we saw. Similar to the British child speaking an Indian language in the historical context of surrogacy under the British rule,[27] the Hebrew God speaking Greek through his angelic instrument and the Indian doctor speaking English become subjects that are almost but never quite part of the Empire. As such, the Hebrew God and the Indian doctor are also hybrid subjects. Like Mary and the Indian surrogate mother, they have also become sites of contradiction. They are unable to fully extract themselves from the workings of the Empire and its dichotomizing racial/ethnic discourse, and their implied stance vis-à-vis the colonizing Other is an ambivalent one. While their ability to speak the language of the Other assigns them a place within the Empire, their respective positionalities as "Greek-speaking Hebrew God" or "Anglicized Indian" undermines their possibility of "passing" within the Empire, of belonging fully to it, or of being fully owned by it—so that it is the condition, both of their limitation, and their freedom. However, the Hebrew God and the Indian doctor each use the real power they enjoy within these imperial constraints, to oppress one of their own. The God of the oppressed colonial subjects and the descendent of oppressed colonial subjects now become the new oppressors within the ongoing cycle of colonial violence. The familiarity of these new oppressors allows them to manipulate the bodies and minds of their women that much more easily. What space of agency or liberation is possible for these women in these straitened circumstances? To that problem we once again turn.

Conclusion

"Women as a group in our society are both produced and inhibited by contradictory discourses," writes Catherine Belsey.[28] Reading Luke's Mary alongside and through the body of the Indian surrogate reveals power structures fighting to dominate, economize, and control the bodies of women, so that these women can emerge as "gestation sites" that produce "powerful saviors" for the powerful Other. At the same time, the new form of colonization depicted in surrogacy constructs enslavement through the lens of freedom. This is true not only for the Indian surrogate, but also for the Lukan Mary, who also experiences simultaneous enslavement and liberation through pregnancy. Both these women are able to transcend their social boundaries and renounce patriarchal power by participating in an act that does not require a physical male.

They are each able to touch the powerful Other, uplift themselves from a lower status, dream of a better future for their children and their people, and take pride in their status as Divine Mothers who gift life to the Other. However, the same act that causes them to feel liberated and gives them agency, simultaneously constructs them as oppressed and exploitated—because of their ability to reproduce. Their socioeconomic inferiority is intimately bound up with their inability to protect themselves from being exploited. Therefore, their hybrid bodies—enslaved and free at one and the same time—embody the violent love of surrogate motherhood and problematize the categories of liberation and oppression that have been used to define these women and confine them to categories of heroine or victim. However, these women are set aside and forgotten once the telos of reproduction is achieved by the powerful Other. Their Divine Motherhood lasts only as long as their reproductive capacity lasts, after which they are pushed back into the shadows from which they had emerged as women daring to dream of a better life. So I would reiterate that the character of Mary cannot be interpreted as a binary subject or dichotomized as hero or victim. The fluidity between the categories of oppression and liberation constructs the love for the Other that is then performed through the violently opened bodies of both surrogates, the Lukan Mary and the Indian woman.

It is "violent love," then, and the willingness to accept an "oppressed liberation" that drives both Mary and the Indian surrogate to open up their bodies for exploitation and violence. It is the love for their children or their people, the love for the infertile Other or the divine Other, the desire for a better life, the desire to belong, the desire to please the Other, and the desire to become Divine that impels these women to engage in a motherhood that never fully enslaves or emancipates them completely. In the end, this "violent love" leaves the Indian surrogate and the Lukan Mary as "victimized heroes," standing up between the categories of oppression and liberation—open, violated, and incomplete, waiting for the material hope now embedded in their bodies to be realized before their eyes.

Conclusion

The character of Mary in the Matthean and Lukan infancy narratives has long been the object of much speculation by both male and female biblical and theological scholars. As women scholars in particular have repeatedly demonstrated, traditional interpretations of Mary's textual performance of motherhood have been androcentric and patriarchal. They have idolized her by constructing her maternal body as pure, virginal, and spiritual, thereby resulting in placing her on a pedestal that is higher than the rest of womankind. As Rosemary Radford Ruether long ago pointed out:

> The female roles have been both sublimated and taken over into male "spiritual" power. Male headship power controls the higher conception, gestation, birth, and suckling, and relates this to a transcendent sphere that negates the "carnal" maternity of women. It then becomes possible to symbolize the female life-giving role as the source of "death," while expropriating the symbols of conception, birth, and nurture to males. Male eschatology is built on negation of the mother.[1]

The effort to dismantle this mythological androcentric construct of Mary has led feminist biblical and theological scholars to make a conscious attempt to create a "Woman's Mary" whose image reflects the lived realities and struggles of ordinary women. In *The Illegitimacy of Jesus,* Jane Schaberg states: "There is power in the Catholic experience of the love of God in the figure of a woman, in the tradition that demonstrates that female language and symbols encompassing the myth and symbols of the Goddess have a transparency toward God. Some feminists have been able to claim for themselves the image of Mary in positive ways, seeing her as one who embodies and personifies the oppressed who are being liberated."[2] However, as I have already argued in this book, the feminist attempt to claim a "gynocentric Mary" often relies on the dichotomization of her textual character into such either/or categories as hero/victim or, liberated mother/oppressed woman. And although such interpretations are pertinent and successful in resisting the androcentric and patriarchal interpretations of Mary, the subjection of Mary's maternal body to binary interpretations, it seems to me, fails to accommodate the complexities present in the lives of real women, not least those living and surviving in globalized economies such as those of India and other regions of the global South. In other words, when we as women do not subject our life experiences or our decisions to binary interpretations, why do we as women readers/scholars impose such dichotomous categories on our textual characters? My book has attempted to address this problem by collapsing the stringent boundaries between hero/victim, love/violence, liberation/oppression, and exploiter/exploited. I have blurred the lines between these categories and constructed Mary's choice to become *a mother to an Other,* particularly in the Lukan infancy narrative, as an ambivalent choice. Specifically, I have argued that such ambivalence comes readily to light when the textual character of Mary is read through and alongside the contextual realities of surrogate mothers living in postcolonial India.

Schaberg observes that "[r]eading as a woman is based on the conviction that experience as a woman is a source of authority for response as a reader, on the assertion that there is continuity between women's experience of social and familial structures and their experience as readers. Women learn to bring their own experience, questions, and concerns to texts, to trust their responses even when they raise questions that challenge prevailing critical assumptions."[3] Although there have been attempts, however, to interpret the textual figure of Mary through the lived realities of women in the Two-Thirds World or women of color in the First World,[4] the majority of such work has been done by white feminist scholars in the First World. As Kwok Pui-lan has observed, "It is necessary to distinguish between a Western habit of 'essentializing' and 'homogenizing' human experience and the self (as most clearly seen in the colonial enterprise) and the womanist and Asian cultural constructions of the self, which are rooted in and understood through the communal experience."[5] Yet, while constructing the human experience as being rooted in community is indeed very important to Asian and womanist scholars, most often as I have shown womanist and Asian feminist readings of Mary also involuntarily fall into an essentialized interpretation that reduces her into one or other of the two categories, hero or victim. As Chandra Talpade Mohanty writes, "Western feminist scholarship cannot avoid the challenge of situating itself and examining its role in . . . a global economic and political framework. To do any less would be to ignore the complex interconnections between First and

Third World economies and their profound effect of this on the lives of women in all countries."[6] When the character of Mary in the infancy narratives is read through the complexities of globalization and capitalism, her maternal consent appears in an ambivalent light.

The five mothers found in Matthew's infancy narrative and the virginal conception of Mary found in Luke's infancy narrative, placed alongside the voices of Indian surrogate mothers as recorded in published interviews and other articles, deconstruct the binary categories of hero/victim, liberation/oppression, love/violence, and exploiter/exploited. I have argued that Mary's maternal performance, when obliquely illuminated by the complexities of globalization, imbues her consent to become a *mother to an Other* with ambivalence, as her character emerges as a victimized-hero whose desire to be liberated is contingent upon her oppression. In the contemporary Indian context, such a promise of liberation is sinister and exploitative, because it promotes "self-slavery" as subaltern female subjects willingly agree to enslave themselves to citizens of an economically superior country in the hope to be free. But can this freedom truly lead to a person's emancipation or is it just an illusion?

In colonial contexts, the power differential between the European Self and the Racial Other is often maintained through the use of binaries. Unlike the classic colonial context, where the exploitation of the Other was regularly justified through appeals to race and economics, the exploitation of the postcolonial subject is masked under the cloak of global capitalism and economic mobility. The Indian surrogate hired by an economically superior couple to carry a genetically unrelated child not only illustrates the subtle ways in which the maternal body of the Other is exploited in the global economy, but also demonstrates the way in which Indian surrogate mothers, recognizing their reproductive potentiality, perform a motherhood that both liberates as well as oppresses their bodies. Deborah L. Spar points out:

> Even if these women had chosen surrogacy over other alternatives; if they had decided on their own that carrying a stranger's child was preferable to sewing shirts or stitching sneakers, one could still argue that their choice was skewed by the inequities of the global trading system. Is it free choice, after all, if a mother of three becomes a surrogate in order to feed her children? When she signs the formal contract, is this woman exercising free will or providing evidence of the desperation caused by inequality? Most critics of surrogacy would insist strongly on the latter. Or as Oliver writes, "in the case of surrogacy, freedom is an illusion."[7]

The mothers in the infancy narratives read through binary lenses reflect only part of the reality of the lives of everyday women. Inserting ambivalence into the biblical text allows for a new definition of motherhood. As I demonstrate exegetically, the new maternal figure that emerges through such a reading deconstructs the traditional definitions of liberation, oppression, choice, and consent and pushes toward a new understanding in which categories of freedom and enslavement can no longer be read through dichotomous lenses. My reading is thoroughly contextual and postcolonial, and in the latter context, where outsourcing and globalization drives the economy, stringent dichotomies do not reflect the reality of everyday people.

As Hardt and Negri argue, "The original moment of violence is that of colonialism: the domination and exploitation of the colonized by the colonizer. The second movement, the response of the colonized to this original violence, can take all sorts of perverted forms in the colonial context."[8] One of the ways postcolonial subjects respond to the new global Empire is through ambivalence. For instance, the Indian surrogate mother "willingly," or ambivalently, agrees to her exploitation hoping against hope that doing so will finally lead to her freedom. Mary's consent to motherhood is regularly interpreted by feminist biblical and theological scholars as symbolic either of her liberation or her victimization. However, I have argued that Mary's decision to become a *mother to an Other* is not merely an altruistic act but is also driven by her selfish love for her people. According to Hardt and Negri, the poor has always been used for its "indispensible presence in the production of common wealth."[9] Mary's poverty highlighted by feminist biblical and theological scholars serves as the link that connects this Holy Mother to the lives of ordinary women, most of all in the global South. Radford Ruether, for example, writes of Mary that "as a woman, specifically a woman from among the poorer classes of a colonized people under the mighty empire of Rome, she represents the oppressed community that is to be lifted up and filled with good things in the messianic revolution."[10] While Ruether's point is well made and to some extent convincing, her interpretation fails to acknowledge the power not only of reproduction but of production that is displayed in the impoverished body of Mary, and is exploited by the patriarchal God and by even Mary herself. Mary produces not just a child, but in and through that child a new configuration of empire—the Empire of God. And this Empire of God will also be a world empire, or a series of them. Out of the body of this poor, powerless, peasant woman is emerging ultimately, then, the wealthiest and most powerful empires the world has ever seen.

In short, Mary's poverty and her reproductive capability becomes a spectacular site of production that is capitalized by a patriarchal God, and it is only through the capitalization of her reproductive capability that the maternal body of Mary is able to experience a brief moment of freedom. As a result, the ambivalent love that slips between the binaries of oppression and liberation is a *violent-love* that oppresses and at the same time liberates the bodies of Mary and the postcolonial Indian surrogate mother. This violent-love is that hyphenated space that drives these mothers to open their bodies up to exploitation and violence. It is the love for their children and their nation, the love for the infertile couple, and God, it is the desire to feel accepted and be loved, it is the desire for a better life, and for justice, that causes these women-mothers to perform an ambivalent motherhood that promises them a conditional freedom that is dependent upon their enslavement to the Other. This *violent-love* or *oppressive-liberation* both imprisons and frees, the maternal bodies of these women, leaving them in a state of perpetual ambivalence, hoping for liberation, but achieving a liberation that is only partial and incomplete, and forever haunted by their enslavement.

Notes

Introduction

1. Adriana Janovich, "Surrogacy a Booming Business in India," *Yakhima Herald-Republic,* August 4, 2012, at http://www.yakima-herald.com/ . . . /surrogacy-a-booming-business-in-india (accessed August 7, 2012).
2. Sadie Stein, "Is Reproductive Tourism Exploiting India's Poor?" *Jezebel,* August 23, 2010, at http://jezebel.com/5619616/is-reproductive-tourism-exploiting-indias-poor (accessed December 11, 2012).
3. Rosemary Radford Ruether, *Sexism and God-Talk: Towards a Feminist Theology* (Boston, MA: Beacon Press, 1983), 152.
4. Michael Hardt and Antonio Negri, *Empire* (Cambridge, MA: Harvard University Press, 2000), 136.
5. Gayatri Chakravorty Spivak, *In Other Worlds: Essays in Cultural Politics* (New York and London: Routledge, 1998), 343.
6. Hardt and Negri, *Empire*, 128.
7. Raywat Deonandan, "The Ethics of Surrogacy," *India Currents*, February 3, 2012, at http://www.indiacurrents.com/articles/2012/02/03/ethics-surrogacy (accessed on October 26, 2012).
8. Chandra Talpade Mohanty, "Under Western Eyes: Feminist Scholarship and Colonial Discourses," *Feminist Review* Vol. 30 (Autumn 1988): 67.
9. Adrienne Arieff, "Having Twins with a Surrogate—in India," *The New York Times*, March 16, 2012, at http://parenting.blogs.nytimes.com/ . . . /having-twins-with-a-surrogate-in-india/ (accessed October 25, 2012).
10. Adriana Janowhich, "Surrogacy a Booming Business in India," *Yakhima Herald-Republic,* August 4, 2012, at http://www.yakima-herald.com/ . . . /surrogacy-a-booming-business-in-india (accessed October 25, 2012).
11. Sagarika Ghosh, "Is Surrogacy Leading to Exploitation of Poor Women?" *CNN-IBN*, June 19, 2012, at (achttp://www. ibnlive.in.com/news/is-surrogacy-leading-to-exploitation-of-poor-women/266801–3.html (accessed October 26, 2012).
12. Sangeeta Dutta, "Relinquishing the Halo: Portrayal of Mother in Indian Writing in English," *Economic and Political Weekly* Vol. 25, Nos. 42/43 (October 1990): 84.

13. Ketu H. Kartrak, *Politics of the Female Body: Postcolonial Women Writers of the Third World* (New Brunswick: Rutgers University Press, 2006), 213.
14. Dutta, "Relinquishing the Halo," 84.
15. Karl Rahner, *Mary Mother of the Lord: Theological Meditations* (New York: Herder and Herder, 1963), 61.
16. Kari Borresen, "Mary in Catholic Theology," in *Mary in the Churches*, ed. Hans Küng and Jürgen Moltmann (*Concilium* 168; New York: Seabury, 1983): 54–55.
17. See Chapter 2, "Mary among Scholars."
18. Hardt and Negri, *Empire,* 145, quoting Homi K. Bhabha, *The Location of Culture* (New York and London: Routledge, 1994), 18.
19. See, for example, Janice Capel Anderson, "Mary's Difference: Gender and Patriarchy in the Birth Narratives," *The Journal of Religion* Vol. 67, No. 2 (1987): 183–202; Elaine Wainwright, "The Gospel of Matthew," *Searching the Scriptures,* Volume 2: *A Feminist Commentary,* ed. Elisabeth Schüssler Fiorenza (New York: Crossroad, 1994), 635–677; Mary Foskett, *A Virgin Conceived: Mary and Classical Representations of Virginity* (Bloomington: Indiana University Press, 2002); Turid Karlsen Seim, "The Virgin Mother: Mary and Ascetic Discipleship in Luke," in *A Feminist Companion to Luke,* ed. Amy-Jill Levine (London and New York: Sheffield Academic Press, 2002), 89–105.
20. See, for example, Itulmeleng J. Mosala, *Biblical Hermeneutics and Black Theology in South Africa* (Grand Rapids, MI: W. B. Eerdmans, 1989); Mary Daly, *Gyn/ecology: The Metaethics of Radical Feminism* (Boston, MA: Beacon Press, 1990); Jane Schaberg, *The Illegitimacy of Jesus: A Feminist Theological Interpretation of the Infancy Narratives.* 20th anniversary ed. (Sheffield: Sheffield Academic Press, 2006); John Dominic Crossan, "Virgin Mother or Bastard Child," in *A Feminist Companion to Mariology,* ed. Amy Jill Levine and Maria Mayo Robbins (London and New York: T&T Clark International, 2005), 37–55.
21. Scholars whom I draw on explicitly or who have informed my analysis include Chandra Talpade Mohanty, *Feminism without Borders: Decolonizing Theory, Practicing Solidarity* (Durham, NC: Duke University Press, 2003); Gayatri Chakravorty Spivak, *A Critique of Postcolonial Reason* (Cambridge, MA: Harvard University Press, 1999); Homi Bhabha, *The Location of Culture*; Arjun Appadurai, "Disjuncture and Difference in the Global Cultural Economy," in *The Globalization Reader,* ed. Frank J. Lechner and John Boli (Malden, MA: Blackwell, 2004), 100–108; Edward W. Said, *Orientalism* (New York: Pantheon, 1978); Hardt and Negri, *Empire*; Kalpana Seshadri Crooks, *Desiring Whiteness: A Lacanian Analysis of Race* (New York: Routledge, 2000); Alfred J. Lopez, *Postcolonial Whiteness* (Albany, NY: State University of New York Press, 2005); Anne McClintock, *Imperial Leather: Race, Gender and Sexuality in the Colonial Contest* (New York: Routledge, 1995); Frantz Fanon, *Black Skin, White Masks,* trans. Richard Philcox (New York: Grove/Atlantic, 2008); Richard Dyer, *White: Essays on Race and Culture* (New York:

Routledge, 1997); Sudhir Kakar, *Intimate Relations: Exploring Indian Sexuality* (Chicago: University of Chicago Press, 1990); Rajeshwari Sunder Rajan, *Real and Imagined Women: Gender, Culture and Postcolonialism* (New York: Routledge, 1993); Judith Butler, *Gender Trouble: Feminism and the Subversion of Identity* (New York: Routledge, 1990); Farhad Dalal, *Race, Color and the Process of Racialization: New Perspectives from Group Analysis, Psychoanalysis and Sociology* (New York: Brunner-Routledge, 2002).

22. Homi K. Bhabha, *The Location of Culture*, 2. Homi Bhabha writes:
    The move away from the singularities of "class" or "gender" as primary conceptual and organizational categories, has resulted in an awareness of the subject positions—of race, gender, generation, institutional location, geopolitical locale, sexual orientation—that inhabit any claim to identity in the modern world. What is theoretically innovative, and politically crucial, is the need to think beyond narratives of originary and initial subjectivities and to focus on those moments or processes that are produced in the articulation of cultural differences. These "in-between" spaces provides the terrain for elaborating strategies of self-hood—singular or communal—that initiate new signs of identity, and innovative sites of collaboration, and contestation, in the act of defining the idea of society itself.

1   Breast, Womb, Empire

1. The words *amah* and *ayah/dhaye* come from the Hindi language, where the former refers to a wet nurse and the latter refers to a nanny or a maternal caregiver of the children. However, as we shall see, many scholars use these terms interchangeably to describe any or all of the duties of the colonial surrogate mothers.

2. As Nupur Chaudhuri notes, "The term 'memsahib' was used originally to show respect for a European married woman..." ("Memsahibs and Motherhood in Nineteenth-Century Colonial India," *Victorian Studies,* Vol. 31, No. 4 [Summer, 1998]: 517). The term *memsahib* literally meaning "Madam Boss" is the feminine derivative of the masculine word *Sahib,* a Hindi word used by native Indians to refer to European men in colonial times. In the contemporary context these titles are used to address men or women in positions of power.

3. Ibid., 530.

4. Indrani Sen, "Colonial Domesticities, Contentious Interactions: Ayahs, Wet-Nurses and Memsahibs in Colonial India," *Indian Journal of Gender Studies,* Vol. 16 (2009): 299.

5. Ann Stoler, "Making Empire Respectable: The Politics of Race and Sexual Morality in 20th Century Colonial Cultures," *American Ethnologist*, Vol. 16, No. 4 (November, 1989): 634.

6. Chaudhuri, "Memsahibs and Motherhood," 517.

7. Ibid., 518.
8. Stoler, "Making Empire Respectable," 640.
9. Laura Mulvey, "Visual Pleasure and Narrative Cinema," in *Feminist Theory: A Reader*, ed. Wendy K. Kolmar and Frances Bartkowski, 2nd ed., (New York: McGraw-Hill, 2005), 299.
10. Ibid., 641.
11. Ibid., 640.
12. Marangoly George, "Homes in the Empire, Empire in the Homes," *Cultural Critique*, Vol. 26 (Winter, 1993–1994): 108.
13. Mulvey, "Visual Pleasure and Narrative Cinema," 299.
14. A Hindi term used to refer to the British Memsahib; it literally means "the white woman/lady."
15. Further on the creation of Anglicized Indians, see Homi K. Bhabha, *The Location of Culture* (New York and London: Routledge, 1994), 121–131 passim.
16. George, "Homes in the Empire, Empire in the Homes," 108–109.
17. Maud Diver, *The Englishwoman in India* (London: Blackwood, 1909), 79.
18. Ibid., 99.
19. Bhabha, *The Location of Culture*.
20. Kate Platt, *The Home and Health in India and the Tropical Colonies* (London: Bailliere, Tindall and Cox, 1923), 21.
21. Sen, "Colonial Domesticities, Contentious Interactions," 301. Alison Blunt in her article titled, "Imperial Geographies of Home: British Domesticity in India, 1886–1925" argues, "racial distancing of the compound reproduced on a household scale the racial distancing of British cantonments and civil lines from the 'native' city." In *Transactions of the Institute of British Geographers*, New Series, 24(4): 428.
22. Antoinette Burton, *Burden of History: British Feminists, Indian Women and Imperial Culture, 1865–1915* (Chapel Hill, and London: University of North Carolina Press, 1994), 35.
23. Ibid., 38.
24. Bhabha, *The Location of Culture*, 122.
25. Anne Flora Steel and Grace Gardiner, *The Complete Indian Housekeeper and Cook: Giving the Duties of Mistress and Servants, the General Management of the House, and Practical Recipes for Cooking in All Its Branches* (London: Heinemann, 1904), 3–4.
26. George, "Homes in the Empire, Empire in the Homes," 111.
27. Diver, *The Englishwoman in India*, 71.
28. Steel and Gardiner, *The Complete Indian Housekeeper and Cook*, 3–4.
29. Ibid., 19.
30. Ibid., 4.
31. Ibid., 19.
32. Ibid., 3.
33. Ibid., 3–4.

34. George, "Homes in the Empire, Empire in the Homes," 109. The term "buk-sheesh" is a Hindi word meaning gift.
35. Diver, *The Englishwoman in India*, 71.
36. Gayatri Chakravorty Spivak, "Breast-giver: For Author, Reader, Teacher, Subaltern, Historian..." in *Breast Stories*, by Mahasweta Devi (Calcutta: Seagull Books, 2002), 78. Gayatri Chakravorty Spivak writes: "Those who read or write literature can claim as little of subaltern status as those who read or write history. The difference is that the subaltern as object is supposed to be imagined in one case and real in another. I am suggesting that it is a bit of both in both cases. The writer acknowledges this by claiming to research (my fiction is also historical). The historian might acknowledge this by looking at the mechanics of representation (my history is fictive)."
37. The term "surrogate mother (hood)" in the contemporary context refers to pregnancy and giving birth. In this context I am using this term by extension to refer to what I see as an analogous phenomenon in colonial India—substitute motherhood of a different but related kind—and thereby establish illuminating connections between the colonial and postcolonial contexts.
38. Spivak, "Breast-giver: For Author, Reader, Teacher, Subaltern, Historian..." 77.
39. Sen, "Memsahibs and Health in Colonial Writings, c. 1840–1930," 254. Sen writes, "Medical handbooks, authored by colonial physicians, sought to give guidance on health matters to Europeans living in remote areas, seeking to bring them within the purview of western medical treatment and control." Indrani Sen, "Memsahibs and Health in Colonial Writings, c. 1840–1930." *South Asian Research* 30, No. 3 (2010),
40. Sen, "Colonial Domesticities, Contentious Interactions," 266.
41. Gayatri Chakravorty Spivak, "A Literary Representation of the Subaltern: A Woman's Text from the Third World," in *In Other World: Essays in Cultural Politics* (New York: Rouledge, 1998), 339. Also see: David Hardiman, "Subaltern Studies' at Crossroads," *Economic and Political Weekly* (February 15, 1986).
42. Ibid., 332.
43. Ann L. Stoler, "Carnal Knowledge and Imperial Power: Gender, Race and Morality in Colonial Asia," in *The Gender/Sexuality Reader: Culture, History, Political Economy*, ed. Roger N. Lancaster and Michaela Di Leornardo (New York: Routledge, 1997), 28.
44. Chaudhuri, "Memsahibs and Motherhood," 527–528.
45. Sen notes that Tilt, a gynecologist who had never been to India but had based his observations on treating women who had returned from India, "identified the hot climate as the primary enemy of the empire" Indrani Sen, "Memsahibs and Health in Colonial Writings, c. 1840–1930." *South Asian Research* 30, No. 3 (2010), 260.
46. A Lady Resident, *The Englishwoman in India: Containing Information for the Use of Ladies Proceeding to, or Residing in, the East Indies, on the Subjects of their*

Outfit, Furniture, Housekeeping, the Rearing of Children, Duties and Wages of Servants, Management of the Stables, and Arrangements for Travelling to which are added Receipts for Indian cookery (London: Smith, Elder 1864), 95.

47. Edward W. Said, *Orientalism* (New York: Vintage Books, 1978), 7, his emphasis.

48. Sen describes the colonial anxiety surrounding the topic of infant mortality; she writes, "Fears about the greater vulnerability of European children (and women) in the tropics were further amplified by the mortality figures which always remained high..." (Sen, "Memsahibs and Health in Colonial Writings")257.

49. *The Pioneer,* October 22, 1880: 5

50. Chaudhuri, "Memsahibs and Motherhood," 529. In the section of her book entitled *Colonial Cultivations of the Bourgeois Self,* Ann Stoler writes:

Foucault makes no room for the fact that these bourgeois bodies were produced in practices never contingent on the will to self affirmation alone. This "body to be cared for, protected, cultivated, and preserved from the many dangers and contacts" required other bodies that would perform those nurturing services and provide the leisure for such self absorbed administering and self-bolstering acts. (153).

51. Brahma is the Hindu God of creation and completes the Trinity along with Vishnu and Shiva within Hinduism.

52. Mahasweta Devi, *Breast Stories*, trans. with introductory essays by Gayatri Chakravorty Spivak (Calcutta: Seagull Books, 2002), 52.

53. Sen, "Memsahibs and Health in Colonial Medical Writings," 267.

54. Ibid., 267, quoting an anonymous 1848 source.

55. A Lady Resident notes, "care should be taken that her own child is taken away by her friends, or she is apt to nurse it by stealth." A Lady Resident, *The Englishwoman in India,* 97.

56. Sen, 323. Also cf. Joseph Ewart, *Goodeve's Hint For the General Management of Children in India,* 6th ed. (Calcutta: Thacker, Spink 1872), 9.

57. Ibid., 9.

58. Allan Cuthbert Sprawson, ed., *Moore's Manual of Family Medicine and Hygiene for India,* 8th ed. Rewritten by the editor with a Foreword by Charles Pardey Lukis (London: J. and A. Churchill, 1916), 493. As notes in her article, "Colonial Domesticities, Contentious Interactions" William Moore was a Bombay based surgeon, 323.

59. R. S. Mair, "Supplement on the Management of Children in India," in *Medical Guide for Anglo-Indians* (New Delhi: Asian Educational Services, 2004, first published in 1878), 328–329. Sen labels this Madras-based physician R. S. Mair as, "one of the harshest in his moral estimate of the *amah* and in fact wrote a virtual advisory against the evils attached to her" 323 in "Colonial Domesticities, Contentious Interactions."

60. Sen, "Colonial Domesticities, Contentious Interactions," 319.

61. Julia Maitland, *Letters from Madras, During the Years 1836–38, by a Lady* (London: John Murray, 1846), 52. Cf. Sen, "Colonial Domesticities, Contentious Interactions," 317.

62. Ibid., 317.

63. Emma Roberts, *Scenes and Characteristics of Hindoostan, with Sketches of Anglo Indian Society.* 2 Vol. (London: W.H. Allen, 1835), 121.

64. Ibid., 121.

65. Sen, "Colonial Domesticities, Contentious Interactions," 318.

66. Joyce Grossman, "Ayahs, Dhayes, and Bearers: Mary Sherwood's Indian Experience and "Constructions of Subordinated Others" *South Atlantic Review* Vol. 66, no. 2 (2001): 24, quoting Sara Suleri, *The Rhetoric of English India* (Chicago: University of Chicago Press, 1992), 80.

67. "Breast-Giver" depicts the tale of a Brahmin woman Jashoda working as a wet nurse for another Hindu family. The milk produced by Jashoda inserted into the market and exchanged for a price allows Jashoda transgress disctinctions of gender, economy, and caste.

68. Devi, *Breast Stories*, 40.

69. Spivak, "Breast-giver: For Author, Reader, Teacher, Subaltern, Historian..." 93.

70. Sen, "Colonial Domesticities, Contentious Interactions," 318.

71. Ibid., 21.

72. Ibid., 33.

73. Stoler, *Carnal Knowledge and Imperial Power*, 156.

74. Chaudhuri, "Memsahibs and Motherhood," 530.

75. Catherine Belsey, "Constructing the Subject: Deconstructing the Text." in *Contemporary Literary Criticism*, ed. Robert Con Davis and Ronal Schleifer, 4th ed. (New York: Addison Wesley Longman Inc, 1998), 379.

76. Chaudhuri, "Memsahibs and Motherhood," 530; citing Major S. Leigh and Alexander S. Kenny, *Tropical Trials: A Hand-book for Women in the Tropics*, which served as a survival guide for British women who found themselves in India and other such places.

77. Stoler, *Carnal Knowledge,* 151–152.

78. Chaudhuri, "Memsahibs and Motherhood," 531.

79. Gayatri Chakrovorty Spivak, *In Other Worlds: Essays in Cultural Politics* (New York and London: Routledge, 1998), 342. Spivak continues:

    The political economy or the sexual division of labor changes considerably by the sale of Jashoda's labor-power, which is specific to the female of the species. One may even call this a moment of transition from one mode of social reproduction to another. Or perhaps one could call it the moment of the emergence of value and its immediate extraction and appropriation. These changes take place within extended domestic economy. One might therefore call it a transition from the domestic to the "domestic."

80. Ibid., 342.

2   Desired Mothers, Discounted Mothers: The Postcolonial Surrogate Mother Emerges

1. Michael Hardt and Antonio Negri, *Empire* (Cambridge, MA: Harvard University Press, 2000), 136.
2. Ketu H. Kartrak, *Politics of the Female Body: Postcolonial Women Writers of the Third World* (New Jersey: Rutgers University Press, 2006), 213.
3. Angela Y. Davis, "Outcaste Mothers and Surrogates: Racism and Reproduction Politics in the Nineties," in *Feminist Theory: A Reader*, ed. Wendy K. Kolmar and Frances Bartkowski (Boston, MA: McGraw Hill, 2005), 509.
4. Ibid., 512.
5. Hardt and Negri, *Empire*, 154.
6. Davis, "Outcast Mothers and Surrogates," 512.
7. Usha Rengachary Smerdon, "Crossing Bodies, Crossing Borders: International Surrogacy between the United States and India," *Cumberland Law Review*, Vol. 39, No. 1 (2008): 16. Also see, Veronica Ions, *Indian Mythology* (New York: P. Bendrick Books, 1983), 58–59.
8. Heléna Ragoné, "Of Likeness and Difference: How Race Is Being Transferred by Gestational Surrogacy," in *Ideologies and Technologies of Motherhood: Race, Class, Sexuality, Nationalism,* ed. Heléna Ragoné and France Winddance Twine (New York and London: Routledge, 2000), 62.
9. Gayatri Chakravorty Spivak. *A Critique of Postcolonial Reason: Toward A History of the Vanishing Present* (Cambridge, MA: Harvard University Press, 1999), 253. Also see: Louis Althusser, *Lenin and Philosophy and Other Essays,* trans. Ben Brewster (New York: Monthly Review Press, 1971), 132–133.
10. Davis, "Outcast Mothers and Surrogates,"512.
11. Ibid., 512.
12. Karl Marx, *Capital: A Critique of Political Economy*, trans. Ben Fowkes (Madison Park, Seattle: Pacific Publishing Studio, 2010), 29.
13. Amrita Pande, "Commercial Surrogacy in India: Manufacturing a Perfect Mother-Worker," *Signs*, Vol. 35, No. 4 (Summer 2010): 969. Tina, a surrogate mother, describing the timetable at a surrogate hostel in Anand, Gujarat, India.
14. Nupur Chaudhuri writes: "According to Emma Roberts (1794–1840), editor of Oriental Observer, these wet nurses are most expensive and troublesome appendages to a family." "Memsahibs and Motherhood in Nineteenth-Century Colonial India," *Victorian Studies,* Vol. 31, No. 4 (Summer, 1988): 529.
15. Amartya Sen, *Development as Freedom* (New York: Anchor Press, 1999), 203.
16. Gayatri Chakravorty Spivak, "Diasporas Old and New: Women in Transnational World" in *Class Issues: Pedagogy, Cultural Studies and the Public Sphere*, ed. Amitava Kumar (New York and London: New York University Press, 1997), 92.
17. I borrow this terms from Amrita Pande's work "Commercial Surrogacy in India."

18. Barbara Ehrenreich and Arlie Russell Hoschschild, eds. *Global Woman: Nannies, Maids, and Sex Workers in the New Economy* (New York: Metropolitan, 2003), 4.

19. Ibid., 4.

20. Pande, "Commercial Surrogacy in India," 969–970.

21. Kate Platt, *The Home and Health in India and the Tropical Colonies* (London: Bailliere, Tindall and Cox, 1923), 138.

22. Lesley A. Sharp, "The Commodification of the Body and ItsParts," *Annual Review of Anthropology*. Vol. 29 (2000): 292. Sharp has observed: "The study of the commodified body is hardly a new proposition, given that the body in its entirety or fragmented form has long been an object of economic, social, and symbolic use in a host of societies."

23. Ibid., 293.

24. Ibid., 294.

25. Hardt and Negri, *Empire*, 43. They write, "Although Empire may have played a role in putting an end to colonialism and imperialism, it nonetheless constructs its own relationships of power based on exploitation that are in many respects more brutal than those it destroyed."

26. Deborah L. Spar, "For Love and Money: The Political Economy of Commercial Surrogacy," *Review of International Political Economy*, Vol. 12, No. 2 (May 2005): 293.

27. Ibid., 293. Also cf. Gillian Hewitson, "The Market for Surrogate Mother Contracts," *The Economic Record*. Vol. 73, No, 222 (September 1997), 212–224.

28. Marx, *Capital: A Critique of Political Economy*, 77. Marx defines labor-power as follows: "labour-power can appear upon the market as a commodity, only if, and so far as, its possessor, the individual whose labour-power it is, offers it or sale, or sells it, as a commodity. In order that he may be able to do this, he must have it at his disposal, must be the untrammelled owner of his capacity for labour, i.e., of his person."

29. Gayatri Chakrovorty Spivak, *In Other Worlds: Essays in Cultural Politics* (New York and London: Routledge, 1998), 347. Spivak is referring to Jashoda, the protagonist in Mahasweta Devi's short story "Breast Giver." Jashoda, a wet nurse is hired to feed the children of her Master Haldarbabu. Additionally, the name "Jashoda" also pronounced "Yashoda" is the name of Lord Krishna's foster mother.

30. Rengachary Smerdon, "Crossing Bodies, Crossing Boundaries," 47. Rengachary Smerdon remarks: "Almost all [fertility clinics in India] require a surrogate to have previously given birth because they question the legitimacy of informed consent unless the surrogate has had the experience of childbirth and delivery and perhaps to provide some assurance that the surrogate can achieve pregnancy." Also see: Anil B. Pinto and Nona Morgan Swank, "Gestational Surrogacy, "in *The Art and Science of Assisted Reproductive Techniques*, ed.

Gautam N. Allahbadia and Rita Basuray Das, (New Delhi: CRC Press, 2004), footnote 206.

31. Marx, *Capital: A Critique of Political Economy, 77.* Marks argues that, "The second essential condition to the owner of money finding labour-power in the market as a commodity is this—that the labourer instead of being in a position to sell commodities in which his labour is incorporated, must be obliged to offer for sale as a commodity that very labour-power, which exisits only in his living self."

32. Trinh T. Minh ha, *Woman, Native, Other: Writing, Postcoloniality and Feminism* (Indianapolis: Indiana University Press, 1989), 37.

33. Pande, "Commercial Surrogacy in India," 978.

34. Elizabeth S. Anderson, "Is Women's Labor a Commodity?" *Philosophy & Public Affairs* Vol. 19, No. 1 (Winter 1990), 82. She writes, "Her [the surrogate mother's] labor is alienated, because she must divert it from the end which the social practices of pregnancy rightly promote—an emotional bond with her child. The surrogate contract thus replaces a norm of parenthood, that during pregnancy one create a loving attachment to one's child, with a norm of commercial production, that the producer shall not form any special emotional ties to her product."

35. Abagail Haworth, "Surrogate Mothers: Wombs for Rent." 3, at www.marie-claire.com/world . . . /news/ . . . /surrogate-mothers-india (accessed on October 15, 2009).

36. Kartrak, *Politics of the Female Body,* 215.

37. Ibid., 215.

38. Lisa Baraitser, *Maternal Encounters: The Ethics of Interruption* (New York and London: Routledge 2009), 4. Lisa Baraitser writes: "The mother" after all, is the impossible subject, par excellence. Caught in an ever widening gap between her idealization and denigration in the contemporary culture, and her indeterminate position as part object, part subject within the Western philosophical tradition, the mother has always been left hopelessly uncertain, with all the death-like and dreadful connotations that the abject possesses. In some senses she is everywhere, our culture saturated with her image in its varied guises, and yet theoretically she remains a shadowy figure who seems to disappear from the many discourses that explicitly try to account for her.

39. Rengachary Smerdon, "Crossing Bodies, Crossing Borders," 53.

40. Mary Warnock, *A Question of Life* (Oxford: Blackwell, 1985), 45.

41. Kritivas Mukherjee, *Rent-a-womb in India Fuels Surrogate Motherhood Debate,* 1 at http://www.geneticsandsociety.org/article.php?id=3386 (accessed on October 15, 2009).

42. Pande, "Commercial Surrogacy in India," 978.

43. Ibid., 987. According to Hindu mythology, Krishna was born as the eighth child of Devaki to the cruel demon king Kamsa. A sage, Narada, predicts that Kamsa will be killed by his nephew, so Kamsa kills his sister's first six children. The eighth child, Krishna, is secretly exchanged for a cowherd's daughter.

Krishna is brought up by the cowherd's wife Yasoda, and most stories surrounding Lord Krishna in his infant years are about the loving bond shared between him and his surrogate mother.

44. Rengachary Smerdon, "Crossing Bodies, Crossing Boundaries," 24. Also see, Richard F. Storrow, "The Handmaid's Tale of Fertility Tourism: Passports and Third Parties in the Religious Regulation of Assisted Conception," Tex. Wesleyan L. Rev. Vol. 12, No. 189 (2005): 204.
45. Haworth, "Surrogate Mothers," 5.
46. Amelia Gentleman, "India Nurtures Business of Surrogate Motherhood," 1 >at http://www.nytimes.com/2008/03/10/world/asia/10surrogate.html (accessed on October 20, 2009). Amelia Gentleman notes: "Under the guidelines issued by the Indian Council of Medical Research, surrogate mothers sign away their rights to any children. A surrogate's name is not even on the birth certificate."
47. Rengachary Smerdon, "Crossing Bodies, Crossing Boundaries," 53. Also cf. Jyotsna Agnihotri Gupta, "Towards Transnational Feminisms: Some Reflection and Concerns in Relation to the Globalization of Reproductive Technologies," Eur. J. Women's Studies Vol. 13, No. 23 (2006): 49. Jyotsna Agnihotri remarks: [s]hould we view these cases as examples of women's agency, self-determination, and solidarity of "global sisterhood" between the fertile/infertile, first world/third world, rich/poor and support them? If only things were that simple!" Such "win-win" type declarations presume that the commissioner and commissioned are on equal footing. But it is debatable whether women are choosing freely to become surrogates, or that their will is socially and economically constructed
48. George Palattiyil, Eric Blyth, Dina Sidhva and Geeta Balakrishnan, "Globalization and Cross-border Reproductive Services: Ethical Implications of Surrogacy in India for Social Work," *International Social Work*, Vol. 53 No. 5 (September 2010): 690. They write: "The market for cross-border reproductive services is becoming increasingly competitive, and surrogacy in India is estimated to be US$445 million-a-year business. Indian surrogates receive US$3000–6000 (compared with an annual income per head around $500), thus making surrogacy a potentially financially attractive option to poor Indian women."
49. Pande, "Commercial Surrogacy in India," 988.
50. Kalpana Seshadri Crooks, *Desiring Whiteness: A Lacanian Analysis of Race* (London and New York, Routledge: 2000), 3–4.
51. Alfred J. Lopez, "Introduction: Whiteness after Empire," in *Postcolonial Whiteness: A Critical Reader on Race and Empire*, ed. Alfred J. Lopez (Albany: State University of New York Press, 2005), 1.
52. Rengachary Smerdon, "Crossing Bodies, Crossing Borders," 52. As Smerdon points out: "Excising the physical act of pregnancy and childbearing from the notion of motherhood necessarily leads to commodification. And for whites, women of color may be easier to commodify. It may be easier to view a woman

of color's womb as merely a component or a toll when that woman's race does not match the child she is bearing."

53. R. S. Mair, "Supplement on the Management of Children in India," in *Medical Guide for Anglo-Indians* (New Delhi: Asian Educational Services, 2004 (first published 1878)), 341. R. S. Mair, the Madras-based physician noted: "The child becomes strongly attached to these servants . . . indeed it is no uncommon thing to find children in India, preferring the society of their native servants to that of their parents. Here lies a danger which must be guarded against by every possible means."

54. Rengachary Smerdon, "Crossing Bodies, Crossing Borders," 30. As Smerdon observes: "Although commercial surrogacy has cropped up in other countries, a contributing factor to the rise in popularity of surrogacy in India is the availability of English-speaking doctors, who can communicate with English-speaking patients and promote surrogacy in the press.."

55. Lopez, *Postcolonial Whiteness*, 4.

56. Maigner Mark, "A Bundle of Joy with Baggage: Indian Surrogacy is Successful but New Parents feel Duped," 1 at http://articles.latimes.com/2011/apr/18/world/la-fg-india-surrogacy-20110418 (accessed on October 26, 2011).

57. Haworth, "Surrogate Mothers," 3.

58. Ragoné, "Of Likeness and Difference," 58–59: Also cf. Rickie Solinger, *Wake Up Little Susie: Single Pregnancy and Race before Roe vs. Wade* (New York and London: Routledge, 1992), 9. It is important to note here how children born to single mothers during the post-World War II years became racialized. Specifically, children born to Euro American single mothers were viewed as "highly valuable," where as a children of color were not, a perspective that regrettably has not significantly changed. The complexity of race in the context of adoption is suggested in the position statement of the National Association of Black Social Workers (NABSW), in which it is recommended that children of color not be placed with Euro-American couples or individuals

59. Rengachary Smerdon, "Crossing Bodies, Crossing Borders," 52–53.

60. Ragoné, "Of Likeness and Difference," 67.

61. Homi K. Bhabha, *The Location of Culture* (New York and London: Routledge, 1994), 107. Homi Bhabha in his book *Location of Culture* observes: "The stereotype, then as the primary point of subjectification in colonial discourse, for both colonizer and colonized, is the scene of a similar fantasy and defense-the desire for an originality which is again threatened by the differences of race, colour and culture."

62. Johar Roshni, "When We Will Be Fair to Women's Skin?"1, at http://www.tribuneindia.com/2003/20031207/herworld.htm (accessed on October 26, 2011)

63. Ibid.

64. Leistikow Nicole, "Skin Lightening Is Coming under Increasing Criticism in India," 1, at http://www.womensenews.org/article.cfm/dyn/aid/1308/context/archive (accessed on October 27, 2011). Nicole Leistikow observes that: "the fairness industry [in India] accounts for 60 percent of skincare sales, bringing $140 million a year."

65. Seshadri Crooks, *Desiring Whiteness: A Lacanian Analysis of Race, 78*
66. Leistikow, "Skin Lightening Is Coming under Increasing Criticism in India,"
    1. Leistikow notes that the advertisements shown as a part of the skin lighten-
    ing campaign exclusively ties whiteness/fairness to economic prospects. She
    writes: "The [Fairness product] ad targeted by the women's association shows
    a woman, whose father had lamented not having a son support the family,
    landing a well-paying job as an airline attendant after using the product.."
67. Shome Raka, "Whiteness and the Politics of Location: Postcolonial
    Reflections," in *Whiteness: The Communication of Social Identity*, ed. Thomas
    K. Nakayama and Judith N. Martin (New Delhi: Sage Publication, 1999),
    118. Raka Shome writes, "In India, there is a politics of skin color-like in many
    Western countries, although it gets played out differently in that it reinscribes
    the structures of sexism, heterosexism, and racism."
68. Ragone, "Of Likeness and Difference," 65. Ragone remarks: "Differences such
    as class, race, and ethnicity appear to be set aside when infertility and child-
    lessness are at issue."

3 Exploited Exploiters, Victimized Victimizers: Reading the Matthean Mothers alongside the Contextual Body of the Indian Surrogate Mother in Postcolonial India

1. Usha Rengachary Smerdon, "Crossing Bodies, Crossing Borders: International
   Surrogacy between the United States and India," *Cumberland Law Review* Vol.
   39, No. 1 (2008): 44–45. Smerdon notes: "Clinics offering surrogacy arrangements to international clients have sprung up in major metropolitan areas
   throughout India, including: Kolkata, Pune, New Delhi, Bhopal, and Indore.
   The clientele appears mostly to be non-resident Indians, constituting as much
   as 70% of the total client base. Indian clinics report that surrogacy arrangements have more than doubled in recent years with demand being driven
   primarily from abroad." It is important to note that the term "Non-Resident
   Indians" (often referred to as NRIs) refers to people born in India (maybe
   even spent a major portion of their life in India) but who now live and work
   abroad.
2. Sagarika Ghosh, "Is Surrogacy Leading to Exploitation of Poor Women?"
   CNN-IBN, June 19, 2012, at: http://www. ibnlive.in.com/news/is-surrogacy-
   leading-to-exploitation-of-poor-women/266801–3.html (accessed August 8,
   2012).
3. Ibid.
4. Santosh Desai, "Towards a Cultural War," *The Times of India,* January 6, 2013,
   at http://blogs.timesofindia.indiatimes.com/Citycitybangbang/entry/towards-
   a-cultural-war (accessed on January 8, 2013). Commenting on the recent gang
   rape incident that took place in India's capital city of Delhi, Desai's article
   attempts to expose the deep seated patriarchy that seems to run among both
   the politicians, and law makers of India. He writes: "The truth is that, however
   inappropriate the statements from politicians, they represent a larger view, and

that should hardly come as a surprise. India is a deeply patriarchal society, and no matter how desirable gender equality is, it is a long and arduous journey that has barely begun."

5. Kishwar Desai, *Origins of Love* (London: Simon & Schuster UK, 2012), 31.

6. Helen Pidd, "Why Is India So Bad for Women?" *The Guardian,* July 23, 2012, at http://www.guardian.co.uk/world/2012/jul/23/why-india-bad-for-women (accessed on August 21, 2012).

7. George Palattiyil, Eric Blyth, Dina Sidhva and Geeta Balakrishnan, "Globalization and Cross-border Reproductive Services: Ethical Implications of Surrogacy in India for Social Work," *International Social Work*, Vol. 53, No. 5 (September 2010): 687.

8. Desai, *Origins of Love,* 74.

9. Fred De Sam Lazro, "Surrogate Mothers in India," *Religion and Ethics Newsweekly,* September 30, at http://www.pbs.org/wnet/religionandethics/episodes/september-30–2011/surrogate-mothers-in-india/9612/ (accessed on October 8, 2012). Emphasis added.

10. Janice Capel Anderson, "Matthew: Gender and Reading," *Semeia*, No. 28 (1983): 8.

11. Amy Jill Levine, "Matthew," in *Women's Bible Commentary: Expanded Edition,* ed. Carol A. Newsome and Sharon H. Ringe (Louisville, KY: Westminster John Knox Press, 1998), 341.

12. For a more detailed discussion, see Jane Schaberg, "Feminist Interpretations of the Infancy Narrative of Matthew," in *The Illegitimacy of Jesus: A Feminist Theological Interpretation of the Infancy Narrative* expanded 20th ed. (Sheffield: Sheffield Phoenix Press, 2006). In this essay Schaberg discusses the "interpretative divide" among feminist biblical and theological scholars. She notes: "Is the belief in a virginal conception somehow compatible with a positive, nonpatriarchal view of female sexuality? Patterson Corrington (*Her Image of Salvation)* thinks not; Schotroff (*Let the Oppressed Go Free)* thinks so, perhaps along with Daly (*Gyn/Ecology*), Ruether (*Sexism and God Talk*), Wainwright ('The Gospel of Matthew'), and Capel Anderson ("Mary's Difference: Gender and Patriarchy in the Birth Narratives"); Levine ('Matthew') does not examine this issue." Continuing further, she asks the question, "How are we to understand a 'fatherless conception' in the light of the rest of Matthew's gospel? Levine gives some strong suggestions here, but I find that the motif of restructuring human relationships makes more sense if I linked to an illegitimate, not a virginal conception." 244. Also cf. Craig. S. Keener, *The Gospel of Matthew: A Socio-Rhetorical Commentary* (Grand Rapids, MI: Eerdmans, 2009), 79. He writes, "Many commentators instead link them [the women in Matthew's genealogy] to charges of either sinfulness [i.e, Schaberg and Mosala] or irregular births [i.e., Wainwright, Levine, Ruether,etc.], suggesting that their names prepare readers for the scandal of the virgin birth in 1:18–25 or counter slanders of Mary's infidelity; as God vindicated these women of old, he would also vindicate Mary." The women in Matthew's geneoalogy are subjected into

dichotomous categories of victimized women or empowered mothers, such interpretations foreclose the opportunity to construct the motherhood performed by these women through a more ambiguous lens.

13. Dorothy Jean Weaver, "Wherever this Good News is Proclaimed: Women and God in the Gospel of Matthew," *Interpretation*, Vol. 65, No. 4 (October 2010), 394.

14. Jerome, *The Fathers of the Church: Commentary on Matthew,* trans. Thomas P. Scheck (Washington, DC: Catholic University of America Press, 2008). Jerome argues: "In the Savior's genealogy it is remarkable that there is no mention of holy women, but only those whom the Scripture reprehends, so that [we can understand that] he who had come for the sake of sinners, since he was born from sinful women, blots out the sins of everyone." 59. Also cf. Jane Schaberg, *The Illegitimacy of Jesus: A Feminist Theological Interpretation of the Infancy Narratives*, expanded 20th ed. (Sheffield: Sheffield Phoenix Press, 2006), 32 and Raymond E. Brown, *The Birth of the Messiah: A Commentary on the Infancy Narratives in the Gospels of Matthew and Luke* (New Haven, CT: Yale University Press, 1993), 71: who points out that this proposal made popular by Jerome regarded, "the four OT women as sinners; and their inclusion foreshadowed for Matthew's readers the role of Jesus as the Savior of sinful men."

15. Brown, *Birth of the Messiah,* 72. The second proposal Brown points was, "one made popular by Luther, has more to recommend it namely, that the women were regarded as foreigners and were included by Matthew to show that Jesus, the Jewish Messiah was related by ancestry to the Gentiles."

16. See especially R. Bloch, "Juda engendra Phar`es et Zara, de Thamar (Matt 1, 3), in *Melanges bibliques rediges en l'honneur de Andre Robert* (Paris: Bloud & Gay, 1957), 381–389. Also cf. A. Paul, *L'Evangile de l'enfance selon saint Matthieu* (Lira la Bible, 17; Paris: Cerf, 1968), 30–37. These authors point out that in the later rabbinic sources the term "Holy Spirit" was used to describe God's irregular use of women in Matthew's genealogy. For a detailed analysis cf. Raymond E. Brown, Karl P. Donfried, Joseph A. Fitzmeyer and John Reumann, eds., *Mary in the New Testament* (New York: Paulist Press, 1978), 81–83 and Brown's *Birth of the Messiah,* 73–74.

17. Janice Capel Anderson, "Mary's Difference: Gender and Patriarchy in the Birth Narratives," *The Journal of Religion*, Vol. 67, No. 2 (1987): 188. She writes, "The first reading associates women, sexuality, and sin. Tamar and possibly Rahab conceive in an anomalous stage outside the bonds of marriage. Tamar and Ruth pursue the levitrate by scandalous means. Rahab was a prostitute. Bathsheba was an adulteress who may have deceived David as well as Uriah." Also cf. Anderson's "Matthew: Gender and Reading," 9.

18. Brown bases his argument on Bloch, "Juda engendra Phar`es et Zara, de Thamar (Matt 1, 3)." In his work Bloch points out that character of Tamar was highly respected in the postbiblical Judaic era. Also cf. Paul, *L'Evangile de l'enfance selon saint Matthieu*, 31–35 and Marshall D. Johnson, *The Purpose of*

the Biblical Genealogies with Special Reference to the Setting of the Genealogies of Jesus (NTSMS 8; Cambridge University, 1969), 159–175. For a detailed analysis see Brown, *The Birth of the Messiah,* 72, footnote 25.

19. Schaberg, *The Illegitimacy of Jesus,* 33.
20. Brown, Donfried, Fitzmeyer, and Reumann, *Mary in the New Testament,* 80. These scholars note: "In such a theory the women have nothing in common with Mary (although in the Third Reich this theory was used to argue that Mary was not a Jew). It is a bit too subtle to argue that the four women represent the Gentile side of Jesus's distaff inheritance, and Mary represents the Jewish side. In general, this theory taken alone, does not seem sufficient to us." Also cf. Brown, *Birth of the Messiah,* who argues, "One would think that the four OT women constitute some preparation for the role of Mary, and yet Mary was not a foreigner." 73. Further on the thesis that Mary was herself a foreigner see R. Seeberg, "Die Herkunft der Mutter Jesu," in *Theologische Fetschrift für* (Leipzig: Deichert, 1918), 13–24.
21. Levine, "Matthew," 340. Also cf. Brown, *Birth of the Messiah,* 73. Brown points out that in postbiblical Jewish literature Ruth and Tamar were not considered foreigners but were depicted as proselytes/converts to Judaism. Brown then raises the question: "If Matthew introduced them into the genealogy to appeal to the Gentile Christian segment of his community and to show these Gentiles that their presence was foreshadowed in the messianic genealogy, how would the Gentiles understand the proselyte status of the women?—or is one to maintain that in a community that had consisted predominantly of Jewish Christians, the Gentile Christians were looked on as proselytes not to Judaism but to Jewish Christianity?" In addition to Brown, Donfried, Fitzmeyer, Reuman and Brown scholars of *Mary in the New Testament* also point out that "Matthew calls no attention to the fact that Uriah was Hittite." 80.
22. Capel Anderson, "Mary's Difference," 188.
23. Schaberg, *The Illegitimacy of Jesus,* 33. Also cf. Brown, *Birth of the Messiah,* 73. Brown notes, "there is something extraordinary or irregular in their union with their partners—a union which, though it may have been scandalous to outsiders, continued the blessed lineage of the Messiah." Also see, Janice Capel Anderson, "Mary's Difference,"188. She points out, "The women foreshadow Mary and prepare the implied reader for a woman's irregular production of the Messiah outside of ordinary patriarchal norms yet within God's overarching plans and an overall patriarchal framework."
24. See also Letty M. Russell, "Wise Women Bearing Gifts," *Cross Currents,* Vol. 53, No. 1 (Spring 2003), 117. Russell observes: "In 1:16 Matthew finally has to mention the *anomaly* in his story. Jesus was born of Mary and not of Joseph and the thirty-nine fathers! He has included Tamar, Ruth, Rahab, and Bathsheba in the genealogy to show that God even uses women to save the people of Israel. These women were *dangerous women* who functioned outside the traditional patriarchal structures to make it clear that God is to fulfill

the divine promise through another dangerous woman named Mary." Also cf. Elaine Wainwright, "The Gospel of Matthew," in *Searching the Scriptures: A Feminist Commentary*, ed. Elisabeth Schüssler Fiorenza (New York: Crossroad, 1994), 643.

25. Schaberg, "Feminist Interpretations of the Infancy Narrative of Matthew," 249. Schaberg's interpretation regarding the illegitimacy of Jesus is shared by another scholar, Itumeleng Mosala. See his, *Biblical Hermeneutics and Black Theology in South Africa* (Grand Rapids, MI: Eerdmans, 1989), 167–169. He argues for an understanding of Mary as "a single mother from the ghettos of colonized Galilee."

26. Frank Reilly, "Jane Schaberg, Raymond E. Brown, and the Problem of the Illegitimacy of Jesus," in *The Illegitimacy of Jesus: A Feminist Theological Interpretation of the Infancy Narrative, Expanded Twentieth Anniversary Edition* (Sheffield: Sheffield Phoenix Press, 2006), 259. Reilly notes, "The substance of the debate between Brown and Schaberg is their exegesis of the conception texts. Brown argued for the virginal conception, reading in his massive commentary on the infancy narratives, *The Birth of the Messiah;* Schaberg acknowledged his influence and dealt with his work as she developed her radically opposed position in *The Illegitimacy of Jesus*. He replied to her arguments in the second edition of the *Birth of the Messiah*; she briefly responded to his criticism of her work on Matthew in the pages of this journal." Reilly is referring to her essay, "Feminist Interpretations of the Infancy Narratives," *Journal of Feminist Studies in Religion*, Vol. 13, No.1 (Spring 1997), 35–62.

27. Brown, *The Birth of the Messiah*, 708. Also cf. note 330, Brown makes the argument: " Given the OT the tendency was to visit the sins of the parents on the children, if Mary had been seduced, would there have been such an insistence on the sinlessness of Jesus (John 8:46; 14:30; 1 Pet 1:19; 3:18; 1 John 3:5,7; heb 4:15)? If Christians knew of a rape of Mary, the portrayed presumptions of family claims (Mark 3:31–35) and of family normality (6:3) are indeed strange."

28. Ibid., 601. Brown writes, "Schaberg's claim that a rapist was Jesus' true father, in my judgment, destroys the theological identity of Jesus intended by Matt in 1:18–25."

29. Ibid., 708.

30. Schaberg, "Feminist Interpretations of the Infancy Narrative of Matthew," 254.

31. Schaberg, *The Illegitimacy of Jesus,* writes: "Tamar was taken by Judah as a wife for his son Er, who was 'wicked in the sight of Yahweh; and Yahweh slew him' (v. 7). Er's brother Onan refused to perform the duty of levitate marriage and produce a male descendant for his brother; instead he practiced coitus interruptus for which he was slain by Yahweh. Tamar's father-in-law, Judah, then refused her his third son, Shelah —Tamar was sent back to live as a widow in her father's house—eventually Tamar understood that Judah wanted to get rid of her permanently, and she acted for the first time on her own. Disguising

herself as a prostitute, she tricked Judah into having intercourse with her, and she became pregnant." (34).

32. Danna Nolan Fewell, "Joshua," in *Women's Biblical Commentary*, ed. Carol A. Newsome and Sharon H. Ringe (Louisville, KY: Westminster John Knox Press, 1998), 72. "From Israel's perspective Madame Rahab is the epitome of the outsider. She is a woman, a prostitute, and a foreigner. As a prostitute she is marginal even in her own culture, and her marginality is symbolized by her dwelling in the city wall, in the very boundary between the inside and the outside."

33. See Elaine Wainwright, *Towards a Feminist Critical Reading of the Gospel according to Matthew* (Berlin and New York: de Gruyter, 1991), 167: "The story is set, however, in a patriarchal context. It begins within a patriarchal family (1:1–15). In Ruth 3, the emphasis shifts from the radical choice made by Ruth to her obedience to her mother-in-law in seeking out a relative of her deceased husband who may perform the duties of the levitate law in her regard (3:1–13). The independent woman who attached herself to another woman unto death and even beyond (1:16–17) is incorporated into the patriarchal family structure (4:1–13)."

34. See Schaberg, *The Illegitimacy of Jesus*, 40: The story of Bathsheba "is the story of a woman taken in adultery, pitied rather than scorned or blamed by the storyteller. She is presented without options, without recourse, without a personal history of significance. She does not act but is acted upon, and then barely reacts."

35. Wainwright, *Towards a Feminist Critical Reading of the Gospel of Matthew*, 162.

36. David M. Gunn and Danna Nolan Fewell, *Narrative in the Hebrew Bible* (New York: Oxford University Press, 1993), 38.

37. Palattiyil, Blyth, Sidhva and Balakrishnan, "Globalization and Cross-border Reproductive Services," 689.

38. Amrita Pande, "Commercial Surrogacy in India: Manufacturing a Perfect Mother-Worker" *Signs*, Vol. 35, No. 4 (Summer 2010): 979.

39. Usha Rengachary Smerdon, "Crossing Bodies, Crossing Borders: International Surrogacy between the United States and India," *Cumberland Law Review* Vol. 39, No. 1 (2008): 56.

40. Pande, "Commercial Surrogacy in India," 976–977.

41. Carol Meyers, "Everyday Life: Women in the Period of the Hebrew Bible," in *Women's Biblical Commentary*, ed. Newsome and Ringe, 255.

42. Wainwright, *Towards a Feminist Critical Reading of the Gospel according to Matthew,* 162, n.29. Also cf. Gerhard Von Rad, *Genesis: A Commentary* (Philadelphia, PA: Westminster Press, 1972), 359. Von Rad argues that Judah, Tamar's father-in-law could have himself fulfilled the levitate duty and made sure that his patrilineal linage would continue. However, as Wainwright argues in 162, n. 31, "If von Rad's suggestion … is correct, that Judah could have fulfilled the duty of levitate, then Schaberg's claim that we have here a

'legitimated illegitimacy' in her book *Illegitimacy of Jesus,* 23, is not as firm. It is rather a legitimate pregnancy achieved by illegitimate means which pushes back patriarchal norms and boundaries."

43. Wainwright, *Towards a Feminist Critical Reading of the Gospel according to Matthew,* 164.
44. Schaberg, *The Illegitimacy of Jesus,* 36.
45. Adrienne Arieff, "Having Twins with a Surrogate—in India," *The New York Times,* March 16, 2012, at http://parenting.blogs.nytimes.com/.../having-twins-with-a-surrogate-in-india/ (accessed on September 18, 2012).
46. Chandra Talpade Mohanty, "Under Western Eyes: Feminist Scholarship and Colonial Discourses," *Feminist Review* Vol. 30 (1988): 79.
47. Wainwright, *Towards a Feminist Critical Reading of the Gospel according to Matthew,* 165.
48. Kishwar Desai, "India's Surrogate Mothers are Risking Their Lives: They Urgently Need Protection," *The Guardian,* June 5, 2012, at http://www.guardian.co.uk/commentisfree/2012/jun/05/india-surrogates-impoverished-die (accessed October 10, 2012)
49. Amy-Jill Levine, "Ruth" in *Women's Biblical Commentary,* ed. Newsome and Ringe, 84.
50. Phyllis Trible, *God and the Rhetoric of Sexuality* (Philadelphia, PA: Fortress Press, 1978), 173.
51. As scholars like Sasson and Campbell have noted in their works, such an implication found in Trible's interpretation has shifted over the years. For example: Jack M. Sassson, *Ruth: A New Translation with a Philological Commentary and a Formalist-Folklorist Interpretation,* The Johns Hopkins Near Eastern Studies 11 (Baltimore, MD and London: Johns Hopkins University Press, 1979), 242–243 and 246–247. Sasson points out that the book of Ruth must be read as a story of family solidarity and universalism. Also see, Edward F. Campbell, *Ruth: A New Translation with Introduction, Notes, and Commentary,* AB 7 (Garden City, NY: Doubleday, 1975), 28–32. For detailed discussion also cf. Wainwright, *Towards a Feminist Critical Reading of the Gospel according to Matthew,* 107, n. 46.
52. As Levine notes in "Ruth," 88: "She [Naomi] advises Ruth to wash, put on perfume and her best dress, and go down to the threshing floor. Marking where Boaz lies down after eating and drinking, Ruth is to join him and uncover his 'feet' (a euphemism for genitals). Naomi adds: 'He will tell you what to do.' (3:4). Both this plan and Ruth's lack of questioning are problematic. First, they are reminiscent of the trickery depicted in Gen. 29:21–30, with Naomi playing the role of Laban, Ruth that of Leah (see 4:11), and Boaz that of Jacob."
53. Palattiyil, Blyth, Sidhva, and Balakrishnan, "Globalization and Cross-border Reproductive Services," 691. Also cf. Neeta Lal, "Regulating the Surrogacy Boom," at http://www.boloji.com/index.cfm?md=Content&sd=Articles&ArticleID=2862: and Imrana Qadeer, "Social and Ethical Basis of Legislation on Surrogacy: Need for Debate," at http://issuesinmedicalethics.org/171co 28.

54. Levine, "Ruth," 88. She writes, "Second, the threshing floor is associated with extramarital sexual activity (see Hos. 9:11)".

55. Abigail Haworth, "Surrogate Mothers: Womb for Rent," *Marie Claire*, July 29, 2007, at http://www.marieclaire.com/world-reports/news/womb-rent-india-5 (accessed September 19, 2012)

56. Smerdon, "Crossing Bodies, Crossing Borders," 4.

57. Schaberg, *The Illegitimacy of Jesus*, 39.

58. Alexander Izchukwu Abasili, "Was It Rape? The David and Bathsheba Pericope Reexamined," in *Vestus Testamentum*, 61 (2011): 1–2. Abasili acknowledges that the scholars stand divided in their interpretation of the David and Bathsheba story. He writes: "Scholars such as George G. Nicol, Randall Bailey, and Hans Wilhelm Hertzberg variously place the burden of seduction on Bathsheba and argue that she was not raped by David. For instance, George G. Nicol argues that Bathsheba by 'bathing in such close proximity to the royal palace was deliberately provocative.' In the same vein, Bailey's interpretation of 2 Sam 11–12 describes Bathsheba as a 'willing and equal partner.' In this connection, he argues that the strong political desire to become the king's wife made Bathsheba take her bath at an auspicious position and time. On the opposite end of the divide, scholars such as Richard M. Davidson, David and Diana Garland, Larry W. Spielman and J. Cheryl Exum argue that Bathsheba was a victim of David's rape and/or abuse. For instance, Richard M. Davidson likened the intercourse between David and Bathsheba to that between an adult and a minor whose consent is of no consequence and concludes that Bathsheba was a victim of David's 'power rape.' "

59. Cf. 2 Sam 15: "Then the Lord struck the child that Uriah's wife bore to David, and it became very ill."

60. Referring to 2 Samuel 11:14: "In the morning David wrote a letter to Joab, and sent it by the hand of Uriah. In the letter he wrote, 'Set Uriah in the forefront of the hardest fighting, and then draw back from him, so that he may be struck down and die.' " Wainwright, *Towards a Feminist Critical Reading of the Gospel according to Matthew*, 168.

61. Elizabeth S. Anderson, "Is Women's Labor a Commodity?" *Philosophy and Public Affairs*, Vol. 19, No. 1 (Winter 1990), 83. Also cf. Kay Longscope, "Standing up for Mary Beth," *Boston Globe,* 5 March 1987, 83; Daniel Goleman, "Motivations of Surrogate Mothers," *New York Times*, January 20, 1987.

62. Palattiyil, Blyth, Sidhva, and Balakrishnan, "Globalization and Cross-Border Reproductive Services," 691.

63. Schaberg, *The Illegitimacy of Jesus*, 39. Also cf. J. A. Wharton, "A Plausible Tale: Story and Theology in II Samuel 9–20, I Kings 2," *Interpretation*, Vol. 35 (1998): 342.

64. Jo Ann Hackett, "1 and 2 Samuel," in *Women's Biblical Commentary*, ed. Newsome and Ringe. Expanded Edition 98.

65. Pande, "Commercial Surrogacy in India," 976.
66. Schaberg, *The Illegitimacy of Jesus*, 41.
67. Raymond E. Brown, "The Annunciation to Joseph (Matt 1:18–25)" in *Worship*, Vol. 61, No. 6 (1987): 483.
68. Schaberg, "Feminist Interpretations of the Infancy Narrative of Matthew," 247.
69. Elaine Wainwright, "Tradition Makers/Tradition Shapers: Women of the Matthean Tradition," in *Word and World*, Vol. 18, No. 4 (Fall 1998): 382–383.
70. Elaine Wainwright, *Shall We Look For Another? A Feminist Reading of the Matthean Jesus* (New York: Orbis Books, 1998), 56. A similar tactic is also used by Schaberg in her book, *The Illegitimacy of Jesus*. 30. She argues that a feminist reading of a text is one that pays attention to the silences in the text. She writes, "This silence is not allowed to prove the absence of women or their nonexistence at the center of foundational events of the Israelite and Christian communities." Her words are drawn from the work of Elisabeth Schüssler Fiorenza, *In Memory of Her: A Feminist Theological Reconstruction of Christian Origins* (New York: Crossroad, 1983), 41. Fiorenza argues that, "Rather than rejecting the argument from silence as a valid historical argument, we must learn to read the silences of androcentric texts in such a way that they can provide 'clues' to the egalitarian reality of the early Christian movement."
71. Frank Reilly, "Jane Schaberg, Raymond E. Brown, and the Problem of the Illegitimacy of Jesus," 263. Reilly observes: "The historic domination of a patriarchal 'virginal conception theology,' including its Mariology and Christology, its ideas of God and of human life, has had enormous negative consequences for women. Many feminists reject the virginal conception and patriarchal theology it represents. Others accept it, but with a feminist interpretation that emphasizes freedom and independence of Mary."
72. Pande, "Commercial Surrogacy in India," 979.
73. Wainwright, *Shall We Look for Another?* 66.
74. Palattiyil, Blyth, Sidhva, and Balakrishnan, "Globalization and Cross-Border Reproductive Services," 691.
75. Pande, "Commercial Surrogacy in India," 975.
76. It is interesting to note that similar to Joseph, the husband of the Indian surrogate is also discouraged from engaging in any form sexual intercourse with his wife during the duration of her pregnancy. Pande describes the environment of the surrogacy hostels and notes, "Husbands are allowed to visit but are encouraged not stay the night, to emphasize the requirement that the surrogate not have any sexual relations during the nine months of pregnancy." Ibid., 981.
77. Anuj Chopra, "Childless Couples Look to India for Surrogate Mothers," in *The Christian Science Monitor*, April 3, 2006, at http://www.csmonitor.com/2006/0403/p01s04-wosc.html/(page) (accessed September 26, 2012).
78. Smerdon, "Crossing Bodies, Crossing Borders," 56. She notes, "In addition, traditional Indian attitudes towards sex and procreation often force a surrogate

to hide her pregnancy and/or invent stories about her pregnancy—for example, saying the baby has died or that they have been away for months on the pretext of visiting relatives."

79. Raymond E. Brown, "The Problem of the Virginal Conception of Jesus," *Theological Studies*,Vol. 33, No. 1 (1972): 14.

80. The interpretations surrounding these texts which reference the family of Jesus have been varied, ranging from siblings, as read by Tertullian, Helvedius and modern Protestants, to stepbrothers, as read by Epiphanius, to cousins, as read by Hegesippus, Jerome, and the principal reformers.

81. Brown, "The Problem of the Virginal Conception of Jesus," 9.

82. Cf. Raymond E. Brown, *The Virginal Conception and Bodily Resurrection of Jesus* (New York: Paulist Press, 1973), 62: "But these 'parallels' consistently involve a type of hieros gamos where a divine male, in human or other form, impregnates a woman, either through normal sexual intercourse or through some substitute form of penetration. They are not really similar to the non-sexual virginal conception that is at the core of the infancy narratives . "

83. Raymond Brown, *Birth of the Messiah A Commentary on the Infancy Narratives in the Gospels of Matthew and Luke (*New Haven, CT: Yale University Press, 1993), 63.

84. Brown, *The Virginal Conception and Bodily Resurrection of Jesus*, 64.

85. Brown, *Birth of the Messiah*, 73.

86. Ibid., 74.

87. Ibid., 118.

88. Joseph Fitzmyer, "The Virginal Conception of Jesus in the New Testament," *Theological Studies*, Vol. 34, No. 4 (1973): 567.

89. For an analysis of the dialogue between Brown and Fitzmyer, see Reilly, "Jane Schaberg, Raymond E. Brown and the Problem of the Illegitimacy," 64.

90. I will deal with this argument in detail when I discuss Jane Schaberg's work in my feminist biblical scholarship section.

91. Ibid., 65.

92. Brown argues that the Spirit that comes upon Mary is similar to the Spirit in Gen 1: 2, suggesting: "The earth was void and without form when that Spirit appeared; just so Mary's womb was a void until through the Spirit God filled it with a child who was His Son" (*Birth of the Messiah,* 314). It is interesting to note that Brown compares Mary's womb to the earth that is sown by God's seed. In making such a comparison Brown seems to rekindle the idea that women's bodies being closer to the earth and nature are therefore inferior.

93. Ibid., 301.

94. Reilly, "Jane Schaberg, Raymond E. Brown, and the Problem of the Illegitimacy of Jesus," 58.

95. Ibid., 75. Cf. Brown, *Birth of the Messiah.* 708, n. 330.

96. Though Jane Schaberg's work will take precedence in my chapter, I begin with Anderson's article as this chronological arrangement will allow me to situate Schaberg's work in context of other feminist scholarship.

97. Capel Anderson, "Mary's Difference," 183.
98. Ibid., 184. See Brown, Donfried, Fitzmyer, and Reumann, eds., *Mary in the New Testament*.
99. Capel Anderson, "Mary's Difference," 185.
100. Ibid., 185.
101. Anderson argues that the genealogy in Matthew ending at 1:16 leaves the implied reader with the question, "How can Jesus trace his descent as Son of Abraham and Son of David through Joseph?" The answer to this question, she points out, is answered in the "initial episode of the birth story" found in Matt: 1:18–25 and helps clarify Jesus' status by alluding to the Hebrew Scriptures, 190.
102. Ibid., 188.
103. Capel Anderson, "Mary's Difference," 190. She argues, "God's control of Mary's reproductive powers and the manner of conception give rise to ambiguity for androcentric gender definition and interpretation of male-female-divine relationships."
104. Ibid., 197.
105. Ibid., 202.
106. Reilly, "Jane Schaberg, Raymond E. Brown, and the Problem of the Illegitimacy of Jesus," 58.
107. Schüssler Fiorenza, *In Memory of Her*, 18. She writes: "Gender analyses assume a binary 'naturalized' relation of the sexes that places them on the same level of meaning and power. As a result these analyses 'naturalize' the grammatical inscription of gender and fail to articulate the asymmetric social relations of domination/submission both between men and women and women and women."
108. Ibid., 19.
109. Ibid.
110. Reilly, "Jane Schaberg, Raymond E. Brown, and the Problem of the Illegitimacy of Jesus," 58.
111. This approach, as we have already seen, has been used by Janice Capel Anderson in "Mary's Difference."
112. Jane Schaberg, *The Illegitimacy of Jesus: A Feminist Theological Interpretation of the Infancy Narratives* expanded 20th anniversary ed. (Sheffield: Sheffield Phoenix Press, 2006) [orig. ed.: San Francisco: Harper & Row, 1987], 27.
113. Ibid., 27.
114. Ibid.
115. Schüssler Fiorenza, *In Memory of Her*, 19–20.
116. Schaberg, *The Illegitimacy of Jesus*, 14–15.
117. Ibid., 15.
118. Ibid. The difference in her reading, as a result, lies in the notion that it presents an "explicit interest in how the sex of a woman reader/interpreter influences the reading of male texts."
119. Ibid., 15.

120. Ibid.
121. Ibid., 58.
122. In making this point, Schaberg differs from Brown who argues that the "divinity" of Jesus is intimately tied into his pure virginal conception.
123. Jane Schaberg, "The Foremothers and the Mother of Jesus," in *A Feminist Companion to the Hebrew Bible in the New Testament*, ed. Athalya Brenner (Sheffield: Sheffield Academic Press, 1996), 150.
124. Ibid., 151.
125. Ibid.
126. Ibid.
127. Wainwright, "The Gospel of Matthew," 640.
128. Ibid., 642.
129. Ibid.
130. Schaberg, "The Foremothers and the Mother of Jesus," 152.
131. Wainwright,"The Gospel of Matthew," 643.
132. Capel Anderson, "Mary's Difference," 199.
133. Wainwright,"The Gospel of Matthew," 643.
134. Jane Schaberg, "Feminist Interpretations of the Infancy Narrative of Matthew," in *A Feminist Companion to Mariology*, ed. Amy Jill Levine and Maria Mayo Robbins (London and New York: T&T Clark International, 2005), 30.
135. Schaberg, *The Illegitimacy of Jesus*, 74.
136. Schaberg, "The Foremothers and the Mother of Jesus," 152.
137. Ibid., 152.
138. Ibid.
139. Ibid., 153.
140. Ibid.
141. Ibid., 154.
142. Ibid., 153.
143. Reilly, "Jane Schaberg, Raymond E. Brown, and the Problem of the Illegitimacy of Jesus," 76.
144. Schaberg, "The Foremothers and the Mother of Jesus," 156.
145. Ibid., 157.
146. Ibid.
147. Schaberg, *The Illegitimacy of Jesus*, 84.
148. Reilly, "Jane Schaberg, Raymond E. Brown, and the Problem of the Illegitimacy of Jesus," 65.
149. Bea Wyler, "Mary's Call," in *A Feminist Companion to the Hebrew Bible in the New Testament*, ed. Athalya Brenner (Sheffield: Sheffield Academic Press, 1996), 141.
150. Ibid., 142.
151. In *Birth of the Messiah,* Brown argues that the verb "to know" in the phrase "I do not know a man" is a Semitism for sexual relations. Brown points out that though this tense is in its present form it must be understood as

describing "a state resultant from a past pattern of behavior, as the OL recognized by using a perfect tense (*novi, cognovi*)." Additionally, Brown observes that the word for "man" is "the specific *aner*, 'male, husband,' not the generic *anthropos*. Here it should not be translated 'husband' since Luke's intent is wider: Mary has not known any man and so is a virgin (1:27)" (289).

152. Wyler, "Mary's Call," 145.
153. Schaberg, *The Illegitimacy of Jesus*, 86.
154. Wyler, "Mary's Call," 145.
155. Reilly, "Jane Schaberg, Raymond E. Brown, and the Problem of the Illegitimacy of Jesus," 69.
156. Schaberg, *The Illegitimacy of Jesus*, 91.
157. Ibid., 91–92.
158. Ibid., 92.
159. Ibid.
160. Ibid., 93.
161. Joseph A. Fitzmyer, *The Gospel According to Luke I-IX* (AB 28; Garden City, NY: Doubleday, 1981), 367.
162. Reilly, "Jane Schaberg, Raymond E. Brown, and the Problem of the Illegitimacy of Jesus," 70.
163. Capel Anderson observes: "As God has chosen a female servant of low estate to bring the Lord into the world and exalted her, so will God overturn the proud, rich, and mighty and exalt the pious, hungry, and lowly…Mary thus serves as spokeswoman and representative of the oppressed servant Israel or the faithful within Israel of low socioeconomic status" ("Mary's Difference," 197). A common point between Anderson and Schaberg is their vision of Mary as a spokesperson for the victimized.
164. Schaberg, *The Illegitimacy of Jesus*, 101.
165. Ibid.
166. Arie Troost, "Elizabeth and Mary—Naomi and Ruth: Gender-Response Criticism in Luke 1–2," in *A Feminist Companion to the Hebrew Bible in the New Testament*, ed. Athalya Brenner (Sheffield: Sheffield Academic Press, 1996), 163.
167. Ibid., 162.
168. John Domnic Crossan, "Virgin Mother or Bastard Child?" in *A Feminist Companion to Mariology*, ed. Amy Jill Levine and Maria Mayo Robbins (London and New York: T&T Clark International, 2005), 54.
169. Schaberg, *The Illegitimacy of Jesus*, 103.
170. Ibid., 103.
171. Troost, "Elizabeth and Mary—Naomi and Ruth," 194.
172. Ibid., 187.
173. Crossan, "Virgin Mother or Bastard Child?" 38.
174. Ibid., 54.
175. Ibid., 55.

176. Ibid.
177. Gail Paterson Corrington, *Her Image of Salvation: Female Saviors and Formative Christianity* (Louisville, KY: Westminster John Knox Press, 1992), 150.
178. Ibid., 154.
179. Ibid.
180. Ibid., 157. Paterson Corrington in her interpretation of Luke's infancy narrative concludes: "I agree with Schaberg that the reference to Mary's low and even humiliated estate together with the links to Elizabeth and to other 'humiliated' women whom God restored through granting or preserving the life of a child-is meant by Luke to fit into his general theological theme: the positive bent of God toward the humiliated and oppressed."
181. Cheryl A. Kirk-Duggan, "Proud Mary: Contextual Constructions of a Divine Diva," in *Blessed One: Protestant Perspectives on Mary*, ed. Beverly Roberts Gaventa and Cynthia L. Rigby (Louisville, KY: Westminster John Knox Press, 2002), 73–74.
182. Ibid., 76.
183. Ibid.
184. Elisabeth Schüssler Fiorenza, *Jesus: Miriam's Child, Sophia's Prophet: Critical Issues in Feminist Christology* (New York: Continuum; London: SCM Press, 1994), 182.
185. Ibid., 183.
186. Itulmeleng, J. Mosala. *Biblical Hermeneutics and Black Theology in South Africa* (Grand Rapids, MI: W. B. Eerdmans Pub, 1989), 167.
187. Ibid., 169.
188. Ibid.

4 Surrogacy as Performance of Violent Love: Reading Luke's Magnificat alongside the Bodies of Indian Surrogate Mothers

1. Louis, Althusser, *Lenin and Philosophy and Other Essays,* trans. Ben Brewster (London: New Left Books, 1971), 169.
2. Sadie Stein, "Is Reproductive Tourism Exploiting India's Poor," *Jezebel*, August 23, 2010, at http://jezebel.com/5619616/is-reproductive-tourism-exploiting-indias-poor (accessed on December 11, 2012)
3. Raywat Deonandan, "The Ethics of Surrogacy," *India Currents: The Complete Indian American Magazine*, February 3, 2012, at http://www.indiacurrents.com/articles/2012/02/03/ethics-surrogacy (accessed on October 25, 2012)
4. Usha Rengachary Smerdon, "Crossing Bodies, Crossing Borders: International Surrogacy between the United States and India," *Cumberland Law Review*, Vol. 39, No. 1 (2008): 24–25. She writes, "In most Western countries, commercial surrogacy is either banned or sharply regulated. For example, Italy, Germany, France, Switzerland, Greece, Spain, Norway, New Zealand, and several Australian states prohibit commercial surrogacy contracts. The

enforcement of surrogacy contracts is sharply limited in Canada, Israel, and the United Kingdom. Several countries have developed these laws after evaluating recommendations of national commissions formed to study the practice. The studies reveal that the recommendations to develop restrictions rest primarily on public policy grounds."

5. Nancy Chodorow, *The Reproduction of Mothering: Psychoanalysis and the Sociology of Gender* (Berkeley: University of California Press, 1978), 14.

6. Ratna Kapur, "No Country for Young Women," *The Hindu*, August 18, 2012, at http://www.thehindu.com/opinion/op-ed/article3785967.ece (accessed on October 29, 2012).

7. Stephanie M. Lee, "Commercial Surrogacy grows in India," *San Francisco Chronicle*, October 20, 2012, at http://www.sfgate.com/health/article/Commercial-surrogacy-grows-in-India-3968312.php (accessed on October 30, 2012). Lee observes: "To qualify, [surrogates] must have one living child, and when they have had five children, either their own or someone else's, they can no longer be a surrogate."

8. Smerdon, "Crossing Bodies, Crossing Borders", 40.

9. Kishwar Desai, *Origins of Love* (London: Simon & Schuster UK, 2012), 26. The word *ghapla* is used in colloquial Hindi to mean confusion, mess or complication.

10. Amrita Pande, "Commercial Surrogacy in India: Manufacturing a Perfect Mother-Worker," *Signs*, Vol. 35, No. 4 (Summer 2010): 989.

11. Ibid.

12. Ibid.

13. Jane Schaberg, *The Illegitimacy of Jesus: A Feminist Theological Interpretation of the Infancy Narratives*, expanded 20th ed. (Sheffield: Sheffield Phoenix Press, 2006), 78.

14. Turid Karlsen Seim, *The Double Message: Patterns of Gender in Luke and Acts* (Nashville: Abingdon Press, 1994) 202.

15. Tat Siong Benny Liew, "Re-Markable Masculinities: Jesus, The Son of Man, and the (Sad) Sum of Manhood?" in *New Testament Masculinities*, ed. Stephen D. Moore and Janice Capel Anderson, (Atlanta: Society of Biblical Literature, 2003), 102; cf. David Halperin, *One Hundred Years of Homosexuality: And Other Essays on Greek Love*, (New York and London: Routledge, 1990), 266.

16. Schaberg, *The Illegitimacy of Jesus,* 80.

17. Ibid., 79.

18. Pande, "Commercial Surrogacy in India," 975.

19. Abigail Haworth, "Surrogate Mothers: Wombs for Rent," *Marie Claire*, July 29, 2007, at www.marieclaire.com/world.../news/.../**surrogate**-mothers-**india** (accessed on October 15, 2009), 5.

20. Chandra Talpade Mohanty, "Under Western Eyes: Feminist Scholarship and Colonial Discourse," in *Feminist Theory: A Reader,* ed. Wendy K. Kolmar and Frances Bartkowski (New York: McGraw Hill, 2005), 377.

21. Amelia Gentleman, "India Nurtures Business of Surrogate Motherhood," *The New York Times,* March 10, 2008, at http://www.nytimes.com/2008/03/10/world/asia/10surrogate.html (accessed on October 10, 2009), 1.

22. Smerdon, "Crossing Bodies, Crossing Borders," 54.

23. Mary F. Foskett, *A Virgin Conceived: Mary and Classical Representations of Virginity* (Bloomington: Indiana University Press, 2002), 124.

24. Turid Karlsen Seim, "The Virgin Mother: Mary and Ascetic Discipleship in Luke", in *A Feminist Companion to Luke,* ed. Amy-Jill Levine (London and New York: Sheffield Academic Press, 2002), 102–103.

25. Deborah L. Spar, "For Love and Money: The Political Economy of Commercial Surrogacy," *Review of International Political Economy* Vol 12, No. 2 (May 2005): 302. Cf. Kelly Oliver, "Marxism and Surrogacy," *Hypatia* Vol. 4 (1989): 99.

26. Haworth, "Surrogate Mothers: Wombs for Rent," 3.

27. E.g., Janice Capel Anderson, "Mary's Difference: Gender and Patriarchy in the Birth Narratives," *The Journal of Religion* Vol 67, No. 2 (April 1997): 191. Capel Anderson notes that similar to her role in the gospel of Matthew, the character of Mary in the Lucan narrative also conceives without a male. She writes: "As in Matthew, when Mary conceives, she is a virgin (1:27, 34). Mary's active acceptance of her role is emphasized. She is a model of faithful response, but her response depends upon God's initiative." Cf. Rosemary Radford Ruether, *Sexism and God Talk: Toward a Feminist Theology with a New Introduction.* (Boston, MA: Beacon Press, 1993), 153. Ruether points out to her readers that Mary's pregnancy, when compared to the pregnancy of Hannah (an older barren woman competing with her husband's younger fertile mistress,) takes a much different turn. She writes: "Her pregnancy does not follow from the proper role of women. Indeed, it puts her under danger as someone who has been making her own choices about her body and sexuality without regard for her future husband—In Luke the decision to have the redemptive child is between her and God. Joseph is not consulted (in Matthew, however, the deal is agreed upon in proper patriarchal fashion between Joseph and God, without consulting Mary). Luke goes out of his way to stress that Mary's motherhood is a free choice." It is important to note that while many male biblical scholars do not focus on the issue of "free choice" in Mary's consent, they nevertheless seek to highlight the obedience and willingness demonstrated in Mary's consent, leading them to interpret her as one of the first disciples to be presented by the author of Luke. Raymond E. Brown, Karl P. Donfried, Joseph A. Fitzmeyer, and John Reumann, eds., *Mary in the New Testament* (New York: Paulist Press, 1978), 125. They write: "This marvelous conception, without male parent, reveals the creative power of God at work but tells us no more about Mary than that she is God's instrument. The real Lucan evaluation of Mary becomes apparent only in 1:38 through her reaction to the angel's Christological revelation—if, as we have seen, 1:32, 33, 35 contains a basic post-resurrectional

proclamation of Christian faith, then Mary is being presented as the first one to hear the gospel."
28. Schaberg, *The Illegitimacy of Jesus,* 123.
29. Ibid., 119.
30. Ibid. Schaberg notes that the "How" in Mary's question to the angel Gabriel is never answered and, in fact, the angel sidesteps the details regarding the exact nature of her conception and focuses on the Holy Spirit as a sign of divine empowerment that will ensure her protection during this delicate time.
31. Ibid., 123.
32. Ibid.
33. Ibid., 124.
34. Ibid., 124–125. Schaberg argues that Mary's question to Gabriel in Luke 1:34, "How will this be, since I have no sexual relations with a husband?" must be interpreted as a declaration of protest that is followed by reassurance. She writes: "The pattern is one of objection followed by reassurance and the giving of a sign, or (in the case of Zechariah) doubt followed by rebuke, and (in the case of Mary) hesitation followed by reassurance" (103).
35. Michael Hardt and Antonio Negri, *Empire* (Cambridge, MA: Harvard University Press), 144.
36. Nilanjana S. Roy, "Protecting the Rightsof Surrogate Mothers in India," *The New York Times,* October 4, 2011. at http://www.nytimes.com/2011/10/05/world/asia/05iht-letter05.html? (accessed on November 6, 2012).
37. Jennifer A. Glancy, "Early Christianity, Slavery and Women's Bodies," in *Beyond Slavery: Overcoming Its Religious and Sexual Legacies,* ed. Bernadette J. Brooten (New York: Palgrave Macmillan, 2010), 143.
38. Schaberg, *The Illegitimacy of Jesus,*123.
39. Sister Josephine Amala Valarmathi, "The Work of Domestic Work," *Samar: South Asian Magazine for Action and Reflection,* November 10, 2008, at http://samarmagazine.org/archive/articles/270 (accessed on November 13, 2012).
40. Schaberg, *The Illegitimacy of Jesus,* 123. Also cf. Sarah B. Pomeroy, *Goddesses, Whores, Wives and Slaves* (New York: Schocken, 1975), 139–140, 191–193, 195–197.
41. Shiela Briggs, "Gender, Slavery, and Technology: The Shaping of the Early Christian Moral Imagination," in *Beyond Slavery*, ed. Brooten
42. Roy, "Protecting the Rights of Surrogate Mothers in India."
43. Catherine Belsey, "Constructing the Subject: Deconstructing the Text," in *Contemporary Literary Criticism*, ed. Robert Con Davis and Ronal Schleifer, 4th ed. (New York: Addison Wesley Longman , 1998), 381. Cf. Louis, Althusser, *Lenin and Philosophy and Other Essays,* trans. Ben Brewster (London: New Left Books, 1971), 169.
44. Colleen M. Conway, "Behold the Man! Masculine Christology and the Fourth Gospel," in *New Testament Masculinities*, ed. Stephen D. Moore and Janice Capel Anderson (Atlanta: Society of Biblical Literature, 2003), 164–165.
45. Karlsen Seim, *The Double Message,* 204.

46. Gayatri Chakravorty Spivak, "'Breast-Giver': For Author, Reader, Teacher, Subaltern, Historian...," in Mahasweta Devi, *Breast Stories* (Calcutta: Seagull Books, 2002), 93–94.
47. Haworth, "Surrogate Mothers: Wombs for Rent," 3.
48. Ibid., 4.
49. Karlsen Seim, *The Double Message*, 203.
50. Devi, *Breast Stories*, 47. "The Breast-Giver" depicts the tale of a Brahmin woman Jashoda, working as a wet nurse for another Hindu family. In making this move, Devi illustrates the way the economic value of a woman, performed by surrogacy, can overturn caste distinctions, and is replaced with class distinctions.
51. Ibid., 62.
52. Devi, *Breast Stories*, 54.
53. Karlsen Seim, *The Double Message,* 205.
54. Haworth, "Surrogate Mothers: Wombs for Rent," 7.
55. Desai, *Origins of Love,* 74.
56. Gail Sexton Anderson, "Surrogacy in India vs. Surrogacy in the United States," *Donor Concierge: A Donor/Surrogate Search and Consultation Service,* July 16, 2012, at http://donorconcierge.com/surrogacy-blog/surrogacy-india-vs-surrogacy-united-states-by-gail-sexton-anderson-edm (accessed on November 14, 2012)
57. Haworth, "Surrogate Mothers: Womb for Rent," 4.
58. Lee, "Commercial Surrogacy grows in India," 3.
59. Schaberg, *The Illegitimacy of Jesus,* 89. For example, some commentators and other scholars argue that the Magnificat in Luke must be interpreted as a battle song. Representative of this position is Paul Winter, "Magnificat and Benedictus—Maccabean Psalms?" *BJRL* Vol. 37 (1954): 328–347. Schaberg argues that while this line of argument seems plausible, it still fails to explain the revengeful tone of voice that is present throughout Mary's song. She writes: "There is a certain violence about it, and a note of revenge. It has been called 'Mary's Song of Victory,' but with the victory interpreted as 'spiritual' and the Lucan meaning unexamined" (89). Other scholars note that such sentiments seem strange because the words are placed in the mouth of a young girl.
60. Schaberg, *The Illegitimacy of Jesus,* 92. Schaberg draws on the work of Robert C. Tannehill, "The Magnificat as Poem," *Journal of Biblical Literature* Vol. 93 (1974): 263–275. She notes that Tannehill argues that the Magnificat must be read as "God's choice of the lowly mother and his overturning of society as *one* act." In this unique poetic vision of the text, "the mother's personal experience is already a fulfillment of the earth-shaking events which are still to come" (91).
61. Schaberg, *The Illegitimacy of Jesus*, 93. Cf. Joseph A. Fitzmyer, *The Gospel according to Luke I–IX* (New York: Doubleday, 1981), 367. This line of argument

goes back at least to Alfred Plummer, *A Critical and Exegetical Commentary on the Gospel according to St. Luke* (New York: Scribner's, 1903), 32.

62. Raymond E. Brown, *The Birth of the Messiah: A Commentary on the Infancy Narratives in the Gospels of Matthew and Luke* (Garden City, NY: Doubleday, 1977; rpt. New Haven, CT: Yale University Press, 1993), 448, n. 12. He writes: "This offering, rather than that of a lamb and a bird, is often adduced as a sign of the poverty of Jesus' parents. However, we are not certain that the alternative offered in Leviticus was still an active custom in Jesus's time."

63. Schaberg, *The Illegitimacy of Jesus,* 93. Cf. Bo Reicke, "Jesus, Simeon, and Anna (Luke 2:21–40)," in *Saved by Hope*, ed. J. I. Cook (Grand Rapids, MI: Eerdmans, 1978), 99.

64. Schaberg, *The Illegitimacy of Jesus*, 94. One of the feminist scholars who shares this sentiment is Rosemary Radford Ruether. In *Sexism and God Talk,* 152, she argues: "This text echoes the Hymn of Hannah, the mother of Samuel. Hannah's favor with God, which issues in the 'elect child,' is seen as God's redemptive favor upon Israel. Hannah's redemption by God from the shame of barrenness is used as an image of God's revolutionary power in history. God reverses the present order of power and powerlessness."

65. Schaberg, *The Illegitimacy of Jesus*, 95.

66. Ibid., 26.

67. Ruether, *Sexism and God Talk,* 152.

68. Elizabeth Johnson, "The Marian Tradition and the Reality of Women," *Horizons* Vol. 12, No. 1 (1985): 133.

69. Some of the other scholars who choose to read the tradition of illegitimacy into the infancy narrative are: Itulmeleng Mosala, *Biblical Hermeneutics and Black Theology in South Africa* (Grand Rapids, MI: W.B. Eerdmans Pub, 1989); Mary Daly, *Gyn/ecology: The Metaethics of Radical Feminism* (Boston, MA: Beacon Press, 1990); John Dominic Crossan, "Virgin Mother or Bastard Child?," in *A Feminist Companion to Mariology*, ed. Amy Jill Levine and Maria Mayo Robbins (London and New York: T&T Clark International, 2005), 37–55.

70. Ruether, *Sexism and God Talk,*152.

71. Ruether, *Sexism and God Talk*, 156. She writes, "Luke's sensitivity to women as members of the poor and the despised, whose faith is vindicated by the messianic prophets, adds an additional dimension to the identification of Mary as liberated Israel in the Magnificat." See also Johnson, "The Marian Tradition and the Reality of Women," 133. In this regard at least, both Ruether and Johnson advance interpretations very similar to those of Fitzmyer, Brown, and other traditionally minded male exegetes.

72. Johnson, "The Marian Tradition and the Reality of Women," 133.

73. Ruether, *Sexism and God Talk,* 155.

74. Ibid., 155.

75. Johnson, "The Marian Tradition and the Reality of Women," 133.

76. Hardt and Negri, *Empire,* 144.

77. Pande, "Commercial Surrogacy in India," 988.
78. Johnson, "The Marian Tradition and the Reality of Women," 133.
79. Pande, "Commercial Surrogacy in India," 988.
80. Ibid., 156.
81. Jean K. Kim notes that "women might be the mothers of the nation, repro-
    ducing its biological future, nurturing the next generation, and teaching the
    mother tongue [yet] women's status has remained that of reproducers rather
    than producers, prized and revered objects of protection rather than agents in
    their own rights." *Woman and Nation: An Intercontextual Reading of the Gospel
    of John from a Postcolonial Feminist Perspective* (Boston, MA: Brill, 2004), 22.
82. Ruether, *Sexism and God Talk*, 157.
83. Ibid., 152.
84. Ibid., 153. Her view is also shared by biblical scholar, Mary F. Foskett, who
    points out: "Although no response is sought by the angel, Mary makes a choice
    in a situation where none is demanded. By offering her consent, the virgin
    asserts her own voice into the scene." This reading allows Foskett to argue
    that Mary's consent defines her as an independent woman. Foskett, *A Virgin
    Conceived*, 124.
85. Mary Daly, *Gyn/ecology: The Metaethics of Radical Feminism*, 84.
86. Ibid., 85.
87. Ibid.
88. Johnson, "The Marian Tradition and the Reality of Women," 118.
89. Elizabeth Johnson, "Truly Our Sister: A Feminist Hermeneutical Disciplinary
    Approach," in *The Many Faces of Mary*, ed. Diego Irarrázabal, Susan Ross, and
    Marie-Theres Wacker (London: SCM Press, 2008), 14.
90. Ibid., 133.
91. Ibid. She writes: "[T]he image of Mary as a virgin has significance as the
    image of a woman from whose personal center power wells up, a woman who
    symbolizes the independence of the identity of woman." Mary's virginity is
    interpreted by both Capel Anderson and Johnson as eluding patriarchal con-
    trol thereby resulting in her independence and ultimately her agency in the
    text.
92. Ibid., 117. Derrida's concept of the hymen, however, has been critiqued by
    other feminist scholars. Roberta Weston, for example, argues that the his-
    tory of the hymen is embedded in patriarchy, and this detail has been over-
    looked by Derrida. "Free Gift or Forced Figure? Derrida's Usage of Hymen in
    'The Double Session,'" in *Language and Liberation: Feminism, Philosophy and
    Language*, ed. Christina Hendricks and Kelly Oliver (Albany: State University
    of New York Press, 1999), 299–321.
93. Beattie, "Redeeming Mary: The Potential of Marian Symbolism for Feminist
    Philosophy of Religion," in *Feminist Philosophy of Religion: Critical Readings*,
    ed. Pamela Sue Anderson and Beverley Clark (New York and London:
    Routledge, 2004), 118.
94. Ibid.

95. Anne Elvey, *An Ecological Feminist Reading of the Gospel of Luke: A Gestational Paradigm* (Lewiston, NY: Edwin Mellen Press, 2005), 116.

96. Ibid., 115. Cf. Jane-Maree Maher, "The Promiscuous Placenta: Crossing Over," in *Contagion: Historical and Social Studies*, ed. Alison Bashford and Claire Hooker (London and New York: Routledge, 2001), 301–315. While the emergence of the placenta for Maher becomes the moment when the oneness of pregnancy is split into two—the fetus gains its own reserves—Kristeva focuses on the umbilical cord which, when cut, becomes the moment of separation between mother and child. Kristeva writes: "Then there is this other abyss that opens up between the body and what had been its inside: there is the abyss between the mother and the child. What connection is there between myself, or even more unassumingly between my body and this internal graft and fold, which, once the umbilical cord has been severed, is an inaccessible other? . . . the abyss between what was mine and is henceforth but irreparably alien." "Stabat Mater" (French original 1983), trans. Leon S. Roudiez, in *The Kristeva Reader*, ed. Toril Moi (London and New York: Routledge, 1986), 178.

97. Elvey, *An Ecological Feminist Reading*, 120–121. However, while Ruether and Foskett read Mary's consent as marking her liberated status, Elvey raises the question, "Can the reader know for sure whether Mary's consent is necessary for the divine will to be done in her?"

98. Ibid., 121.

99. Deborah Sawyer, "Hidden Subjects: Rereading Eve and Mary," *Theology and Sexuality*, Vol. 14, No. 3 (2008): 306.

100. Ibid., 315.

101. Cf. Ann Loades, "The Virgin Mary and the Feminist Quest," in *After Eve*, ed. Jane Martin Soskice (Basingstoke: Marshall Pickering, 1990), 163. She writes: "The language of perfection is thus largely transferred to the Church, a somewhat problematical move, but . . . Mary is still in contrast with 'Eve'— all other women—and it does not take much expertise to discover how they are to be viewed." In other words, Christian women are socially conditioned to see themselves as reflections of Eve (sexual and impure) who are unable but still must try to reach the goddess status of Mary.

102. Sawyer, "Hidden Subjects," 319.

103. Ibid.

5   The Synoptic Marys and the Synoptic Hierarchies

1. Yolanda Dreyer, "Gender Critique on the Narrator's Androcentric Point of View of Women in Matthew's Gospel," in *HTS Teologiese Studies/Theological Studies* Vol. 67, No. 1 (2011): 2–3. Also cf. Craig. S. Keener, *The Gospel of Matthew: A Socio-Rhetorical Commentary*, (Grand Rapids, MI: Eerdmans , 2009), 88.

2. Jean Dean Kingsbury, "The Birth Narrative of Matthew," in *The Gospel of Matthew in Current Study*, ed. David E. Aune (Grand Rapids, MI: Eerdmans Publishing, 2001), 158.
3. Wilhelmus J. C. Weren, "The Five Women in Matthew's Genealogy," in *Catholic Biblical Quarterly*, Vol. 59, No. 2 (April 1997): 304.
4. Elaine Wainwright, *Shall We Look for Another? A Feminist Reading of the Matthean Jesus* (New York: Orbis Books, 1998), 58.
5. Dale C. Allison Jr. "Divorce, Celibacy and Joseph (Matthew 1:18–25 and 19:1–12)," *Journal for the Study of New Testament* Vol. 49 (1993): 4. Dale C. Allison illustrates the relevant point but does not parse this line of thought any further. He states: "In 1:19–25 we are told that Mary became pregnant through the Holy Spirit, that Joseph first learned of her pregnancy without learning of its supernatural cause, and that therefore Joseph determined to obtain a certificate of divorce."
6. Amy Jill Levine, "Matthew," In *The Women's Bible Commentary,* ed. Carol A. Newsom and Sharon H. Ringe. 2nd ed. (Louisville, KY: Westminster John Knox Press, 1998), 341. As Amy Jill Levine notes: "Matthew explains the virgin birth as the prophetic fulfilment of Isa 7:14. Although the Hebrew version of Isaiah states simply that a 'young woman' has conceived, the Greek version of this passage (the Septuagint) which Matthew follows, translates the term for 'young woman' as *parthenos,* or 'virgin'."
7. Deepali Gaur, "Rent-A-Womb: Surrogacy in India on the Rise," January 25, 2008, at rent-a-womb-surrogacy-in-india-on-the-rise (accessed October 5, 2012).
8. Amrit Dhillon, "Mothers for Hire," September 7, 2012, at http://www.theage.com.au/national/mothers-for-hire-20120906–25hi1.html (accessed October 5, 2012). As one journalist reports: A failed business venture is the reason why Neetu Sangar, 32, is sitting in the Delhi Research Centre of Dr Anoop Gupta, a pioneer of IVF in India. The cavernous waiting rooms, humming with the sound of air conditioners and fans, are packed with childless couples. Gupta's own room is like a thoroughfare as couples come and go, talking about embryos. Sangar is one of Dr Gupta's surrogates. Even though surrogacy is only five percent of his work, he has delivered more than 300 surrogate babies in the past few years. Pale and thin, Sangar is four months pregnant with twins in her second surrogacy for a Singaporean couple. In her first, she delivered twins to a Lebanese couple. Her motive is to be able to give her two children an education and a happier life. What happened to the 300,000 rupees she earned from the first pregnancy? She looks down at the ground, sheepishly. She speaks in a whisper, embarrassed about being overheard: "My husband started a business—selling water purifiers. It didn't work out and we lost the money. That's why I'm here again." Gupta asks Sangar to stand up and he praises her as a "decent, clean woman" to the couple who are the potential commissioning parents.

9. Dorothy Jean Weaver, "Whenever This Good News Is Proclaimed: Women and God in the Gospel of Matthew," *Interpretation* Vol. 65, No. 4 (October 2010): 395. As Weaver observes: Joseph's response could mean not only "disgrace" for Mary, but also the ultimate failure of Abraham's family line to reach its God-intended climax in the birth of "the Messiah" (1:1, 16,17,18). However, Joseph knows nothing of God's messianic plans for Jesus. Joseph responds as he must. While he ponders the unthinkable legal response of "public disgrace for Mary (1:19b), he is a righteous man" (1:19a) who opts instead for a private divorce (1:19c).

10. Pande, "Commercial Surrogacy Grows in India," *San Francisco Chronicle,* October 20, 2012, 974.

11. Divya Gupta, "Inside India's Surrogacy Industry" December 6, 2011, at http://www.guardian.co.uk/world/2011/dec/06/surrogate-mothers-india (accessed October 5, 2012) Divya Gupta interviewed a surrogate mother named Ranju Rajubhai: When an accident left 32-year-old Ranju Rajubhai's husband severely burned and unable to work, surrogacy seemed the answer to the couple's problems. "I thought I'll be doing a good deed, my work will also get done and [the couple] will also get a baby," says Rajubhai who is due in a month. Like all the women signed on by Akanksha, Rajubhai will receive $6,225, the equivalent of seven years wages for her husband. "I will get my husband's surgery done [for his burns]," she says. "I also want to buy a house. It costs [$14,500 -$18,500] these days. One pregnancy won't be enough, so I am thinking of coming back."

12. Jerome H. Neyrey, "Jesus, Gender, and the Gospel of Matthew," in *New Testament Masculinities,* ed. Moore and Anderson (Atlanta: Society of Biblical Literature, 2003), 60.

13. Michael Hardt and Antonio Negri, *Empire* (Cambridge, MA: Harvard University Press, 2000), 121, their emphasis.

14. Deborah L. Spar, "For Love and Money: The Political Economy of Commercial Surrogacy," *Review of International Political Economy* Vol. 12, No. 2 (May 2005): 302.

15. Nelson M. Rodriguez, "Emptying the Content of Whiteness: Toward an Understanding of the Relation between Whiteness and Pedagogy," in *White Reign: Deploying Whiteness in America*, ed. Joe L. Kincheloe, Shirley R. Steinberg, Nelson M. Rodriguez, and Ronald E. Chennault (New York: St. Martin's Press, 2000), 39. Also see Richard M. Dyer, *White: Essays on Race and Culture* (New York and London: Routledge,1998).

16. Helen Roberts and Francis Hardy, "Our 'rent a womb' Child from an Indian Baby Farm: British Couple Paying £20,000 for a Desperately Poor Single Mother to Have Their Child," *Mail Online*, August 31, 2012, at http://www.dailymail.co.uk/femail/article-2196538/Our-rent-womb-child-Indian-baby-farm-British-couple-paying-20-000-desperately-poor-single-mother-child.htm (accessed on November 26, 2012).

17. Homi K. Bhabha, *The Location of Culture* (New York and London: Routledge, 1994), 101. Homi Bhabha writes: "[C]olonial discourse produces the colonized as a social reality which is at once an 'other' and yet entirely knowable and visible. It resembles a form of narrative whereby the productivity and circulation of subjects and signs are bound in a reformed and recognizable totality. It employs a system of representation, a regime of truth, that is structurally similar to realism."

18. Hardt and Negri, *Empire*, 145.

19. Kishwar Desai, *Origins of Love* (London: Simon & Schuster UK, 2012), 74.

20. Kalpana Seshadri-Crooks, *Desiring Whiteness: A Lacanian Analysis of Race* (London and New York: Routledge, 2000), 21.

21. The word *saala* in Hindi literally means "wife's brother"; however, in India this word is used as an expletive. *Banjo* is another slang word used in Hindi and literally it means "sister f***er." In the Indian context, this word is even more volatile than its English counterpart, "mother f***er"

22. Ibid., 39.

23. Alfred J. Lopez, "Introduction: Whiteness after Empire," in *Postcolonial Whiteness: A Critical Reader on Race and Empire*, ed. Alfred J. Lopez (Albany: State University of New York Press, 2005), 20. Alfred J. Lopez argues: This notion of whiteness as an explicit and implicit cultural ideal—of beauty, desirability, virtue, purity—lingers in the postcolonial world in surprising ways, and presents a formidable obstacle for both subjects of color and whites who find themselves marginalized in some other way (by nationality, ethnicity, gender, sexuality, etc.), who either strive for an unattainable ideal (Bhabha's "almost but not quite.") or must learn to assert their own cultural difference in the face of the universalized white norm.

24. Desai, *Origins of Love*, 74.

25. Amrit Dhillon, "The Indian Obsession for Fairer Skin Sinks to a New Low," *National Times,* May 23, 2012, at http://www.smh.com.au/opinion/society-and-culture/the-indian-obsession-with-fairer-skin-sinks-to-a-new-low-20120522-1z300.html (accessed November 26, 2012).

26. Alfred J. Lopez, *Posts and Pasts: A Theory of Postcolonialism* (Albany: State University of New York Press, 2001), 86.

27. As Nupur Chaudhuri notes in her article, "Memsahibs and Motherhood in Nineteenth Century Colonial India," *Victorian Studies* Vol. 31, No. 4 (Summer, 1998): 530, citing Major S. Leigh and Alexander S. Kenny, *Tropical Trials: A Hand-book for Women in the Tropics*: "Hunt and Kenny emphasized in tropical Trials that by learning the local language a child's little mind will soon become contaminated with ideas and expressions that would utterly horrify the mother did she herself understand the language of the country. Because of their own ignorance of native languages, most British mothers could not follow their children's conversation with their servants. This made many mothers insecure, and they often became anxious to send their children to Britain for this reason as well as for physical health."

28. Catherine Belsey, "Constructing the Subject: Deconstructing the Text," in *Contemporary Literary Criticism,* ed. Robert Con Davis and Ronald Schleifer. 4th ed. (New York: Addison Wesley Longman Inc., 1998), 382.

Conclusion

1. Rosemary Radford Ruether, *Sexism and God Talk: Toward a Feminist Theology* (Boston, MA: Beacon Press, 1983), 143–144.
2. Jane Schaberg, *The Illegitimacy of Jesus: A Feminist Theological Interpretation of the Infancy Narratives, Expanded Twentieth Anniversary Edition.* Sheffield: Sheffield Phoenix Press, 2006), 25.
3. Ibid., 28.
4. To name a few: Mary Foskett, *A Virgin Conceived: Mary and Classical Representations of Virginity* (Bloomington: Indiana University Press, 2002); Itulmeleng Mosala, *Biblical Hermeneutics and Black Theology in South Africa* (Grand Rapids, MI: W.B. Eerdmans; Cheryl A. Kirk-Duggan, "Proud Mary: Contextual Constructions of a Divine Diva," in *Blessed One: Protestant Perspectives on Mary* (London: Westminster John Knox Press, 2002).
5. Kwok Pui-lan, *Postcolonial Imagination and Feminist Theology* (Kentucky: Westminster John Knox Press, 2005), 36.
6. Chandra Talpade Mohanty, *Feminism Without Borders: Decolonizing Theory, Practicing Solidarity* (London: Duke University Press, 2003), 20.
7. Deborah L. Spar, "For Love and Money: The Political Economy of Commercial Surrogacy" *Review of International Political Economy* Vol. 12, No. 2 (May 2005): 302, quoting Kelly Oliver, "Marxism and Surrogacy," *Hypatia* Vol. 4 (1989): 99.
8. Michael Hardt and Antonio Negri, *Empire* (Cambridge, MA: Harvard University Press), 131.
9. Ibid., 157. Hardt and Negri continue, "The poor is distinguished no longer only by its prophetic capacity but also by its indispensable presence in the production of common wealth, always more exploited and always more closely indexed to the wages of rule. The poor itself is power. There is World Poverty, but there is above all World Possibility, and only the poor is capable of this."
10. Ruether, *Sexism and God Talk,* 156–157.

Bibliography

A Lady Resident. *The Englishwoman in India: Containing Information for the Use of Ladies Proceeding to, or Residing in, the East Indies, on the Subjects of their Outfit, Furniture, Housekeeping, the Rearing of Children, Duties and Wages of Servants, Management of the Stables, and Arrangements for Travelling to which are added Receipts for Indian cookery.* London: Smith, Elder, 1864.

Abasili, Alexander Izchukwu. "Was it Rape? The David and Bathsheba Pericope Reexamined." *Vestus Testamentum* Vol. 61 (2011).

Allison, Dale C. "Divorce, Celibacy and Joseph (Matthew 1:18–25 and 19:1–12)." *Journal for the Study of New Testament* Vol. 49 (1993).

Althusser, Louis. *Lenin and Philosophy and Other Essays.* Trans. Ben Brewster. New York: Monthly Review Press, 1971.

Anderson, Elizabeth S. "Is Women's Labor a Commodity?" *Philosophy & Public Affairs* Vol. 19, No. 1 (Winter 1990).

Anderson, Gail Sexton. "Surrogacy in India vs. Surrogacy in the United States." *Donor Concierge: A Donor/Surrogate Search and Consultation Service*, July 16, 2012: http://donorconcierge.com/surrogacy-blog/surrogacy-india-vs-surrogacy-united-states-by-gail-sexton-anderson-edm (accessed November 14, 2012).

Anderson, Janice Capel. "Mary's Difference: Gender and Patriarchy in the Birth Narratives." *The Journal of Religion* Vol. 67, No. 2 (1987).

Anderson, Janice Capel. "Matthew: Gender and Reading." *Semeia* Vol. 28 (1983).

Anderson, Janice Capel and Stephen D. Moore. "Matthew and Masculinity." In *New Testament Masculinities*, ed. Stephen D. Moore and Janice Capel Anderson. Atlanta: Society of Biblical Literature, 2003.

Arieff, Adrienne. "Having Twins with a Surrogate—in India." *The New York Times,* March 16, 2012: http://parenting.blogs.nytimes.com/ . . . /having-twins-with-a-surrogate-in-india/ (accessed October 25, 2012).

Baraitser, Lisa. *Maternal Encounters: The Ethics of Interruption.* New York and London: Routledge, 2009.

Beattie, Tina. "Redeeming Mary: The Potential of Marian Symbolism for Feminist Philosophy of Religion." In *Feminist Philosophy of Religion: Critical Readings*, ed. Pamela Sue Anderson and Beverley Clark. New York and London: Routledge, 2004.

Belsey, Catherine. "Constructing the Subject: Deconstructing the Text." In *Contemporary Literary Criticism,* ed. Robert Con Davis and Ronald Schleifer. 4th ed. New York: Addison Wesley Longman Inc., 1998.

Benveniste, Emile. *Problems in General Linguistics.* Miami: University of Miami Press, 1971.

Bhabha, Homi K. *The Location of Culture.* New York and London: Routledge, 1994.

Bloch, R. "Juda engendra Phar`es et Zara, de Thamar (Matt 1, 3)." In *Melanges bibliques rediges en l'honneur de Andre Robert.* Paris: Bloud & Gay, 1957.

Borresen, Kari. "Mary in Catholic Theology." In *Mary in the Churches, Concilium 168,* ed. Hans Küng and Jürgen Moltmann. New York: Seabury, 1983.

Boslooper, Thomas. *The Virgin Birth.* Philadelphia, PA: The Westminster Press, 1962.

Briggs, Sheila. "Gender, Slavery, and Technology: The Shaping of the Early Christian Moral Imagination." In *Beyond Slavery,* ed. Bernadette J. Brooten. New York: Palgrave Macmillan, 2010.

Brown, Raymond E. "The Annunciation to Joseph (Matt 1:18–25)." *Worship* Vol. 61. No. 6 (1987).

Brown, Raymond E. *The Birth of the Messiah, A Commentary on the Infancy Narratives in the Gospels of Matthew and Luke.* Garden City, NY: Doubleday, 1977; rpt. New Haven, CT: Yale University Press, 1993.

Brown, Raymond E., Karl P. Donfried, Joseph A. Fitzmyer, and John Reumann, eds. *Mary in the New Testament.* New York: Paulist Press, 1978.

Brown, Raymond E., Karl P. Donfried, Joseph A. Fitzmeyer, and John Reumann, eds., *Mary in the New Testament.* New York: Paulist Press, 1978.

Brown, Raymond E. *The Virginal Conception and Bodily Resurrection of Jesus.* New York: Paulist Press, 1973.

Brown, Raymond E. "The Problem of the Virginal Conception of Jesus." *Theological Studies* Vol. 33, No. 1 (1972).

Burton, Antoinette. *Burden of History: British Feminists, Indian Women and Imperial Culture, 1865–1915.* Chapel Hill: University of North Carolina Press, 1994.

Butler, Judith. *Gender Trouble: Feminism and the Subversion of Identity.* New York and London: Routledge, 1990.

Campbell, Edward F. *Ruth: A New Translation with Introduction, Notes, and Commentary.* Anchor Bible 7. Garden City, NY: Doubleday, 1975.

Chaudhari, Nupur. "Memsahibs and Motherhood in Nineteenth-Century Colonial India." *Victorian Studies* Vol. 31, No. 4 (Summer 1998).

Chodorow, Nancy. *The Reproduction of Mothering: Psychoanalysis and the Sociology of Gender.* Berkeley: University of California Press, 1978.

Chopra, Anuj. "Childless Couples Look to India for Surrogate Mothers." *The Christian Science Monitor,* April 3, 2006: http://www.csmonitor.com/2006/0403/p01s04-wosc.html/(page) (accessed September 26, 2012).

Conway, Colleen M. "Behold the Man! Masculine Christology and the Fourth Gospel." In *New Testament Masculinities,* ed. Stephen D. Moore and Janice Capel Anderson. Atlanta: Society of Biblical Literature, 2003.

Corrington, Gail Patterson. *Her Image of Salvation: Female Saviors and Formative Christianity*. Louisville, KY: Westminster John Knox Press, 1992.

Crooks, Kalpana Seshadri. *Desiring Whiteness: A Lacanian Analysis of Race*. London and New York: Routledge, 2000.

Crossan, John Dominic. "Virgin Mother or Bastard Child?" In *A Feminist Companion to Mariology*, ed. Amy Jill Levine and Maria Mayo Robbins. London and New York: T&T Clark International, 2005.

Daly, Mary. *Gyn/ecology: The Metaethics of Radical Feminism*. Boston, MA: Beacon Press, 1990.

Datta, Damayanti. "Infertility on the Rise." *India Today*, July 5, 2010: http://indiatoday.intoday.in/story/infertility-on-the-rise/2/103037.html (accessed on October 26, 2012).

Davis, Angela Y. "Outcaste Mothers and Surrogates: Racism and Reproduction Politics in the Nineties." *Feminist Theory: A Reader*, ed. Wendy K. Kolmar and Frances Bartkowski. Boston, MA: McGraw Hill, 2005.

Deonandan, Raywat. "The Ethics of Surrogacy." *India Currents,* February 3, 2012: http://www.indiacurrents.com/articles/2012/02/03/ethics-surrogacy (accessed on October 26, 2012).

Desai, Kishwar. "India's Surrogate Mothers Are Risking Their Lives. They Urgently Need Protection." *The Guardian,* June 5, 2012: http://www.guardian.co.uk/commentisfree/2012/jun/05/india-surrogates-impoverished-die (accessed on October 10, 2012).

Desai, Kishwar. *Origins of Love*. London: Simon & Schuster UK Ltd, 2012.

Desai, Santosh. "Towards a Cultural War." *The Times of India,* January 6, 2013: http://blogs.timesofindia.indiatimes.com/Citycitybangbang/entry/towards-a-cultural-war (accessed on January 8, 2013).

Devi, Mahasweta. *Breast Stories*. Trans. with introductory essays by Gayatri Chakravorty Spivak. Calcutta: Seagull Books, 2002.

Dhillon, Amrit. "Mothers for Hire." *The Age*, September 7, 2012: http://www.theage.com.au/national/mothers-for-hire-20120906–25hi1.html (accessed October 5, 2012).

Dhillon, Amrit. "The Indian Obsession for Fairer Skin Sinks to a New Low." *National Times*, May 23, 2012: http://www.smh.com.au/opinion/society-and-culture/the-indian-obsession-with-fairer-skin-sinks-to-a-new-low-20120522–1z300.html (accessed November 26, 2012).

Diver, Maud. *The Englishwoman in India*. London: Blackwood, 1909.

Dreyer, Yolanda. "Gender Critique on the Narrator's Androcentric Point of View of Women in Matthew's Gospel." *HTS Teologiese Studies* Vol. 67, No. 1 (2011).

Dutta, Sangeeta. "Relinquishing the Halo: Portrayal of Mother in Indian Writing in English." *Economic and Political Weekly* Vol. 25, Nos. 42/43 (October 1990).

Dyer, Richard M. *White: Essays on Race and Culture*. New York and London: Routledge, 1998.

Ehrenreich, Barbara and Arlie Russell Hoschschild, eds. *Global Woman: Nannies, Maids, and Sex Workers in the New Economy*. New York: Metropolitan, 2003.

Elvey, Anne. *An Ecological Feminist Reading of the Gospel of Luke: A Gestational Paradigm*. Lewiston, NY: Edwin Mellen Press, 2005.

Ewart, Joseph. *Goodeve's Hint For the General Management of Children in India*. 6th ed. Calcutta: Thacker, Spink, 1872.

Fewell, Danna Nolan. "Joshua." In *The Women's Biblical Commentary*, eds. Carol A. Newsom and Sharon H. Ringe. 2nd ed. Louisville, KY: Westminster John Knox Press, 1998.

Fitzmyer, Joseph A. *The Gospel According to Luke I-IX*. Anchor Bible 28. Garden City, NY: Doubleday, 1981.

Fitzmyer, Joseph A. "The Virginal Conception of Jesus in the New Testament." *Theological Studies* Vol. 34, No. 4 (1973).

Foskett, Mary F. *A Virgin Conceived: Mary and Classical Representations of Virginity*. Bloomington: Indiana University Press, 2002.

Gaur, Deepali. "Rent-A-Womb: Surrogacy in India on the Rise," January 25, 2008: rent-a-womb-surrogacy-in-india-on-the-rise (accessed October 5, 2012).

Gentleman, Amelia. "India Nurtures Business of Surrogate Motherhood," *New York Times*, March 10, 2008: http://www.nytimes.com/2008/03/10/world/asia/10surrogate.html (accessed on October 20, 2009).

George, Marangoly. "Homes in the Empire, Empire in the Homes." *Cultural Critique* Vol. 26 (Winter 1993–1994).

Ghosh, Sagarika. "Is Surrogacy Leading to Exploitation of Poor Women?" *CNN-IBN*, June 19, 2012: http://www. ibnlive.in.com/news/is-surrogacy-leading-to-exploitation-of-poor-women/266801-3.html (accessed August 8, 2012).

Glancy, Jennifer A. "Early Christianity, Slavery and Women's Bodies." In *Beyond Slavery: Overcoming its Religious and Sexual Legacies*, ed. Bernadette J. Brooten. New York: Palgrave Macmillan, 2010.

Gnuse, Robert. "Dream Genre in the Matthean Infancy Narratives." *Novum Testamentum* Vol. 32 (1990).

Goleman, Daniel. "Motivations of Surrogate Mothers." *New York Times*, January 20, 1987.

Grossman, Joyce. "Ayahs, Dhayes, and Bearers: Mary Sherwood's Indian Experience and Constructions of Subordinated Others." *South Atlantic Review* Vol. 66, No. 2 (2001).

Gunn, David M. and Danna Nolan Fewell. *Narrative in the Hebrew Bible*. New York: Oxford University Press, 1993.

Gupta, Divya. "Inside India's Surrogacy Industry." December 6, 2011: http://www.guardian.co.uk/world/2011/dec/06/surrogate-mothers-india990 (accessed October 5, 2012).

Gupta, Jyotsna Agnihotri. "Towards Transnational Feminisms: Some Reflection and Concerns in Relation to the Globalization of Reproductive Technologies." *European Journal of Women's Studies* Vol. 23 (2006).

Hackett, Jo Ann. "1 and 2 Samuel." In *The Women's Biblical Commentary*, ed. Carol Newsom and Sharon H. Ringe. 2nd ed. Louisville, KY: Westminster John Knox Press, 1998.

Haimowitz, Rebecca and Vaishali Sinha. "Made in India": http://www.madeinindiamovie.com/the-film.html (accessed October 5, 2012).

Halperin, David. *One Hundred Years of Homosexuality: And Other Essays on Greek Love*. New York and London: Routledge, 1990.

Hardt, Michael and Antonio Negri. *Empire*. Cambridge, MA: Harvard University Press, 2000.

Haworth, Abagail. "Surrogate Mothers: Wombs for Rent." *Marie Claire,* July 29, 2007: www.marieclaire.com/world…/news/…/surrogate-mothers-india.

Hewitson, Gillian. "The Market for Surrogate Mother Contracts." *The Economic Record* Vol. 73, No. 22 (September 1997).

Ions, Veronica. *Indian Mythology*. New York: P. Bendrick Books, 1983.

Jacobson, Edith. *The Self and the Object World*. New York: International University Press, 1964.

Janovich, Adriana. "Surrogacy a Booming Business in India." *Yakhima Herald-Republic*, August 4, 2012: http://www.yakima-herald.com/…/surrogacy-a-booming-business-in-indiaCached (accessed August 7, 2012).

Jerome. *The Fathers of the Church: Commentary on Matthew*. Trans. Thomas P. Scheck. Washington, DC: Catholic University of America Press, 2008.

Johar, Roshni. "When Will We Be Fair to Women's Skin?" *The Tribune*, December 7, 2003: http://www.tribuneindia.com/2003/20031207/herworld.htm (accessed on October 26, 2011).

Johnson, Elizabeth. "The Marian Tradition and the Reality of Women." *Horizons* Vol. 12, No 1 (1985).

Johnson, Elizabeth. "Truly Our Sister: A Feminist Hermeneutical Disciplinary Approach." In *The Many Faces of Mary*, ed. Diego Irarrazabal, Susan Ross, and Marie-Theres Wacker. London: SCM Press, 2008.

Johnson, Marshall D. *The Purpose of the Biblical Genealogies with Special Reference to the Setting of the Genealogies of Jesus*. New Testament Studies Monograph Series, 8. Cambridge: Cambridge University Press, 1969.

Kapur, Ratna. "No Country for Young Women." *The Hindu*, August 18, 2012: http://www.thehindu.com/opinion/op-ed/article3785967.ece (accessed on October 29, 2012).

Karlsen Seim, Turid. "The Virgin Mother: Mary and Ascetic Discipleship in Luke." In *A Feminist Companion to Luke,* ed. Amy-Jill Levine. London: Sheffield Academic Press, 2002.

Kartrak, Ketu H. *Politics of the Female Body: Postcolonial Women Writers of the Third World*. New Brunswick, NJ: Rutgers University Press, 2006.

Keener, Craig. S. *The Gospel of Matthew: A Socio-Rhetorical Commentary*. Grand Rapids, MI: Eerdmans, 2009.

Kim, Jean K. *Woman and Nation: An Intercontextual Reading of the Gospel of John from a Postcolonial Feminist Perspective*. Boston, MA: Brill, 2004.

Kingsbury, Jean Dean. "The Birth Narrative of Matthew." In *The Gospel of Matthew in Current Study*, ed. David E. Aune. Grand Rapids, MI: Eerdmans, 2001.

Kirk-Duggan, Cheryl A. "Proud Mary: Contextual Constructions of a Divine Diva." In *Blessed One: Protestant Perspectives on Mary*, ed. Beverly Roberts Gaventa and Cynthia L. Rigby. Louisville, KY: Westminster John Knox Press, 2002.

Kristeva, Julia. "Stabat Mater" (French original 1983). Trans. Leon S. Roudiez. In Toril Moi, ed., *The Kristeva Reader*. London and New York: Routledge, 1986.

Lee, Stephanie M. "Commercial Surrogacy grows in India." *San Francisco Chronicle*, October 20, 2012: http://www.sfgate.com/health/article/Commercial-surrogacy-grows-in-India 3968312.php (accessed on October 30, 2012).

Lacan, Jacques. *The Seminars of Jacques Lacan, Book I: Freud's Papers on Technique*, ed. Jacques-Alain Miller. Trans. John Forrester. New York: Norton. 1988.

Lazro, Fred DeSam. "Surrogate Mothers in India." *Religion and Ethics Newsweekly*, September 30: http://www.pbs.org/wnet/religionandethics/episodes/september-30–2011/surrogate-mothers-in-india/9612/ (accessed on October 8, 2012).

Leistikow, Nicole. "Indian Women Criticize Fair and Lovely Ideal." *The World*, April 28, 2003: http://www.womensenews.org/article.cfm/dyn/aid/1308/context/archive (accessed on October 27, 2011).

Levine, Amy Jill. "Matthew." In *The Women's Bible Commentary*, ed. Carol A. Newsom and Sharon H. Ringe. 2nd ed. Louisville, KY: Westminster John Knox Press, 1998.

Levine, Amy-Jill. "Ruth." In *The Women's Bible Commentary,* ed. Carol A. Newsom and Sharon H. Ringe. 2nd ed. Louisville, KY: Westminster John Knox Press, 1998.

Liew, Tat Siong Benny. "Re-Markable Masculinities: Jesus, The Son of Man, and the (Sad) Sum of Manhood?" In *New Testament Masculinities*, ed. Stephen D. Moore and Janice Capel Anderson. Atlanta: Society of Biblical Literature, 2003.

Loades, Ann. "The Virgin Mary and the Feminist Quest." In *After Eve*, ed. Jane Martin Soskice. Basingstoke, UK: Marshall Pickering, 1990.

Longscope, Kay. "Standing up for Mary Beth." *Boston Globe*, March 5, 1987.

Lopez, Alfred J. "Introduction: Whiteness After Empire." In *Postcolonial Whiteness: A Critical Reader on Race and Empire*, ed. Alfred J. Lopez. Albany: State University of New York Press, 2005.

Lopez, Alfred J. *Posts and Pasts: A Theory of Postcolonialism*. Albany, NY: State University of New York Press, 2001.

Maher, Jane-Maree. "The Promiscuous Placenta: Crossing Over." In *Contagion: Historical and Cultural Studies,* ed. Alison Bashford and Claire Hooker. New York and London: Routledge, 2001.

Maigner, Mark. "A Bundle of Joy with Baggage: Indian Surrogacy Is Successful but New Parents Feel Duped." *Los Angeles Times*, April 18, 2011: http://articles.latimes.com/2011/apr/18/world/la-fg-india-surrogacy-20110418 (accessed on October 26, 2011).

Mair, R. S. "Supplement on the Management of Children in India." In *Medical Guide for Anglo-Indians*. New Delhi: Asian Educational Services, 2004 (first published in 1878).

Maitland, Julia. *Letters from Madras, during the Years 1836–38, by a Lady.* London: John Murray, 1846.

Marx, Karl. *Capital: A Critique of Political Economy.* Trans. Ben Fowkes. Madison Park: Pacific Publishing Studio, 2010.

Meyers, Carol. "Everyday Life: Women in the Period of the Hebrew Bible." In *The Women's Bible Commentary,* ed. Carol A. Newsom and Sharon H. Ringe. 2nd ed. Louisville, KY: Westminster John Knox Press, 1998.

Minh ha, Trinh T. *Woman, Native, Other: Writing, Postcoloniality and Feminism.* Indianapolis: Indiana University Press, 1989.

Mohanty, Chandra Talpade. "Under Western Eyes: Feminist Scholarship and Colonial Discourses." *Feminist Review* Vol. 30 (1988).

Mohanty, Chandra Talpade. *Feminism without Borders: Decolonizing Theory, Practicing Solidarity.* Durham, NC: Duke University Press, 2003.

Mosala, Itulmeleng, J. *Biblical Hermeneutics and Black Theology in South Africa.* Grand Rapids, MI: Eerdmans, 1989.

Mukherjee, Kritivas. "Rent-a-womb in India Fuels Surrogate Motherhood Debate." *The Washington Post,* February 4, 2007: http://www.geneticsandsociety.org/article.php?id=3386 (accessed on October 15, 2009).

Mulvey, Laura. "Visual Pleasure and Narrative Cinema." In *Feminist Theory: A Reader,* ed. Wendy K. Kolmar and Frances Bartkowski. 2nd ed. New York: McGraw-Hill, 2005.

Nast, Heidi. "Mapping the 'Unconscious': Racism and the Oedipal Family." *Annals of the Association of American Geographer* Vol. 90, No. 2 (June 2000).

Newton, Esther. *Mother Camp: Female Impersonators in America.* Chicago: University of Chicago Press, 1972.

Neyrey, Jerome H. "Jesus, Gender, and the Gospel of Matthew." In *New Testament Masculinities,* ed. Stephen D. Moore and Janice Capel Anderson. Atlanta: Society of Biblical Literature, 2003.

Oliver, Kelly and Christina Hendricks. *Language and Liberation: Feminist, Philosophy and Language.* Albany, NY: State University of New York Press, 1999.

Oliver, Kelly. "Marxism and Surrogacy." *Hypatia* Vol. 4 (1989).

Palattiyil, George, Eric Blyth, Dina Sidhva and Geeta Balakrishnan. "Globalization and Cross-border Reproductive Services: Ethical Implications of Surrogacy in India for Social Work." *International Social Work* Vol. 53, No. 5 (September 2010).

Pande, Amrita. "Commercial Surrogacy in India: Manufacturing a Perfect Mother-Worker." *Signs* Vol. 35, No. 4 (Summer 2010).

Paul, André. *L'Evangile de l'enfance selon saint Matthieu,* Lira la Bible, 17. Paris: Cerf, 1968.

Pidd, Helen. "Why Is India so Bad for Women?" *The Guardian,* July 23, 2012: http://www.guardian.co.uk/world/2012/jul/23/why-india-bad-for-women (accessed on August 21, 2012).

Platt, Kate. *The Home and Health in India and the Tropical Colonies.* London: Bailliere, Tindall and Cox, 1923.

Plummer, Alfred. *A Critical and Exegetical Commentary on the Gospel according to St. Luke.* New York: Scribner's, 1903.

Pomeroy, Sarah B. *Goddesses, Whores, Wives and Slaves.* New York: Schocken, 1975.

Pui-lan, Kwok. *Postcolonial Imagination and Feminist Theology.* Kentucky: Westminster John Knox Press, 2005.

Rad, Gerhard von. *Genesis: A Commentary.* Philadelphia, PA: The Westminster Press, 1972.

Ragoné, Heléna. "Of Likeness and Difference: How Race is Being Transferred by Gestational Surrogacy." In *Ideologies and Technologies of Motherhood: Race, Class, Sexuality, Nationalism,* ed. Heléna Ragoné and France Winddance Twine. New York and London: Routledge, 2000.

Rahner, Karl. *Mary Mother of the Lord: Theological Meditations.* New York: Herder and Herder, 1963.

Reicke, Bo. "Jesus, Simeon, and Anna (Luke 2:21–40)." In *Saved by Hope,* ed. J. I. Cook. Grand Rapids, MI: Eerdmans, 1978.

Reilly, Frank. "Jane Schaberg, Raymond E. Brown, and the Problem of the Illegitimacy of Jesus." In *The Illegitimacy of Jesus: A Feminist Theological Interpretation of the Infancy Narrative.* Expanded 20th ed. Sheffield: Sheffield Phoenix Press, 2006.

Roberts, Emma. *Scenes and Characteristics of Hindostan, with Sketches of Anglo Indian Society.* 2 vols. London: W.H. Allen, 1835.

Roberts, Helen and Francis Hardy. "Our 'Rent a Womb' Child from an Indian Baby Farm: British Couple Paying £20,000 for a Desperately Poor Single Mother to Have Their Child." *Mail Online,* August 31, 2012: http://www.dailymail.co.uk/femail/article-2196538/Our-rent-womb-child-Indian-baby-farm-British-couple-paying-20–000-desperately-poor-single-mother-child.htm (accessed on November 26, 2012).

Rodriguez, Nelson M. "Emptying the Content of Whiteness: Toward an Understanding of the Relation between Whiteness and Pedagogy." In *White Reign: Deploying Whiteness in America,* ed. Joe L. Kincheloe, Shirley R. Steinberg, Nelson M. Rodriguez, and Ronald E. Chennault. New York: St. Martin's Press, 2000.

Roy, Nilanjana S. "Protecting the Rights of Surrogate Mothers in India." *The New York Times,* October 4, 2011: http://www.nytimes.com/2011/10/05/world/asia/05iht-letter05.html (accessed on November 6, 2012).

Ruether, Rosemary. *Sexism and God Talk: Toward A Feminist Theology with A New Introduction.* Boston, MA: Beacon Press, 1993.

Russell, Letty M. "Wise Women Bearing Gifts." *Cross Currents* Vol. 53, No. 1 (Spring 2003).

Said, Edward W. *Orientalism.* New York: Vintage Books, 1978.

Sassson, Jack M. *Ruth: A New Translation with a Philological Commentary and a Formalist-Folklorist Interpretation.* Johns Hopkins Near Eastern Studies, 11. Baltimore: Johns Hopkins University Press, 1979.

Sawyer, Deborah. "Hidden Subjects: Rereading Eve and Mary." *Theology and Sexuality* Vol. 14, No. 3 (2008).

Schaberg, Jane. "The Foremothers and the Mother of Jesus." In *A Feminist Companion to the Hebrew Bible in the New Testament,* ed. Athalya Brenner. Sheffield: Sheffield Academic Press, 1996.

Schaberg, Jane. "Feminist Interpretations of the Infancy Narrative of Matthew." In *A Feminist Companion to Mariology*, ed. Amy Jill Levine and Maria Mayo Robbins. New York: T&T Clark International, 2005.

Schaberg, Jane. *The Illegitimacy of Jesus: A Feminist Theological Interpretation of the Infancy Narratives*. Expanded 20th anniversary ed. Sheffield: Sheffield Phoenix Press, 2006.

Schüssler Fiorenza, Elisabeth. *In Memory of Her: A Feminist Theological Reconstruction of Christian Origins*. New York: Crossroad, 1994.

Schüssler Fiorenza, Elisabeth. *Jesus: Miriam's Child, Sophia's Prophet: Critical Issues in Feminist Christology*. New York: Continuum; London: SCM Press, 1994.

Seeberg, R. "Die Herkunft der Mutter Jesu." In *Theologische Fetschrift für* G. Nathanael Bonwetsch zu seinem siebzigsten Geburtstage, ed. H. Achelis. Leipzig: Deichert, 1918.

Seim, Turid Karlsen. *The Double Message: Patterns of Gender in Luke and Acts*. Nashville: Abingdon Press, 1994.

Sen, Amartya. *Development as Freedom*. New York: Anchor Press, 1999.

Sen, Indrani. "Memsahibs and Health in Colonial Writings, c. 1840–1930." *South Asian Research* Vol. 30, No. 3 (2010).

Sen, Indrani. "Colonial Domesticities, Contentious Interactions: Ayahs, Wet-Nurses and Memsahibs in Colonial India." *Indian Journal of Gender Studies* Vol. 16 (2009).

Sharp, Lesley A. "The Commodification of the Body and its Parts." *Annual Review of Anthropology* Vol. 29 (2000).

Sherwood, Mary Martha. *The Works of Mrs. Sherwood*. 16 Vols. New York: Harper, 1834–1858.

Shome, Raka. "Whiteness and the Politics of Location: Postcolonial Reflections." In *Whiteness: The Communication of Social Identity*, ed. Thomas K. Nakayama and Judith N. Martin. New Delhi: Sage Publication, 1999.

Smerdon, Usha Rengachary. "Crossing Bodies, Crossing Borders: International Surrogacy between the United States and India." *Cumberland Law Review* Vol. 39, No. 1 (2008).

Solinger, Rickie. *Wake up Little Susie: Single Pregnancy and Race before Roe vs. Wade*. New York and London: Routledge, 1992.

Spar, Deborah L. "For Love and Money: The Political Economy of Commercial Surrogacy." *Review of International Political Economy* Vol. 12, No. 2 (May 2005).

Spar, Deborah L. *The Baby Business: How Money, Science and Politics Drive the Commerce of Conception*. Boston, MA: Harvard Business School Press, 2006.

Spivak, Gayatri Chakravorty. "Breast-Giver": For Author, Reader, Teacher, Subaltern, Historian…." In *Breast Stories*, ed. Mahasweta Devi. Calcutta: Seagull Books, 2002.

Spivak, Gayatri Chakravorty. "Diasporas Old and New: Women in Transnational World." In *Class Issues: Pedagogy, Cultural Studies and the Public Sphere,* ed. Amitava Kumar. New York: New York University Press, 1997.

Spivak, Gayatri Chakravorty. *A Critique of Postcolonial Reason: Toward a History of the Vanishing Present*. Cambridge, MA: Harvard University Press, 1999.

Spivak, Gayatri Chakrovorty. *In Other Worlds: Essays in Cultural Politics*. New York and London: Routledge, 1998.

Sprawson, Allan Cuthbert, ed. *Moore's Manual of Family Medicine and Hygiene for India*. 8th ed. rewritten by the editor with a Foreword by Charles Pardey Lukis. London: J. and A. Churchill, 1916.

Steel, Anne Flora and Grace Gardiner. *The Complete Indian Housekeeper and Cook: Giving the Duties of Mistress and Servants, the General Management of the House, and Practical Recipes for Cooking in all Its Branches*. London: Heinemann, 1904.

Stein, Sadie. "Is Reproductive Tourism Exploiting India's Poor?" *Jezebel*, August 23, 2010: http://jezebel.com/5619616/is-reproductive-tourism-exploiting-in-dias-poor (accessed December 11, 2012).

Stoler, Ann Laura. "Carnal Knowledge and Imperial Power: Gender, Race and Morality in Colonial Asia." In *The Gender/Sexuality Reader: Culture, History, Political Economy,* ed. Roger N. Lancaster and Michaela Di Leornardo. New York and London: Routledge, 1997.

Stoler, Ann Laura. *Carnal Knowledge and Imperial Power*. Berkeley: University of California Press, 2002.

Stoler, Ann. Laura. "Making Empire Respectable: The Politics of Race and Sexual Morality in 20th Century Colonial Cultures." *American Ethnologist* Vol. 16, No. 4 (November, 1989).

Storrow, Richard F. "The Handmaid's Tale of Fertility Tourism: Passports and Third Parties in the Religious Regulation of Assisted Conception". *Texas Wesleyan Law Review* Vol. 12 (2005).

Suleri, Sara. *The Rhetoric of English India*. Chicago: University of Chicago Press, 1992.

Trible, Phyllis. *God and the Rhetoric of Sexuality*, Philadelphia, PA: Fortress Press, 1978.

Troost, Arie. "Elisabeth and Mary-Naomi and Ruth: Gender-Response Criticism in Luke 1–2." In *A Feminist Companion to the Hebrew Bible in the New Testament*, ed. Athalya Brenner and Sheffield: Sheffield Academic Press, 1996.

Valarmathi, Sister Josephine Amala. "The Work of Domestic Work." *Samar: South Asian Magazine for Action and Reflection*, November 10, 2008: http://samarma-gazine.org/archive/articles/270 (accessed on November 13, 2012).

Wainwright, Elaine. "The Gospel of Matthew." In *Searching the Scriptures*, Volume 2: *A Feminist Commentary*, ed. Elisabeth Schüssler Fiorenza. New York: Crossroad, 1994.

Wainwright, Elaine. "Tradition Makers/Tradition Shapers: Women of the Matthean Tradition." *Word and World* Vol. 18, No. 4 (Fall 1998).

Wainwright, Elaine. *Shall We Look for Another? A Feminist Reading of the Matthean Jesus*. New York: Orbis Books, 1998.

Wainwright, Elaine. *Towards a Feminist Critical Reading of the Gospel According to Matthew*. Berlin and New York: De Gruyter, 1991.

Walker, Megan. "Mary of Nazareth in Feminist Perspective: Towards a Liberating Mariology." In *Women Hold up Half the Sky: Women in the Church in Southern Africa*, ed. Denise Ackermann, Jonathan A. Draper and Emma Mashinini. Pietermaritzburg, South Africa: Cluster Publications, 1991.

Warner, Marina. *Alone Of All Her Sex: The Myth and the Cult of the Virgin Mary*. New York: Macmillan, 1976.

Warnock, Mary. *A Question of Life*. Oxford: Blackwell, 1985.

Weaver, Dorothy Jean. " 'Wherever this Good News is Proclaimed': Women and God in the Gospel of Matthew." *Interpretation* Vol. 65, No. 4 (October 2010).

Weren, Wilhelmus J. C. "The Five Women in Matthew's Genealogy." *Catholic Biblical Quarterly* Vol. 59, No. 2 (April 1997).

Wharton, J. A. "A Plausible Tale. Story and Theology in II Samuel 9–20, I Kings 2." *Interpretation* Vol. 35 (1998).

Witherington, Ben, III. *Women in the Earliest Churches*. Cambridge: Cambridge University Press, 1988.

Wyler, Bea. "Mary's Call." In *A Feminist Companion to the Hebrew Bible in the New Testament*, ed. Athalya Brenner. Sheffield: Sheffield Academic Press, 1996.

Yeats, W. B. "The Mother of God." In *The Collected Poems of W. B. Yeats*, ed. Richard J. Finneran. London and New York: Scribner, 1973.

Index

Abraham, 45, 47
active, 98, 107–8, 111, 121, 125–6,
   172n27
agency, 93, 99–102
Althusser, Louis, 20, 91, 106
altruism, 21, 26–7, 30, 32, 41, 63, 100,
   132, 142
amah/ayah/dhaye, 1, 9–12, 15–16,
   21–2, 24–5, 34, 36, 147n1
ambiguity, 15, 42, 45, 64, 110, 133
ambivalence, 16, 23, 68, 92–3, 103,
   113, 115, 117, 120, 126–7, 131–2,
   140–3
   ambivalent motherhood, 42, 46,
   50–8, 93, 107, 125
Anderson, Elizabeth, 28, 63
Anderson, Gail Sexton, 111–12
Anderson, Janice Capel, 45, 48, 72–5,
   79, 85, 122, 172n27
androcentrism, 45–8, 51, 66–7, 73–6,
   78–9, 80, 103, 113, 116, 139–40,
   165n70, 167n104
Annunciation, 66, 71, 82–3, 97
Arieff, Adrienne, 55–6
Artificial Insemination, 26

Balakrishnan, Geeta, 33, 44, 60, 68
Baraitser, Lisa, 30, 154n38
Bathsheba, 46–9, 51, 61–7, 73, 159n17,
   160n24, 162n34, 164n58
Beattie, Tina, 121–2
Belsey, Catherine, 106, 136
Bhabha, Homi, 93, 103, 118, 125,
   133

Bible, 44, 49, 52, 58, 72, 76, 83. *See
   also individual Gospel authors*
Birsa Munda, 8
Blyth, Eric, 33, 44, 60, 68
breast, 1, 8, 11, 12, 16, 36, 134
breast-giver, 8
"Breast-Giver" (Devi), 9, 11, 13,
   151n67, 153n29, 174n50
Briggs, Sheila, 105–6
British Empire, 1–2, 5, 10, 16, 22, 25,
   36, 39, 131
British memsahib. *See* memsahib
Brown, Raymond, 48, 49, 50, 66, 69,
   73, 81, 82

capitalism, 18, 27–9, 38, 42, 92, 95–6,
   106, 128, 131–2, 141–2
Chaudhuri, Nupur, 1, 10–11, 147n2,
   152n14, 180n27
Chodorow, Nancy, 92
choice, 23, 29, 32, 100, 102, 104, 120,
   131, 142
Chopra, Anuj, 69
Christianity, 49–50, 70–6, 81, 86, 102,
   109, 118, 121, 134
colonialism, 2–3, 34, 38–9, 131,
   135–6, 142
   colonial anxieties, 2, 8, 10–11,
   14–16, 150n48
   colonial Empire, 1, 4–5, 9, 15–16,
   23–4, 26–7
   colonized, 1–2, 4–11, 16, 23, 25,
   33–6, 89, 120, 133, 142, 156n61,
   180n17

CPSIA information can be obtained
at www.ICGtesting.com
Printed in the USA
LVHW10*1438120918
589882LV00004BA/15/P